CONTENTS.

—⚬⚭⚬—

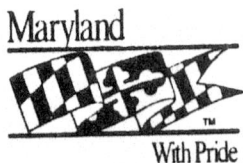

Maryland

With Pride

THE EAST-HAVEN REGISTER:
in Three Parts

PART I

CONTAINING A HISTORY OF THE TOWN OF EAST-HAVEN, FROM ITS FIRST SETTLEMENT IN 1644, TO THE YEAR 1800. ALSO AN ACCOUNT OF ITS BOUNDARIES, IRON WORKS AND MILLS, DIVISION OF LANDS, CONTROVERSIES WITH NEW-HAVEN AND BRANFORD, TOWN CHARTERS, ECCLESIASTICAL AFFAIRS, SCHOOLS, POPULATION AND TAXES, LOSSES BY WAR, NATURAL HISTORY AND CURIOSITIES, ROADS AND PUBLIC LANDS.

PART II

CONTAINING AN ACCOUNT OF THE NAMES, MARRIAGES, AND BIRTHS, OF THE FAMILIES WHICH FIRST SETTLED, OR WHICH HAVE RESIDED IN EAST-HAVEN, FROM ITS SETTLEMENT IN 1644, TO THE YEAR 1800.

PART III

CONTAINING AN ACCOUNT OF THE DEATHS IN THE FAMILIES NAMED IN THE SECOND PART, FROM THE YEAR 1647 TO THE END OF THE YEAR 1823.

Compiled by Stephen Dodd
Pastor of the Congregational Church in East-Haven

HERITAGE BOOKS
2014

HERITAGE BOOKS

AN IMPRINT OF HERITAGE BOOKS, INC.

Books, CDs, and more—Worldwide

For our listing of thousands of titles see our website
at
www.HeritageBooks.com

A Facsimile Reprint
Published 2014 by
HERITAGE BOOKS, INC.
Publishing Division
5810 Ruatan Street
Berwyn Heights, Md. 20740

Originally published
New-Haven:
Published for the Author, and sold by A. H. Maltby & Co. No. 4,
Glebe Building.
T. G. Woodward & Co. Print.
1824

International Standard Book Numbers
Paperbound: 978-1-55613-845-4
Clothbound: 978-0-7884-9351-5

PREFACE.

THIS little work, now offered to the patronage of the public, derives its importance from the *times* and *subjects* of which it treats, rather than from its size or execution. The affairs of a *township* so small as East-Haven, cannot be expected to furnish materials for a narrative, or for a statistical account, so interesting as those of large towns, and especially those which were first colonized, and were concerned in the transactions of the first settlements of New-England. Yet it should be recollected, that some small towns, and the maritime towns in particular, were once constituent parts of the first colonies. This is true of East-Haven. It was a part of the ancient colony of New-Haven; and was connected with that colony and town, in all its domestic and foreign concerns, about 140 years. In this town also, the Quinipiack tribe of Indians had their planting ground, their forts, their place of burial, and their last place of residence. Here, too, the first Iron-works in Connecticut were established, and continued for about 25 years; and made *Stoney River* a place of business, for both New-Haven and Branford. These ancient affairs, with some events of a more recent date,—events, too, that grew out of the labours, trials, and perseverance of the first generations of the colony,—and the rise and progress of the Church and worship of God in the town, possess sufficient importance to engage the attention of, at least, the descendants of the ancient colonists, who bequeathed to their posterity the precious fruits of their toils and sufferings. An acquaintance also with the genealogy of their families, and with the progress of disease and death among them, cannot certainly be an object of indifference. These matters are, however, so local, that it is not expected they will excite much interest among those who have never had any connection with the town, or with its inhabitants. The patronage of this publication, therefore, will be chiefly derived from East-Haven families. But no suitable remuneration for the labour of the compiler, is expected from the small patronage which it will receive.

The Records of the village of East-Haven commence in the year 1680. But these are imperfect. The records of the Church, previous to the ordination of the Rev. Mr. Street in 1755, are lost: and the oldest monuments in the present cemetery, are dated 1712. These records and monuments were all read. Then the records of New-Haven Colony, of the Town and Probate offices of New-Haven, were examined, and also the monuments of the old cemetery of that town. Some materials were gleaned from the Town and Church records of Branford, North-Branford, Northford, North-Haven, and Wallingford. Several documents were drawn from the Secretary of State's office: and considerable information of a family nature, was derived from the aged people of this town. Yet, among so many names and dates, and so many subjects, errors and imperfections will doubtless be discovered : and some may find fault with the style and manner of execution. In reply, the compiler would only observe, that he has done the best he could to render the work accurate, amusing, and useful.

In respect to the dates, there is no difference observed between the old, or *Julian style*, and the new, or *Gregorian style*. The *new style* was adopted in the British dominions, in the year 1752. All the dates in this work, previous to the 14th of September of that year, are *old* style ; and all the dates after the 14th of September, 1752, are *new* style. It was also customary to begin the year on the 25th of March. Between the 1st of January and the 25th of March, a part of the preceding year and a part of the new year were reckoned. Thus, Jan. 30, 1689, was written 1688—9, or 1688/9. But this mode of reckoning does not affect the dates as used in this work. The year is uniformly treated as beginning on the 1st day of January.

STEPHEN DODD.

East-Haven, Sept. 1824.

ERRATA.

Page 13, line 2d from bottom, for *in* read *it.*

14, line 8th from bottom, for *argued* read *agreed.*

20, line 5th from top, for *Hassukque* read *Hassuakque.*

20, line 16th from bottom, for *Tapponshaske* read *Tappanshasiske.*

22, line 16th from top, after *called,* dele the word *of.*

26, line 17th from bottom, transpose the word *grant* to the beginning of the line.

48, line 20th from top, read Jared and Samuel *Potter.*

83, line 13th from top, for *watty* read *walty.*

83, line 19th from bottom, for *their* read *these.*

85, line 12th from top, for *Umbesa* read *Umbesec.*

88, line 19th from top, add a g at the end of the line.

EAST-HAVEN REGISTER.

—❧—

CHAPTER I.

New-Haven purchased and settled:—Then the tract on the East side of the River—the Cove—Stoney River and South-end, Foxon—and Dragon.

DURING the reign of James I. and Charles I. kings of England, the Puritans were subjected to a destructive oppression, and a furious persecution for conscience sake; and seeing no end to their sufferings, projected settlements in the wilderness of America, as a place of retreat for the Church of God, and where the salvation and freedom of themselves and of their posterity might be promoted and secured. Hence large companies left their native land and crossed the Atlantic. Among them were persons of wealth, learning, and distinguished piety and eminence.

On the 26th July, 1637, Rev. John Davenport, Mr. Samuel Eaton, Theophilus Eaton, Edward Hopkins, Thomas Gregson, and their company arrived at Boston. They were invited to continue there, or in that vicinity. This proposal they rejected, for they were determined to settle a new colony. Accordingly, in the fall of that year, Mr. Eaton and others explored the country along the sea-coast, west of Connecticut river, and finally fixed upon Quinipiack, as the place of their settlement. On the 30th March, 1638, the company sailed from Boston, and in about two weeks arrived safe at the place of their destination.

On the 18th April, the first Lord's day after their arrival, the people attended public worship under a large oak, and Mr. Davenport preached to them from Matth. vi. 1. Soon after their arrival, they held a day of fasting and prayer; at the close of which, they solemnly entered into a plantation

2

covenant, binding themselves, "*that as in matters that concern the gathering and ordering of a Church, so also in all
publick offices which concern civil order ; as choice of Ma-
gistrates and officers, making and repealing laws, dividing
allotments of inheritance, and all things of like nature, they
would all of them, be ordered by the rules which the scrip-
ture held forth to them.*" By this covenant they were regulated the first year.

On the 24th Nov. 1638, Theophilus Eaton, Esq. Mr. Davenport, and other English planters, made their first purchase of Momauguin, sachem of that part of the country, and
his counsellors. The English promised to protect Momauguin and his Indians from their enemies, and that they
should have sufficient planting ground between the harbor
and Saybrook fort. This ground was located in East-Haven, from the Old Ferry point or Red-Rock, to the Solitary-
Cove, on the west—on the north, the road from the ferry
to Stoney-River—on the east, from the said road along the
foot of Grave or Fort-Hill and the road that runs from
Bridge-Swamp to the Cove. The purchasers also gave the
sachem and his counsellors—"*12 coats of English cloth,* 12
alchemy spoons, 12 *hatchets,* 12 *hoes, two dozen of knives,* 12
porringers, and 4 *cases of French knives and scissors.*"
This contract was signed by Momauguin and his council
on the one part, and Theophilus Eaton and John Davenport
on the other part. Thomas Stanton was interpreter. By
the oppression of the Mohawks and Pequods, this tribe was
then reduced to about 40 men.

On the 11th Dec. 1638, they purchased another large
tract, which lay principally north of the former purchase.
This was bought of Montowese, son of the great Sachem at
Mattabeseck, (now Middletown.) It was 10 miles long,
north and south, and 13 miles in breadth. It extended 8
miles east of the river Quinipiack, and 5 miles west of it.
For this tract they gave 13 coats, and allowed the Indians
ground to plant, and liberty to hunt on it. These purcha-
ses "included all the lands within the ancient limits of the
old towns of New-Haven, Branford, and Wallingford, and
almost the whole contained within the present limits of those
towns, and of the towns of East-Haven, Woodbridge, Che-
shire, Hamden and North-Haven."

On the 4th June 1639, all the free planters of Quinipiack
convened in a large barn of Mr. Newman's, and formed their

Constitution. Sixty-three names were subscribed to it on that day, and about fifty more were added soon after. A-mong the subscribers who settled in East-Haven, or were concerned in that settlement, were William Andrews, Jasper Crayne, Thomas Gregson, William Touttle or Tuttle, Garvis Boykim, John Potter, Matthew Moulthrop, Matthias Hitchcock, and Edward Patterson. To these were added Thomas Morris and John Thompson.

On the 7th March, 1644, the colony Constitution was revised and enlarged; and then were added the names of Matthew Rowe and John Tuthill: And in July following, Alling Ball, Edmund Tooly, Thomas Robinson, sen. and jun., William Holt, Thomas Barnes, and Edward Hitchcock : And in August, Peter Mallory and Nicholas Augur. On the 4th April, 1654, George Pardee, John Potter, jun. ; and in May, Matthew Moulthrop, jun., were added.

Feb. 7, 1657, John Davenport, jun. Jonathan Tuthill, and John Thompson subscribed : May 1st, 1660, Nathaniel Boykim, and Thomas Tuttle.—Thomas Morris was admitted a free inhabitant 3d July, 1648; John Chedsey, 19th Feb. 1658 ; George Pardee, 16th June, 1662 ; and Robert Augur in 1674.

The town was named New-Haven in 1640. The first division of lands was made within the town plat, and that vicinity, for home lots. But several enterprizing farmers turned their attention to the lands on the east side of the Quinipiack, and began to settle there, when the second division was made.

In 1639, Thomas Gregson petitioned for his second division at Solitary-Cove, and on the 5th August, 1644, 133 acres were alottted to him at that place. There he placed his family—the first in East-Haven. The next year he was appointed agent for the colony to the Parliament in England, to obtain a patent. In 1647, Mr. Gregson, and Capt. Turner, and Mr. Lamberton, and five or six more of the principal inhabitants, sailed for England, in a ship of 150 tons ; and were all lost.—Jane, the widow of Thomas Gregson, in 1677, gave a deed for 33 acres of the Cove farm to her daughter Phebe, who had married Rev. John Whiting, of Hartford, which he sold 18th July, 1678, to George Pardee. And the remainder of the farm was sold to George Pardee, jun. soon after it was divided among the heirs, in 1716.

In 1640, lots were laid out on the East side the river. The proportion for the second division was 20 acres of upland for 100l. estate, and 2½ acres for every poll in the family. And on 4th Nov. 1642, the town voted " that those who have their farms at the river called Stoney-River, shall have liberty to make a sluice in the river for their own convenience." Fifty acres of meadow on the east side, was granted to Rev. Mr. Samuel Eaton, 29th Aug. 1640. " Benjamin Linge and William Tuttle are allowed to have their meadow when Mr. Eaton hath his first 50 acres, viz. in the fresh Meadow towards Totokett, and Mr. Crayne is to have his also there."—Jasper Crayne had his lot and house on the east side of the green ; William Tuttle on the south side of the fresh meadows. I cannot ascertain the spot where Benjamin Linge built. These were men of wealth, and much employed in public affairs.

Jasper Crayne sold his farm of 16 acres, to Matthew Moulthrop, 7th Sept. 1652, and removed to Totokett; and from thence his son Jasper removed to Newark, 1667. William Tuttle had five sons, all of whom sold their patrimony and removed, except Joseph ; some of whose descendants still remain in the town. Benjamin Linge died without children, and Col. Dixwell, one of King Charles' judges, married his widow.

In 1649, " It was ordered that Mr. Davenport, pastor of the Church, shall have his meadow, and the upland for his second division, both together, on the East side of the East-River, where himself shall choose, with all the conveniency the place can afford for a farme, together with the natural bounds of the place, whether by creeks or otherwise." He accordingly laid out a tract of land of about a mile square, and containing about 600 acres, above Dragon.

In 1650, Alling Ball became his farmer, and was exempted from militia service, while he continued in Mr. Davenport's employment.

The following list of polls and estates, by which the first division was regulated, will show the relative wealth of some of those who first had their farms in this town :

Mr. Davenport	3 polls	£1000
William Tuttle	7	450
Jasper Crayne	3	480
Thomas Gregson	6	600
Benjamin Linge	2	320

William Andrews	2	150
John Cooper	3	30
John Potter	4	25
Matthias Hitchcock	3	50
Matthew Moulthrop	1	10
Edward Patterson	1	40
Richard Berkley	4	20

In 1643, pieces of eight were reckoned at five shillings and eight pence. Wampum, in 1640, was fixed at six for a penny.

Totokett being settled about this time, in 1649, a difficulty arose concerning the boundary between the two towns,* which was committed to an arbitration; but it appears that the business was still unfinished in 1659.

In 1644, a bridge was built over Stoney-river on the road to Totokett, by William Andrews, for which he charged the town of New-Haven £3. 8. 9.

The ferry at Red-Rock, had been kept by Francis Brown; but in 1650, George Pardee took it, and he was afterwards allowed to build a house there at his own expense. And in 1670 the ferry farm was granted to him, which was left by him to his son George, and continues still in the possession of his descendants. The rates of ferriage established in 1671, were as follows: For a man and horse, sixpence. If the horse swam over, three pence. Afterwards it was reduced to fourpence,—and a footman, twopence.

In 1651, William Tuttle, and Benjamin Linge, and Matthew Moulthrop, obtained 14 acres of the fresh meadow. They and the Governor had 20 acres of it. John Potter and Ellis Mew, also obtained 20 acres of in. In 1662, John Potter, obtained a piece of land upon which to set his

---

* Sept. 5, 1640. The General Court, at New-Haven, made a grant of Totokett to Mr. Samuel Eaton, brother of Governor Eaton, upon the condition of his procuring a number of his friends from England, to make a settlement in that tract of country. Mr. Eaton failed in fulfilling the conditions.—About three years after, the subject was acted upon thus: " Totokett, a place fit for a small plantation, betwixt New-Haven and Guildford, and purchased from the Indians; was granted to Mr. Swayne and some others in Wethersfield, they repaying the charges, which are betwixt £12 and 13, and joining in one jurisdiction with New-Haven and the forenamed plantations, upon the same fundamental agreement settled in Oct. 1643, which they duly considering accepted."
The settlement began in 1644.   [*N. Haven records.*]

blacksmith shop. About the same time, John Tuttle, jun. sold to him his house and home lot—it was the same on which Josiah Bradley now lives. And about the same time William Luddington died, and his widow bought of John Tuttle, jun. land at Stoney-river, which was a part of his patrimony.

John Cooper came to Stoney-river about the time of the building of the Iron works, of which he appears to have been the agent and overseer.

In 1662, Samuel Heminway appeared and obtained land for a home lot, which was not far from the furnace. Thomas Barnes bought of John Harriman south of Muddy-river, 1662—and in 1664, petitioned the town for a piece of land at the Iron works, for Ralph Russel, which, by the advice of the townsmen was granted. That lot is now occupied by Thomas Barnes. John Russel, his brother, come here a-bout the same time, but I cannot ascertain the spot he loca-ted. William Fowler owned land on the east side, and in 1676 he confirmed by deed to John Austin, land, that he had previously bought of widow Jones. Anna, widow of William Andrews, sold to Matthew Moulthrop, sen. a piece of land at Fowler's Cove, 1667. This name, and that of Fowler's Creek, were both derived from William Fowler, who owned land or meadow adjacent to both places.

The purchase and settlement of the great neck, or South-end, appears next in order.

William Andrews, John Cooper, Sergt. Richard Berkley, Isaac Whitehead, and Nathaniel Merriman, petitioned for land beyond Solitary-Cove, in 1645, but their petition was not granted. In 1649, William Andrews alone applied for the same tract, but failed. In 1651, Richard Berkley re-newed the application for himself. But the town refused to grant him the land, because other men had also applied for it.

On the 3d Dec. 1651, the application was again renewed, and it was finally " *argued and ordered that,* William An-drews, Richard Berkley, Matthias Hitchcock, Edward Pat-terson, and Edward Hitchcock, shall have the neck of land by the sea-side, beyond the Cove, and all the meadows be-longing to it below the Island with a rock upon it. They are to have the neck entire to themselves by paying to the Town one penny an acre for 500 acres, for every rate ; and for their meadows as other men do. They are to settle

and dwell upon it at spring next, and improve it by way of
farming for getting corn, and breeding of Cattle, and not to
dispose of it by letting or selling, without the Town's consent. And if they, or any of them should remove out of the
plantation within five years, they are to leave the lands to
the Town, (if they will accept it) they paying for improve-
ments as it is then worth, being appraised by indifferent
men. And if their cattle do damage by eating the meadows the farmers now have at Stoney River, it is agreed, (Mr.
Linge and Mr. Tuttle being present) that a fence shall be
made to secure it from their cattle, which is to be made and
maintained betwixt them ; that is, the farmers on the neck
half, and the farmers at Stoney River (who are concerned
in it) the other half.

" Further the farmers upon the neck promise (that seeing
they have the neck entire to themselves) if any of their cattle get out of the pasture without the neck, they will make
a fence to keep them in."

The taxes laid upon this land seem to have constituted a
kind of rent, and being considered by the tenants as very
burdensome, they petitioned for relief, but could obtain no
abatement.

William Andrews sold his share in the neck to James
Denison and John Asbill, 1663. John Asbill sold his
part to J. Denison, 1689. Thomas Smith married the
daughter and only child of Edward Patterson ; and so became possessor of his share. In 1662, Richard Berkley sold
his share to Thomas Harrison ; and the same year, Harrison sold his share at South-end and land at Muddy river,
to John Thompson. The Hitchcock family sold their part,
and all died or removed from East-Haven.

The South-end men still feeling uncomfortable under
their one-penny tax ; on the 3d May 1689, Thomas Smith,
James Denison, Eliakim Hitchcock and John Thompson,
proposed to the town a final payment, instead of the yearly
rent for their lands, which was referred to the towns-men :
And on the 4th November, " In pursuance of the town order made in May last, the towns-men having treated with
the five South-end men about the neck of land, for which
they were to pay £25 in money, declared that the said men
are willing to pay £15 in money to the town, to clear off the
incumbrance, and the yearly payment aforesaid ; the town
making over the said neck of land by their grant, or deed

in writing to them the said five men, their heirs and assigns forever according to law, and with mention of full bounda-ry thereon."

" The town after some debate voted their acceptance of said £15 in money tendered by the said South-end men, to be by them, or their order, paid to Mr. Baker of Boston, to-wards payment for the bell bought of said Baker, some time in May next. And they ordered that any two of the townsmen are appointed to sign and seal a deed or deeds to the South-end men, for settlement of right and title to them accordingly."

Tradition states, that this bell is the same now used in the Court House in New-Haven.

According to this agreement and vote of the town, on the 7th Dec. 1689, Moses Mansfield and Abraham Dickerman, two of the townsmen of New-Haven, gave a deed, for the consideration of £15 in money, to John Thompson, Thomas Smith, James Denison, Eliakim Hitchcock, and Nathaniel Hitchcock—" bounded on the south and south-west by the sea, and on the east with Stoney river, from the mouth of it to a stake by the side of the said river, with a heap of stones at it. And from thence to a white oak, marked with N. H. and stones at the root. And thence Westerly bounded by the meadows of John Russel, widow Mew, William Lud-dington, John Austin, Matthew Moulthrop, and John Pot-ter, into the middle of Huckleberry swampe, and soe unto Fowler's meadow westerly, and so along by the meadows of Hartfordshire suburbs quarter, and so unto the east end of a pond by the beach called the *black pond.*"—*N. H. Rec.*

On the 16th March, 1671, Thomas Morris, a shipbuilder, bought the little neck. Having Gregson's farm on the north and the meadows along Fowler's creek on the east. His design was to carry on ship building, the timber there being very suitable for that purpose. But two years afterwards death put an end to all his purposes.

The lots about Dragon point, between the Davenport and Ferry farms, were laid out, but lay dormant several years. The transaction relative to that subject stands thus on record :

13th Feb. 1670. " The town by vote granted that those that have land on the east side about Dragon point shall have liberty to lay their lots together, and to begin at which end they please. And the townsmen are hereby appointed to settle it with them, both in respect to convenient high-ways, and also how far their lots shall run in length from the river." In 1703 these lots were occupied.

Next to the Brown farm, Matthew Rowe, jun. had his farm. Alling Ball obtained a farm north of the Davenport farm. Eleazar Morris, jun. settled on the hill east of the Ball farm. John Austin appears on record in 1673; and six years after obtained a piece of land overflowed by the Forge pond. He built on the north side of the road, west of the Green. In 1683 Isaac Bradley came into the village from Branford, and bought a building lot next to the river, of sergt. John Potter, and north of his house. He was a carpenter. In 1681 deacon John Chedsey, a tanner and shoemaker, settled on the north side of the Green, on a three square lot of about three acres, between John Potter and John Austin. And afterwards ten acres were granted him by the village, on the west side of the fresh meadows, which ever since has been known by the name of Chedsey's field, and Chedsey's hill. In March 1683 he " proposed to the village to have a third division of land among us equal to ten heads and £100 estate, which he doth apprehend to be 60 acres; and for the future he will be engaged to pay to-wards the expenses of the village after the rate of £200 rateable estate, until his estate shall amount to £200, and then to rise as his estate shall rise."

In 1683 the village made a third division of land; and passed the following order, viz.: " Thomas Pinion, Robert Dawson, William Roberts, Joseph Abbot, and James Tailor, on their motion to the village, are to have no third division with the rest of the inhabitants; but shall have their land next to that land we obtained from Branford, as follows. Thomas Pinion, Robert Dawson and William Roberts, be-ing married men, shall have 30 acres each man. And Jo-seph Abbott and James Tailor shall have 20 acres each man, provided each of the aforesaid five men do build upon the said land a tenantable house within three years of the pres-ent date."

The lots granted by the village to the five men above-mentioned, were confirmed by a town vote of New-Haven. The lots lay on Foxon's farms, north and south, across the river, and the road as it now runs. That plain was called *Foxon's farms* from the circumstance of its being the resi-dence of an Indian sagamore, named *Foxon*. It is on re-

cord of the date of 1644. " The people of Branford com-
plained that the Indians set trapps in the cattle's paths;
and a Marshall was sent from New-Haven to warn *Uncas,*
or his brother, or *Foxon,* to come and speak to the Governor
about it." In 1658 the inhabitants of the village petitioned
the town, " that a line might be run from the rear corner of
Mr. Davenport's farm towards the town to *Foxon's Week-
wam,* and so Stoney river be their bounds on the east;"
from which it appears that Foxon's residence was on the
plain, not far from the river. From an inspection of a number of other documents, I find that Foxon's farms was on
the plain between the house of Jared Grannis and Capt.
Chedsey, and the river and the swamps at the foot of the
hill north and west.

Thomas Goodsell, from Branford, was admitted an inhabitant of New-Haven in April, 1692, and soon after built
the house now occupied by the widow and son of Azariah
Bradley; and is the oldest house in East-Haven. Edmund
Tooley built on the lot south of sergt. John Potter. Edward Vickar lived east of the furnace dam. William Luddington, jun. lived on the southeast corner of the road opposite the pumpkin lot, and the place was afterwards owned
by Gideon Potter and by Isaac Mallory. Samuel Thompson built on the corner lot west of the present meeting-
house; and it is probable that his father, John Thompson,
lived there before him. Thomas Robinson's house was opposite the present meeting house, on the south side of the road.
Samuel Russel lived on the lot now owned by Thomas
Barnes. Capt. John Russel built west of Mullen hill. The
lot of Matthew Moulthrop, the third, is now in the possession of the Shepard family. John Luddington was located
in Bridge swamp, and his son James succeeded him, and he
sold to Jedediah Andrews. Thomas Smith, jun. built near
where John Forbes now lives, and his son Thomas built between him and Capt. John Russel's.

CHAP. II.

Concerning the Boundaries of the Town.

WE shall now proceed to take a view of the boundaries
of the town. The dividing line between New-Haven and
Branford had not been definitely ascertained and fixed at

the time New-Haven sold Totokett; which left much room for uneasiness and altercation. It is a prevailing tradition, and supported too by collateral records, that the original line ran along the east side of Branford hills. And it appears from the petition of the village to New-Haven, and the grant of New-Haven to the village in 1679, and the subsequent grant by Branford, of the half mile, to the village; that Branford actually held in possession more land, than was contained in the original purchase from New-Haven in 1644, and that was not paid for. Branford claimed as far as the Furnace pond. So early as 1649 a difficulty on this subject appeared, which was submitted to arbitration, but without effect. In 1656 New-Haven made a grant of the Furnace farm to the Iron company, and 12 acres to the collier; both within the line claimed by Branford, though Branford was treated as having some interest in the Iron works. About the year 1660 Branford proposed to New-Haven to have the line run between them. And after a long delay the business was acted upon in the following manner, as appears from the Colony records, Hartford, 14th May, 1674.

" This Court ordereth that the agreement between New-Haven and Milford, Branford and Wallingford, about their bounds, be recorded with the records of the Court, and is as followeth."

" Whereas there has been a difference between the inhabitants of New-Haven and the inhabitants of Branford about the dividing bounds between each plantation, and the inhabitants of New-Haven aforesaid having chosen and empowered James Bishop, jun. Thomas Munson, William Andrews, John Mosse, and John Cooper, senr. on their part, and the inhabitants of Branford aforesaid having chosen and empowered Mr. John Wilford, Thomas Blackley, Michael Tayntor, Thomas Harrison and Samuel Ward on their part, to issue the sayd difference in reference to the sayd bounds, the sayd persons abovenamèd (excepting John Cooper, in whose roome Mr. William Tuttle was desired by the authority of New-Haven) being mett together this fifth day of October 1669, and a full debate and consideration of the case for the preserving of love and peace and the preventing of trouble for the future between them that have hitherto been loving neighbours, have condescended so far each to other as to agree about the premises as followeth, viz. That from the river formerly called in an agreement Tapamshashack (with the exception of meadows therein expressed) the great pond at the head of the Furnace shall be the bounds so far as it goes; and from the head of the said pond that a straight line be drawn to the east end of a Hassukque meadow out of which a brooke called Hercules brooke runnes into muddye river, and from the east end of the sayd meadowe to runn a north lyne, with the just variation according to the country unto the end of the = bounds of Branford aforesayd, that is, ten miles from the sea according to the order of the General Assembly. In testimonie whereof we have set too our hands the day and year above written.

John Wilford	Samuel Bishop
Tho: Blackley	Thomas Munson
Michael Tayntor	William Andrews
Tho: Harrison	William Tuttell
Samuel Warde	John Mosse.''

In another instrumemt of a later date the bounds are thus described.

" Whereas the General Court of Connecticut Colony, have formerly granted unto proprietors, inhabitants of the town of New-Haven in the sayd Colony, all those lands both meadows and uplands with all their appurtenances within these abutments following, viz. on the sea or sound ; on the south, from the mouth of Oyster river, to the mouth of Scotch Cap, or Stoney River, untill it come to the brooke called Tapponshaske (only in that line is not included the meadow that is laid out to New-Haven proprietors, on the east side the sayd river according to former agreement with Branford) and so the sayd brooke is the bounds to the Furnace dam, and thence the great pond to the head of it, and thence a line eastward half a mile to a white oak, marked with H. T. B. and stones laid at the foot of it."

Colony Records, entered 7th Jan. 1685.

Branford bounds are mentioned in another instrument, of a later date, after the half mile was set off. " Upon the sea upon the south, and on the New-Haven bounds on the west, at Scotch Cap, or Stoney River, until it comes to the brooke Tappanshasick, (only in that line is not included the meadow, which is laid out to proprietors on the east side of the sayd River, and hath been agreed upon,) and that sayd brooke is the bounds to the Furnace dam, and thence the

great pond to the head of it, and thence a line eastward half
a mile to a station, which is a white oak, marked H. T. B."
The east line of the half mile, had not yet been run and
marked. The village, therefore, moved the matter to Branford, and having agreed, their Committees met and came to
the following result :

"We the subscribers being appointed to measure off the
half mile agreed upon with New-Haven, as by record may
appear, to the inhabitants of East-Haven village, in pursuance thereof on the 14th April, 1713, then meeting with
East-Haven Gentlemen at the head of the Furnace pond, and
after full debate and consideration of the premises, we began at the first bound mark at the head of sayd pond, near
the middle of sayd pond, and run a line eastwardly, square
from the old line, which was the dividing line between
New-Haven and Branford, an 160 rods to an heap of stones,
on the east side of a small hill, at the upper end of Brushy
plane ; thence a line northward, according to agreement, to
a Walnut Tree marked with B B, and stones at the root,
which Tree is 160 rods eastward from the Antient bounds
Tree ; near Hercules' meadow, and from the aforesaid
Walnut Tree, still northward according to agreement, to
the head of the bounds to a White Oak Tree, with letters
on it and stones at the root, which is 160 rods eastward
from the Antient corner at the head of the bounds between
New-Haven and Branford. It is agreed, that the above-
mentioned bounds shall stand and abide to be the bounds
between Branford and East-Haven. As witness our hands.

John Russel, Samuel Russel, Daniel Collins, Alling Ball, Samuel Hotchkiss,	*Committee of East-Haven.*
Nathaniel Harrison, Nathaniel Johnson, John Lindsley,	*Committee of Branford.*

Voted in Town-meeting, Branford, 4th Jan. 1714."

The 29th Dec. 1679, the village, among other things, petitioned New-Haven for their parish or village bounds to
extend as far north as Muddy River ; in answer to which
they say—"That their bounds shall be the north side of
Alling Ball's Farme, by a line from the River as his line
runs, untill it meets with Branford line, above Foxon's."

3

Thus the bounds of the town were all fixed. But after several families on the half mile were set off to North-Haven Society, the line in that quarter was changed. In 1716, the General Court granted the northern parish in New-Haven, to be a distinct Eclesiastical Society. And in May 1718, the Assembly gave them permission to enter into a church state. A number of East-Haven families living on the half mile, were so far from public worship that they requested the privilege of uniting with North-Haven Society, which was granted as follows :

"New-Haven, Oct. 1737—In the memorial of Samuel Jacobs, Daniel Finch, Benjamin Barns, Isaac Blakeslee, Nathaniel Hitchcock, William Rogers, Abel Smith, Joseph Moulthrop, and Caleb Hitchcock, inhabitants in New-Haven, shewing this Assembly that they are settled within the bounds Parish of East-Haven, on a certain tract of land, called of the the half mile, in the Northeast corner of said Society and remote from the publick worship of God in said Parish, praying this Assembly to discharge them from the said East Socity, and annex them to the North Society in said Town, so as to include the said memorialists, and no other inhabitants ; bounding so far South, as to include Benjamin Barnes' Farm, and so Eastward to the east part of said half mile between Mr. Mather's and Mr. Abraham Heminway's land, and so north to Wallingford Town line, between Branford and said half mile, including all the lands east of the said North Society, within said bounds."—[*Colony Records.*]

When North-Haven became a town in 1786, that society line became, of course, the line between the two towns, across the half mile ; and all the *half mile* above that line was taken from the town of East-Haven and annexed to the town of North-Haven. And this alteration of the line on the half mile, accounts for the crookedness of the north line of this town. The whole line between the two towns was surveyed 11th March, 1789:

"Beginning at a heap of stones at Branford line, northeast of the house of Abner Thorpe; thence 4 degrees north 78 rods to the middle of the high way or thereabouts to a heap of stones ;—thence in the high way 47 rods south 5 degrees west to a heap of stones; thence in the line of Jonathan Barnes' farm west 8 degrees north 80 rods, to the old New-Haven line to a heap of stones ; thence 4¼ degrees west of south, 80 rods ;—thence south 2½ degrees west, 80 rods, to a heap of stones; thence south 3 degrees west 80 rods to a heap of stones; thence in the same line 80 rods more to a lage white oak tree marked; thence west 11 degrees south 80 rods; still in the same course 80 rods more; thence west 13 degrees south 80 rods; thence west 14 degrees south 80 rods; thence west 12 degrees south 70 rods, to the bend in the Ball farm, and from said bend 10 rods to another monument; thence west 6 degrees and 8 minutes south to the East River; erecting monuments at the distance of every 80 rods, with marked stones at each monument from the white oak Tree to the River; the number of monuments or 80 rods distance is 12, and 49 rods. 11th March, 1789."

Josiah Bradley,
Stephen Smith,
Isaac Chedsey,
Ephraim Hummiston,   } *Committee.*
Joshua Barnes,
Levy Ray,

This is now, 1824, the condition of the bounds of the town of East-Haven.

CHAPTER III.

Concerning the Iron Works and Mills.

THE transactions relative to the Iron Works are contained in sundry resolutions and orders. This was, probably, the first establishment of the kind within the present bounds of the state. This business was introduced in the following manner:

"General Court, N. H. 12th Nov. 1655.

"The Towne was acquainted that there is a purpose, that an *Iron Worke* shall be set up beyond the farmes at Stoney River, which is considered will be for a publique good; and Mr. Goodyear declared that Mr. Winstone and himself did intend to carry it on; only he desired now to know what the Town desired in it; much debate was about it; but no man engaged in it at present; but divers spoke, that they would give some worke towards making the Damm, whose names and number of days worke were taken, which amounted to about 140 days: so it issued for that time."

"29th Nov. 1655.—The Governor informed the Towne that this meeting was called to consider something further about the Iron Worke, sundry who engaged to worke, last Court, have not yet performed, tho' all others have; and it was now concluded that those that are now behinde, should be called upon to perform what they promised.—It was also now desired that men would declare, who will engage in the worke, and what estate they will put in. But few speaking to it, it was desired that those who are willing would meet at the Governor's this afternoon at 2 o'clock, to declare themselves therein, and it was now propounded whether the Towne will give up their right in the place, and what accommodation is necessary for the best conveniency of the said *Iron Worke*; in this case all the Towne voted to give a full libertie for the *Iron Workes* to go on, and also for wood, water, ironplace, oares, shells for lime, or what else is necessary for that worke, upon the Towne lands upon that side of the great river, called the East River; provided, that no man's proprietie, laid out, or to be laid out, be entered upupon, nor no planter prohibited, from cutting wood, or other conveniency upon the said common, in an orderly way ; and that Branford doe make the like grant, according to their proportion they have in the worke, that future questions about this thing may be prevented.

" 19th May, 1656. Upon motion of Mr. Goodyear and John Cooper in behalf of the Collier that comes to burn coal for the Iron workes; he had 12 acres of land granted him as his own, if the Iron workes go on, and he stay three years in the worke. Provided that all minerals there be reserved, and that he attend all orders of the Towne for the present, and in disposing of said lands hereafter, if it shall so fall out, to have it. The place propounded for is a piece of land lying betwixt the Great Pond, and the Beaver Meadows, a 100 or 2 acres, about 2 miles from the Iron worke. Against which grant or place none objected, so as to hinder the same."

This is now called *the Farm.* It was first in the possession of Theophilus Eaton the Governor. It was given to his daughter Mary, who married Valentine Hill, merchant, Dover—Pisquataqua. He sold it to Nathaniel Micklethwaite, merchant, London, 2 Nov. 1660—for £230 sterling, or $1022 22. He sold it to Thomas Clark of Boston for £100 lawful money, 28th Feb. 1665.—And in the Township of New-Haven.—The farm contained 300 acres of upland and 60 acres of meadow.

" 14th Sept. 1657. The Governor informed the Court

that Mr. Winthrop has let out his part of the Iron workes
to two men in Boston, Capt. Clarke and Mr. Payne, as they
have agreed."

This plan met with a general disapprobation. Debating
followed. It was contended, that as this establishment was
made for the purpose of trade ; there was danger of the entire alienation of the trade and the property. And there
would also be a collection of disorderly persons, which
would corrupt the morals of the neighborhood, and cause
great trouble in the Town. The subject was referred to the
Court, and the Townsman John Cooper to consider of it,
upon what terms to let out the workes, and whether they
should cut wood upon our ground."

That reference reported thus :

"An agreement made by the Committee appointed to
consider about the Iron workes, was read to the Towne and
by vote confirmed and ordered to be entered."

"At the Governor's house, 1 Dec. 1657."

"1. It is agreed that the Iron Workes propounded to
and allowed by this Towne, and to which they granted several priveleges, was, and is only for this Furnace now made
in the place intended, and expressed, as appeareth by the
records, with a Forge, or two, if necessary for the Iron which
this furnace produceth, which are to be improved by the
Townes jointly within the limits allowed by this Court.

"2. This Iron worke and all the privileges thereunto belonging, were intended and granted for the good of New-
Haven and Branford, for bringing and setting up trade
there, which in whole or in a great measure they are like
to be deprived of, if any part of it be alienated either to
strangers, or others out of their jurisidiction. They, therefore, think it not safe, that any part of it be sold, or leased
out, without particular and express law and licence from
the Towne, or Jury, or a Committee, as is appointed for
house lots or lands.

"3. That our neighbors and friends of Branford provide
and supply their part of wood, which is 3-8th parts, with
other things of a like nature, from the land within their own
limits, and that New-Haven do the like for their 5-8th parts.

"4. That all servants, women and others employed in
any respect about the Iron workes, shall attend and be subject to all orders and laws already made, or which shall be
made and published by this towne, or jurisdiction, as other
men.

" 5. That the grant made by the Iron workes be forthwith delivered to the Secretary here, that it may be read and considered; as the grant made by New-Haven shall be to them; that the two plantations may receive and bear their due proportion in profits and charges, as was at first provided for."

How far these resolutions were carried into effect does not appear. But about eight years afterwards, Benjamin Linge prosecuted John Cooper, agent of the Iron works, for the damage he had sustained from the water of the dam. And the people employed there being many of them corrupt foreigners and strangers, were so immoral and vicious as to require the frequent interposition of the civil authority.

"The General Court, therefore, ordered that complaint should be made to Capt. Clark about the disorderly persons that came to the Iron works. And also ordered that the master, clerk, or overseer, and other officers, shall not admit any without a certificate from persons of known reputation, under the penalty of 40 shillings for every offence; and if any come or tarry there without such recommendation and permission, shall be liable to the penalty of forty shillings."

And as a further check to these increasing evils, Matthew Moulthrop, sen. was appointed conservator of the morals of the people about the Iron works.

Of so much consequence was this establishment, that after the union of New-Haven with Connecticut, a special was made to grant the people employed in the work, to free them from taxes for 7 years, as appears from the following order.

"13th May, 1669, Upon the petition of Mr. William Andrews, on behalf of Capt. Thomas Clark, master of the Iron works of New-Haven, for encouragement of the said worke, for the supply of the country with good Iron, and well wrought according to art, this Court do confirm a grant formerly made by New-Haven: That the said persons and estates constantly or only employed in the said work, shall be and are hereby exempt from paying country rates for 7 years next ensuing."—[*Conn. Col. Rec.*]

At this period, and until the business was relinquished, Thomas Clark of Boston appears to have been the principal owner. Business was carried on here both from New-Haven and Branford. It continued until about 1679 or '80. Why the business was relinquished cannot now be satisfactorily ascertained. The furnace was supplied with bog ore from North-Haven. It was chiefly carted, but sometimes brought from bog-mine wharf by water, round to the point below the furnace; and from that circumstance the point to this day is called *Bogmine.* There was a great mortality in the village in the year 1679, when Ralph Russell, and some other principal workmen died, which may have obstructed the operation; and, probably, the expense was too great to realize sufficient profits. It is a tradition in the Russell family, that the death of the principal workmen produced this change.

Jasper Crane and John Cooper were overseers and agents. Richard Post was founder; and John Russell was potter in the furnace.

On the 19th August, 1680, Thomas Clark sold to sergt. John Potter, " All that farm lying and being within the township of New-Haven, and near and adjoining to a brook called by the name of Stoney brook, which Thomas Clarke bought of Nathaniel Micklethwaite of the city of London, merchant, containeth by estimation 300 acres of upland, be it more or less, and 3 score acres of meadow, be it more or less, adjoining thereto; excepting always all the uplands that hath been formerly sold from the said farme or Iron workes, reserving only all the Iron worke plates of Iron, and the moveables to himself, that are upon the premises." John Potter was to pay £40 per annum for 21 years, in wheat, pork and peas."

The farm soon passed into the hands of William Rosewell, whose only daughter and heir married Gurdon Saltonstall, afterwards the Governor of Connecticut.

Sergt. John Potter did not resume the Iron business, as was contemplated when he bought the farm. But in the year 1692, he and Thomas Pinion petitioned New-Haven for liberty to build a Bloomary on the *first spring*, or brook towards Foxon. In April, " some of the townsmen having viewed the brooke that runs into Stoney river at the place, or thereabouts, which was moved for by John Potter, formerly, to set up a Bloomary; the town by vote approved of his design of a Bloomary; and for his encouragement allow him the use of said brooke, and 20 acres of land, not exceeding 30, near the *first spring*, the west side of Stoney river; and grant him the liberty of what Iron mines there are within the town bounds, and the use of what wood he needs in the commons for the work, if it proves effectual. And the aforesaid land is to be laid out and bounded to him.

by the surveyor, and one or two of the Townsmen. Always
preserving the necessary highways if there be any."—[*N.
H. Rec.*]

This Bloomary was established, but I cannot find how
long it was in operation.

The site of the Furnace was sequestered for a grist-mill,
as appears from the following curious document on East-Haven records:

"Articles of agreement made between the Inhabitants of
Stoney River of the one party, and Samuel Heminway of
the other party, 2 July, 1681, is as followeth, concerning
setting up of a Grist-Mill at the Furnace Dam.

1. "The said Village doth for his encouragement give the
Furnace Dam, with the use of the water damed therewith,
and do promise to defend the said Heminway in the possession thereof, (so far as in their power) without let or moles-
tation from any, either New-Haven or Branford, or any other; reserving liberty for John Potter to have a convenient
place for water from the same pond, to set up and manage a
Bloomary Furnace of Iron, if the said Potter shall at any
time, hereafter, see cause to enter upon such a design."

2. "The said Village doth give to the said Heminway the
land that lies next to his house between Stoney River and
the Farme, to the quantity of an acre or two, if it may be
spared from the highways, as they shall see good to set out
to him, and 16 or 17 acres of land elsewhere, that may be
convenient for the said Heminway.

3. "The said Village do free the said Grist Mill from
paying taxes to the said Village or Town.

4. "The Inhabitants of the said Village do engage to
bring the corn that they would have ground into meal, to the
said Mill.

5. "The said Inhabitants do engage to perform the whole
work of what is necessary for the setting down said Mill,
and to repair it, that the Dam may be secure from breaches
at the setting down said Mill. But the said Heminway is
to secure it at his own charges for the future, when some
extraordinary, or unexpected accident shall happen to it.

6. "The said Inhabitants of the said Village do engage to
assist him to raise the Mill Stones, and to get them to the
said Mill, and to give the said Samuel Heminway liberty to
use what timber and stones may be needful for building and
repairing the said Mill, as shall be most convenient for him
in that business.

" And in consideration of the premises, the said Samuel Heminway doth engage as followeth:

1. " That the said Heminway will, before the next winter, in November next ensuing, set up a sufficient Grist Mill, at the above place, and keep the said mill in good repair, fit to make good and sufficient meal of corn, that is dry and fit for grinding.

2. "That he the said Heminway will set up a house over the Mill sufficient to secure the inhabitants' corn from damage by the neighbours hogs, or other creatures, that might otherwise devour it—within his compass.

3. "That the said Heminway or somebody for him, shall attend at the said Mill, one day in a fortnight, if there be need, to grind for the inhabitants their corn. And shall spend more time, and give attendance on the same, if need be, that is, till he hath ground all that is brought to be ground the said day.

4. " That the said Heminway will take no more toll for the grinding our corn into meal than what the law allows.

5. " That he will either keep this mill himself, or if he shall let it to any other, it shall be to such an one as the Inhabitants of the Village shall approve of.

6. " The said land, the said Village do give to the said Heminway, to be for the use of said Mill, and so continue, except the 16 or 20 acres given him.

"'The first article is thus to be so understood that the said Heminway doth engage to bear his share with the other Inhabitants of the said Village in any damage that may fall by the Dam or Stream, or by any trouble for the same, by New-Haven or Branford or any other. And as for the land about the house, mentioned in this agreement, it be understood, that the said Heminway is to have what can be spared there from highways and across on the other side of the pond.

" The abovesaid articles of agreement concerning the Mill, made between the said Samuel Heminway and the Inhabitants of said Village, 2d July, 1681, is confirmed by Vote to be their doings."—[*E. H. Rec.*]

The grant of 16 or 17 acres, the town of New-Haven refused to ratify.

About 25 years after this transaction, the sons of Samuel Heminway, viz. John and Abraham, obtained a grant of the Mill privilege from Branford, as follows:

" Branford, 23 Augt. 1706.—At a meeting of the Propri-

etors, warned according to law, John and Abraham Heminway, of New-Haven Iron works, desire us to grant them liberty to erect a Dam on the Furnace pond, where it formerly was, and to get stone, and timber and earth to erect the
same, on our side."

1. " We having considered the public benefit such a Mill
may be, doe on the terms following grant the desire of the
said John and Abraham Heminway, viz. that they shall
raise the said Dam no higher than it was formerly, nor no
higher, than shall be allowed by Mr. William Maltbie, Deacon John Rose, Sergt. Nathaniel Foot, of Branford, when
they shall view said Mill place."

2. " John and Abraham Heminway and all who shall after them possess and improve said Mill, shall at all times,
hereafter, grind what corn shall come from this Towne, in
turn, as it shall come to said Mill, not preferring others before them."

3. " The said John and Abraham Heminway, their heirs
and assigns, shall erect and maintayne a sufficient Mill at
said place, at all times, hereafter forever; upon those aforesaid conditions, we grant the request of said John and Abraham Heminway. But if they or any, who shall at any time
hereafter possess said mill, shall refuse or neglect to perform
any or all the abovementioned conditions, then this grant
shall be void and of no effect, that we, or our successors, may
set up a Mill ourselves for the public benefit on this side."

Voted, and passed Test, by Wm. Maltbie, Clerk.—[*Branford Rec.*]

The manner of expression in this document intimates that
the mill had not been erected by their father, as was expected when he obtained the village grant.

The water privilege where the forge stood was disposed
of afterwards. Samuel Heminway applied to the town of
New-Haven for it and obtained the following order :

" April 26th, 1687. Samuel Heminway moved to have
liberty to set a fulling mill where the forge formerly stood.
After much debate the towne granted liberty to the said
Heminway to set up a fulling mill in the forementioned
place, provided that he make no dam that shall make a pond
to raise the water above two feet deep upon Austin's highway. And that he consider beforehand, whether such a
dam, but of such a height as aforesaid, will answer his purpose."

Upon this grant, and one that was made by the village in

1706, John and Abraham Heminway, and John Marsh, jointly, erected a fulling mill in 1709, on the premises.

In 1684 it was contemplated to build a saw-mill on the first spring. That plan was relinquished, and one was built on Claypit brook, below Danforth's swamp, which was abandoned many years ago.

—ഛை—

CHAP. IV.

The General History of the town continued—the half mile obtained—divisions of land—town Charters, &c.

A NEGOCIATION had been carried on with Branford, concerning land that lay within their bounds, that they had not paid for, and that New-Haven had granted to the village. Branford, finally, promised them land. But the execution of that promise was delayed; the village grew impatient and and passed the following order :

" At a formal meeting of the village, 15th Feb. 1681, it was propounded that we might choose men to treat with Branford about the land in their bounds that was given to us and is now in contention. After some debate it was ordered and appointed, that John Potter, Samuel Heminway, John Thompson, Nathaniel Hitchcock, Alling Ball, jun. and Matthew Moulthrop, them or any four of them were empowered to treat that matter with our friends of Branford as to land or line, and finish it."

This vote was predicated on a grant from New-Haven in Dec. 1679 as follows, viz. :—" For the Quinipiack land now within the town of Branford, and was at first bought by us, and never payed for by Branford to us, that the Towne would grant unto them our right, the better to enable them to treat with Branford for enlargement on the purchase money due, with the consideration that New-Haven hath been long out of purse."

The same month that the village passed the before-mentioned vote, Branford acted on the subject thus :

" Whereas there is a difference between the Towne of Branford and the Ironworke farmers (or inhabitants of New-Haven) concerning the propriety of lands in Branford bounds. At a Towne meeting in Branford, Feb. 1681, the Towne have unanimously agreed to leave the case depending to a Committee. And the Towne have made choice of and appointed Mr. William Rosewell, Mr. Edward Barker, Thomas Harrison, William Hoadly, and Eleazer Stent, a Committee for the issue of the case aforesaid, and they do give them full power, in the behalf of the Towne, either by composition with the farmers, (or New-Haven inhabitants) or to manage the said case at General Court, either by themselves, or any other attorney or attorneys, as they see cause, and to be at what charge they cause in the management thereof. They do also desire and appoint the said Committee, to take into their custody whatsoever writings or conveyances, may be had (or copies of them) that concern the Towne.—And do engage to reimburse what charges the committee shall be at in the whole case."

But as an attempt to settle the controversy failed, the Village proceeded to the use of some high-toned language on the subject, which was met by Branford in the annexed resolution:

" Whereas the Ironworke farmers have given us notice that if we do not grant them land, then they will run a line in our bounds. At a Towne meeting in Branford, 8th July, 1681 ; the inhabitants of the Towne did answer and declare by vote that the farmers have no right to do with the running of any line or lines in our bounds, or within our Township, and, therefore, do protest against any such proceeding, as an invasion of our just rights and privileges, and further do forbid them or any of them to enter upon our Towne bounds with any such design, if they do, be it at their peril."

The case was brought before the General Court the next fall, and that body adopted some measures to promote an adjustment of their difficulties.

" At a General Court held at Hartford, 13th Oct. 1681.

" Whereas there is a difference between Branford and the farmers on the East side, about the line between New-Haven and sayd Branford, or New-Haven purchase of the Indians, this Court do request the Deputy Governor, and Mr. Andrew Leete, and Mr. Samuel Eales to take some pains to examine the case, and to endeavour an accommodation between them, and if they cannot attayn an issue, they are to make report how they find it to the next Court, where both parties are to attend for issue, and the sayd Towne of Branford, and the farmers, are to attend to this affayre, when they shall be appointed by the Deputy Governor ; they, viz. the Committee, are also to consider whether there be any obligation that doth lie upon New-Haven, that doth hinder this people from building a Dick at the East side or South-end."—[*Col. Rec.*]

This arrangement of the General Court had a happy effect. The parties came to a settlement of their difficulties, and Branford gave the village a deed, dated 8th May, 1682, for that tract of land called the *half-mile*, in which it was stipulated, that " the line shall run and be as formerly, from the sea to the head of the Furnace pond," &c. as it is described in the bounds already mentioned.

The 9th May, in behalf of the Village, Samuel Heminway, James Denison, John Potter, Matthew Moulthrop, John Thompson, and Nathaniel Hitchcock, gave a quitclaim to Branford, for lands within their bounds. The Committee appointed by the General Court reported their proceedings, which, by a formal vote, were accepted and ratified.

" Hartford, May, 1682. The Gentlemen of New-Haven and Branford had agreed about the purchase of their lands which they were appoynted by the Court to issue ; and Major Treat, William Leete, and Mr. Eales were desired to assist them in, Oct. last."—[*Col. Rec.*]

After the Village had obtained their Village grant from the General Court to become a society, they proceeded to transact local business, separately from the town of New-Haven. They seem to have apprehended that their Parish grant involved some authority for the choice of Village officers, and for the laying out and disposing of land within their Parish bounds. This course brought upon themselves and New-Haven a long scene of confusion and trouble, and not a little expense.

17th Jan. 1683. The Village granted to Deacon John Chedsey 3 acres on the north side of the green, for a home lot. And also one acre to Joseph, son of Ralph Russel, next to Stoney river, which he soon sold to John Potter, and John Potter the same day conveyed it to Isaac Bradley, on which he built his house. They also granted home lots to Thomas Pinion, John Luddington, James Taylor, and William Roberts, between the road that goes to Alling Ball's farm and the highway that leads to the fresh meadows. And it was confirmed by the town.

" At a meeting of the Village, 19th March, 1683, it is agreed by vote that in laying out the third division we will follow the method of New-Haven, viz. 20 acres for each hundred pounds in the list, and 4 acres to each child, and 20 acres to each family, tho' their heads and estates do not amount thereunto." And under date 26th Nov. 1683, " It

4

was agreed to lay out the one half of said third division upon
Stoney river, and the other half where it will be most con-
venient; and begin the lots as to their order upon the land
next to the five men's land at Foxon. John Potter and
Matthew Moulthrop were appointed to lay out the lots, and
John Thompson and Nathaniel Hitchcock were sizers."

After the arrangements for the third division were made,
they voted to lay out the third division, "by the list of the
estates we give in to the payment of the minister this present year, with the addition of our persons' heads, not there
given in, because not rated, but here to be added, as in the
following list alphabetically arranged."

Matthew Moulthrop and Eliakim Hitchcock, according
to appointment, made out the list as follows :

Joseph Abbot	Polls 1	List £16	10	0	*20 acres.
John Austin	6	110	0	0	46
Alling Ball	3	26	0	0	20
Alling Ball, jun.	4	56	0	0	$27\frac{1}{4}$
Thomas Carnes	2	7	0	0	20
John Chedsey	10	100	0	0†	
Robert Dawson	6	16	0	0	*30
James Denison	8	150	0	0	62
Joseph Dickerson	1	3	0	0	20
Samuel Heminway	10	147	0	0	$69\frac{1}{2}$
Eliakim Hitchcock	8	88	0	0	$49\frac{3}{4}$
Nathaniel Hitchcock	6	112	0	0	$46\frac{1}{2}$
John Luddington	1				4
William Luddington	3	52	10	0	$24\frac{1}{2}$
Widow Ann Mew	1	42	10	0	20
Matthew Moulthrop	8	150	0	0	62
George Pardee	5	66	0	0	$35\frac{1}{4}$
Thomas Pinion	6	67	0	0	*30
John Potter	11	178	0	0	$73\frac{5}{4}$
William Roberts	4	11	0	0	*30
John Rose	5	71	10	0	$34\frac{1}{4}$
Thomas Smith	8	101	0	0	$52\frac{1}{4}$
James Tailor	1	3	0	0	*20
John Thompson	6	147	0	0	$53\frac{3}{4}$
Edmond Tooley	1				4
Edward Vickars	2	23	0	0	22
Polls	127	£1694	00	0	
A Minister's lot					50
A lot for the first Minister					50—$976\frac{1}{2}$

† John Chedsey drew, but his estate not being all listed, the quantity of land is not mentioned.   * These five had their land at Foxon.

With this small population, and with this small property, they supported a minister of the Gospel about four years.

"On the 26th Nov. 1682, the Village appointed M. Moulthrop, John Potter, John Thompson and Samuel Heminway, to revise the Village Records, and to select such as were useful to be preserved, and draw them up according to law. At a meeting 22d Jan. following, the Committee presented and read what they judged needful to stand upon record, which was approved and accepted by Vote, and the whole to be entered on their Ledger." Samuel Heminway was appointed Clerk. He was a neat, handsome penman.

Their public expenses, and some other embarrassments, were so great, that some began to cherish the idea that they should not be able to proceed, and especially as their crops had recently failed. They therefore took a vote, 29th March, 1684, " whether they should go forward in building up the Village." Nineteen men being present, they all voted to proceed.

At this meeting John Thompson, Matthew Moulthrop, and Samuel Heminway were chosen selectmen. And in August, John Thompson and Samuel Heminway were chosen collectors of rates, and George Pardee constable. And they continued to choose Village officers, and presented them to New-Haven for confirmation.

The proceedings of the Village in dividing land, gave offence to New-Haven, and they appointed a Committee to confer with the Village on the subject. The Village also appointed a Committee, to go to New-Haven and inform their Committee of all their proceedings.

But in 1685, they appear to have relinquished their Village privileges, and returned to their former connection with New-Haven; for about this time they requested New-Haven to furnish them with a further division of land, which was referred to a special Committee, whose report was accepted and recorded, as follows:

" In answer to the inhabitants of New-Haven, the Committee appointed by the Towne to consider their proposals about the third division, order as followeth:

" 1. That in laying out the remainder of the third division, not yet taken up by the said inhabitants, being approved planters, it be laid out to them in quantity according to the list of estates in 1679, by appointed sizers, and Enos Tamadge for the Towne.

" 2. That the grants which have been made by the late Village Company to any of them, having a right to the third division as aforesaid, be accounted as part of such remainder of third division, except eight acres granted and laid out as appendix to the Mill.

" 3. That they lay out the said remainder upon and out of the half mile of lands, or addition from Branford, as far as their granted bounds, provided that they lay it out as to others of the Towne, viz. one half mile in depth, and lying together, and not in particular tracts or parcels; and if there be not enough found there, then to make up their quantity elsewhere within the bounds formerly granted, provided, that the Towne commons, as formerly appointed, be stated by the now appointed sizers and surveyors, who are to view and lay out the said proportions of third division, and the remainder for commons.

" 4. As to the grants of land made to sundry particular persons by the East side inhabitants, we see not cause at present to confirm; but before we so do, we expect that now, having laid down the Village designs, and being returned to their former station for power and privilege with ourselves as one plantation, that they plainly declare themselves in so doing without reservation, not to go off from us when they please, or judge themselves in a capacity for it without the Towne's approbation in that case.

" 5. We appoint Mr. Bishop, Capt. Mansfield, and Thomas Kimberly sizers, and Enos Tamadge surveyor: and at the charge of the East side inhabitants: and we desire their answer to these premises in writing under their hands."

[*N. H. Rec.*]

I cannot find any reply to these resolutions; but from this time their affairs seem to have proceeded without any particular controversy, until 1703, when the Village moved to resume their Village grant of 1680. The Village bore their proportion of town and colony charges, and endured great hardships and dangers, in attending public worship at New-Haven. After the termination of King Philip's war, the Indians were frequently in a state of commotion. Some powerful tribes that were under the influence of the French in Canada, frequently assumed a hostile attitude. In 1689, the town prepared a flying army, which stood ready to march at a moment's warning. A patrol of four horsemen was continually scouring the woods. And all the militia were obliged to carry their arms with them to public worship, pre-

pared for battle. The Indians near the Village were sometimes employed as scouting parties, and in other respects as
useful auxiliaries. The following anecdote received from
the oldest man now living in the town, and received by him
from his father, may be worth preserving:

A friendly Indian warrior was requested to act as centi-
nel in the Gap, north of Mullen hill. He consented, and for
this purpose borrowed Mr. Heminway's gun, and was assu-
red it was well loaded. Without examination, he took the
gun and repaired to his post. He soon perceived two enemy
Indians descending into the valley from the Pond Rock,
and advancing toward the Gap. They passed him, and
when he had them in range, intending to kill both at one shot,
he attempted to fire, but his gun only flashed, for it was not
charged. The spies, without observing it, passed on across
the fresh meadows, and mingled with the friendly Indians
about Grave hill. The disappointed warrior was enraged,
and threatened to kill Mr. H. for deceiving him in order
that *he* might be killed. Mr. H. was innocent of the charge:
for he had charged the gun himself, but some other person
had discharged it without his knowledge, and priming, left
it in the usual place in that condition. With the discovery
of this fact, the warrior was finally pacified. But in a day
or two, one of these spies was found dead on the Indian land,
—and supposed to have been killed by the enraged warrior.

The people on the East side were exposed to many dangers and inconveniences in attending public worship at New-
Haven. The year 1690 was sickly, and they lost a number of their useful men. Under all these circumstances, it
was natural for them to desire relief.

After they returned to their former connection with New-
Haven Society, Deacon John Chedsey, John Potter and John
Austin, obtained liberty of New-Haven, to buy one quarter
of an acre of the Indians at the Ferry place, to build housing
for their horses, when they went to New-Haven. They obtained a deed for the land, 4th March, 1686, which was signed by Narranshanott, George Sagamore, Maug, and Kehow.
They paid six shillings for it. And it was afterwards called
Stable point.

Nothing further appears on record of a special nature, respecting the Village, until the close of the year 1703. The
following extracts from the Village records, will show the
course of their affairs at that period.

"At a Village Meeting, 23d Decr. 1703. The inhabi

4 *

tants voted that they would take up their Village grant; and to that end chose Capt. Alling Ball, Lieut. Samuel Hotchkiss, Samuel Heminway, Sergt. John Potter, William Luddington, Ensign John Russel and George Pardee, for a Committee to manage the concerns of the Village, in order to a settlement according to the General Court's grant. And informed New-Haven of their design."

" In April, 1704, Caleb Chedsey was chosen Moderator, and Ebenezer Chedsey was chosen Clerk."

" 20th Nov. 1704. They voted that all the undivided land within the Village bounds shall be equally divided unto each of the present inhabitants, according to the heads and estates in 1702, when we were in a Village way, according to N. Haven grant, excepting persons that are tenants."

"The Committee appointed to search for land reported that they judged there were yet 1200 acres of undivided land."

" 30th March, 1705, they agreed to lay out a half division of land, according to the list in 1702; and to draw lots who should pitch first, and next, &c.; and none shall pitch on the half mile gained from Branford. George Pardee was chosen to draw lots. Samuel Thompson and Samuel Hotchkiss, jun. were chosen surveyors of the half division."

The following table will show their names, population, and estates in 1702, and the quantity of land divided to each person:

	Polls	List	acres
Joseph Abbot	3	£75 00 00	9 acres.
David Austin	3	74	13½
Joshua Austin	1	59	9¼
Capt. Alling Ball	6	93	21¼
Isaac Bradley	9	62	24
Caleb Chedsey	6	72	19½
Daniel Collins	4	42	12¼
James Denison	6	143	26¼
Robert Dawson	4	53	13¼
Thomas Goodsell	9	128	30¾
Eliakim Hitchcock	9	152	35¼
Nathaniel Hitchcock	2	55	9½
Lieut. Samuel Hitchcock	7	60	20
Joseph Holt		18	2
John Howe	7	50	20½
Samuel Heminway	7	104	24½
John Heminway	3	53	11¼
Widow Priscilla Thompson	1	10	3

Samuel Thompson	3	59	$11\frac{1}{4}$
William Luddington	11	54	27
Henry Luddington	4	25	10
John Moulthrop	6	62	$18\frac{1}{4}$
Matthew Moulthrop	6	53	$17\frac{1}{4}$
Samuel Moulthrop	1	34	$5\frac{1}{4}$
Eleazer Morris	8	131	28
Ebenezer Chedsey	7	53	19
Joseph Mallory	7	29	17
Widow Ann Mew	1	6	2
John Potter, sen.	3	77	13
John Potter, jun.	6	60	18
Samuel Potter	1	36	$5\frac{1}{4}$
George Pardee	9	148	32
William Roberts	8	21	18
John Russel	7	55	$19\frac{1}{2}$
Thomas Smith	6	107	22
Thomas Smith, jun.	5	12	10
John Thompson	7	106	24
John Luddington	1		2
Thomas Pinion	4	52	13
Joseph Granniss		48	8
William Bradley	1	18	

Polls 200   £2550 00 00 $835\frac{3}{4}$ acres.

Joseph Tuttle, John Miles, and Daniel Collins were made inhabitants in 1706.

The town of New-Haven was offended with the proceedings of the Village, respecting the laying out of land, and while the Village petition for the renewal of Parish privileges, was pending before the General Assembly, passed some angry resolutions, manifesting their unwillingness to admit the Village to Society privileges, and forbade the people south of Muddy river, and north of the Village line, to pay any longer to the support of the ministry there; but to return to New-Haven.

"April 24, 1705. The Townsmen moved the Towne to consider whether the Towne look on the grant formerly made by New-Haven, doth give them power to take up again a Village on the east side, and whether the right of soil in the bounds of said Village belongs to the inhabitants there. The Towne by vote declare that they look upon the said former grant for a Village on that side to have been some time since, and by sundry applications and matters of record, are super-

ceeded and cancelled, and that those neighbours may not law-
fully resume and manage a Village affairs without a new
grant and allowance orderly made to them ; and that the
right of undivided and common land within the former grant
in no wise is, or ever was, granted to the inhabitants of said
Village, but is, and must remain at the disposal of the Towne
of New-Haven, as much as any other tracts of common land,
lying within the established boundary of New-Haven Towne.
And whereas in said former grant the farmers on that side,
northward of the Village bounds, were allowed to pay to the
Ministry settled in said Village till farther orders. The
Towne likewise doth order that those inhabitants, hencefor-
ward pay to the support of the Ministry in New-Haven platt,
untill that matter shall be otherwise ordered by said Towne.''
                                                    [*N. H. Rec.*]
The right of soil in the undivided land, did, indeed, belong to the town of New-Haven. And the Village had no
right to make a division of common land, except the half-
mile. That belonged to the Village by a deed from Branford, predicated on a special grant of New-Haven to that
effect. New-Haven had no right of soil in the half-mile.
The Village, however, obtained from the General Assembly, a renewal of their Parish grant, which they had received
in 1680. And they proceeded to manage their religious affairs in their own way.
New-Haven attempted to tax the Village as before, which
was resisted by the Village. And on the 24th April, 1707,
" The Village voted that 600 acres on the lower end of the
half-mile should be sold to defend lawsuits against New-Haven, particularly when distressed for taxes. And that the
purchasers should sue at the next County Court, after New-
Haven had strained for taxes." William Luddington, John
Russel, John Moulthrop, Joseph Tuttle, Daniel Collins, and
Jacob Robinson, took the 600 acres on those conditions, and
divided it among themselves. This tract lay between the
Pond, and Bull-swamp bridge. Caleb Parmerly, Caleb
Chedsey, and Isaac Penfield afterwards settled on it.
Some attempts to quiet this controversy were made, but
without effect. In October, of this year, the Village proposed to New-Haven to take their whole right of lands within
the Village bounds, and maintain their own poor. The next
year, according to advice of the General Assembly, a Committee of twelve was appointed by both parties, and the articles of agreement proposed by the General Assembly, partly

consented to, i. e. to take the common lands within their bounds and support their own poor. Some of the Village people, however, protested against any propositions that might infringe their old rights.

While these events were passing, the Village, 13th June, 1707, "Agreed to sequester a piece of land for a burying place, on the south side of the pond, on the Forthill so called, as much as may be spared from highways and watering cattle." Previous to this time they had buried their dead chiefly at New-Haven; but some were buried on the west side of the green.

In September, the village granted to Joshua Austin a piece of land near the springs, for beating the drum for public worship, and other public occasions.

About this time also, there was a difference between the Village and the South-end men, respecting the last division of land; but this was adjusted by admitting them to a full proportion with the rest.

To accomplish their object respecting further privileges the village proceeded thus:

"15th Feb. 1707. Sergt. John Potter and Joseph Tuttle were directed to attend a Town-meeting at New-Haven, and obtain their consent that this Village may be settled a distinct Towne."

The following spring the Village petitioned the General Assembly for that object, which was granted.

"May, 1707. This Assembly, considering the petition of the East Village of New-Haven do see cause to order that they shall be a Village distinct from the Towne of New-Haven, and invested and priviledged with all immunities and priviledges that are proper and necessary for a village, for the upholding of the public worship of God, as also their own civil concerns; and in order thereunto doe grant them libertie of all such officers so chosen as aforesaid and sworn as the law directs, shall be inabled with power and authoritie as fully and effectually for their limits or bounds as is already granted them, as any such officers of any Towne what soever: As also the said Village have libertie to have a school amongst themselves, with the privilege of the fortie shillings upon the £100 estate as every Towne hath by lawe, and also free their own village charge, and maintain their own poor as all towns are obliged to doe, and be fully freed from paying any taxes to the Towne of New-Haven, and shall be called by the name of East-Haven."—[*Col. Rec.*]

This is a very ample charter for all the common privileges, and immunities and duties of a Town. The right of choosing a representative is not, indeed, specified, but is implied in the "immunities and priviledges of a Towne."— They are furnished with the officers and powers of a Town, and the specific duties of a Town are imposed. So the people considered the grant, and acted upon it by immediately choosing town officers, laying rates, and taking the charge of their own poor. And had the Village still co-operated with New-Haven in dividing their common lands, instead of assuming the right of dividing themselves, probably, they would not have been molested. But New-Haven was displeased, as appears from the following document:

"16th Sept. 1707. The Towne taking into their consideration, that, notwithstanding all fair and friendly endeavours have been used by our Committee, for a good agreement between us and our neighbours at the Ironworkes, that they have yet given us causeless trouble and charge, in that they have four times summoned us to answer them before the General Court, and in May last, have moved the said General Court that they may have the privileges of a seperate Towne, and be freed from payment of Towne rates here, and also that they have unjustly entered upon, and granted sundry parcels of land, being our right and property, to the great prejudice of the Towne, and more particularly of some of their neighbours, do, therefore, by their vote declare, that altho' we have ever, hitherto, been willing, not only to grant them liberty, but all due encouragement to be a seperate society for carrying on the worship of God; yet the above proceedings being not only injurious to our right, property, and privilege, secured to us by law, and our patent; but are also accompanied with great disturbance of the peace, and much disorder, which is likely to increase if not prevented, that, therefore, we may in no measure be satisfied therewith; but do order the Townsmen, with good advice in all proper methods of law, to endeavour the prevention thereof, and to secure our interest. Being informed also that the listers cannot obtain the bills of persons and estates from the aforesaid inhabitants of the Ironworkes, who refuse to deliver the same, on pretence that Towne privileges were conferred upon them seperately by the General Court, in May last, that, therefore, our said listers are not capable to perfect their list, and to give the sum total thereof, according to an act of the General Assembly, in October last past, the Towne considering thereof, do declare that the sum total of their list cannot be known, and desire it should not be presented, 'till it be perfected according to law."

In the year 1708, Gurdon Saltonstall was elected Governor. He had married the only child of William Rosewell, and of course came into the possession of the Furnace farm, on which he fixed his residence. It is a common tradition among the aged people of this town, that he constantly opposed their town privileges; and being a man of great influence, he had abundant opportunity to injure them. The most ancient man of this town, of excellent memory and judgment, and who was once conversant with the people of that generation, related to me the following anecdote, which will show the spirit of the times relative to East Haven affairs.

The people of the Village kept large flocks of geese; many of which found their way to the Furnace pond, and frequently passed over to the Governor's farm. The Governor being vexed with this invasion of *his rights*, proclaimed a defensive war, attacked and routed the feathered army, making a great slaughter among them. The owners of the geese thought that this was a "*cruel and unnecessary war*," and were, in turn, greatly offended. And such was the effect upon the minds of the inhabitants generally, that at the next election for Governor, not a single vote from East Haven appeared for Saltonstall. After this discovery, the singular acts were passed by the General Assembly which destroyed their Charter.

Whether these representations respecting the hostility and influence of the Governor be correct, or not, it is certain that a most singular legislative legerdemain followed; and which, whenever adopted, is sufficient to ruin any charter, or fritter down any law, into perfect nonsense. It is similar in effect, to that exercise of power by which the Kings of England revoked charters, and disannulled laws, and rendered every privilege and all property totally insecure.

The controversy continued. And the General Assembly undertook to explain the act containing the town charter of East-Haven.

"New-Haven, Oct. 1710. This Assembly taking into consideration an Act passed in the General Court held at Hartford, 8th May 1707, granting several privileges to the Village called (in the said Act) East-Haven, do declare up on the same, that there is nothing contained in the said Act that concerns property of lands, or that excludes the said Village from being within the Township of New-Haven; nor that intends to give the said Village the liberty of choosing deputies distinct from the Town of New-Haven."

[*Col. Rec.*]

"5th Feb. 1711. Caleb Chedsey, Sergt. John Potter, John Howe, Samuel Russel, Ab. Heminway, and Samuel Thompson, were chosen to goe to New-Haven and discourse with the Committee there, about the differences they speak of between them and us, and to make return to the Village, and not to conclude of any thing respecting the aforesaid matters, without the approbation of the Village."

Nothing, however, was accomplished by this attempt at explanation. The Commentary of the General Assembly did not even diminish the magnitude of the controversy. East-Haven pursued their own course, and New-Haven threatened and prosecuted the people for their taxes.

In 1716, East-Haven again cited New-Haven before the General Assembly, in hope that they should be able to maintain their town privileges on the charter of 1707. But contrary to their expectations, this application only brought forth a commentary on the commentary last mentioned.

"New-Haven, Oct. 1716. Upon consideration of the petition of the inhabitants at the Village of East-Haven, this Assembly find upon examination that the last act of this Assembly, dated Oct. 1710, determines them to have no other powers than those that are common to other parishes, and, therefore, are of opinion that the law does not put the care of the poor into their hands, but into the Town of New-Haven."—[*Col. Rec.*]

Ρ In December of the same year, New-Haven "Voted to clear the inhabitants of East-Haven Village of all taxes to the Ministry or School, so long as they support the same according to the laws of this Colony." And appointed a Committee to settle with them about civil matters; and if they could not settle, they were determined to prosecute.

In January, 1708, the Village found themselves in debt to their Minister and meeting-house, and in order to cancel those debts, they voted to sell the half-mile. "The division to begin near Mr. Pierpont's and so come down. The land to be laid out in two tiers of lots, with a six rod road thro' the middle; and the land was valued at one shilling and eight pence per acre. And proportioned at

the rate of 5 acres to the £100 estate, and one acre to the
poll. The land was apportioned as follows, and the money
was paid to Caleb Chedsey, Treasurer."

Joseph Abbot,	9 acres.	Mat. Moulthrop,	17 acres.
David Austin,	13 ½	Samuel Moulthrop,	5
Joshua Austin,	8	Ebenezer Chedsey,	19 ¼
Capt. Alling Ball,	21 ¼	Joseph Mallory,	17
Isaac Bradley,	24	John Potter,	29
Caleb Chedsey,	19 ½	George Pardee,	32
Daniel Collins,	15	William Roberts,	18
Robert Dawson,	13	John Russel,	19
Thomas Goodsell,	30	Wid. Mary Potter,	2
Samuel Hotchkiss,	18	Samuel Russel,	15
Joseph Holt,	2	Thomas Smith,	14
John Howe,	20	John Thompson,	24
John Heminway,	23	Thomas Pinion,	13
Ab'm Heminway,	12	Joseph Grannis,	8
Wid. P. Thompson,	3	William Bradley,	2
Samuel Thompson,	16 ⅓	Widow Hotchkiss,	1
Wm. Luddington,	27		
Henry Luddington,	10		538 ½ acres.
Serg't J. Moulthrop,	18		

They also granted lots of land in other parts of the village
upon the petition of individuals.

" The Selectmen were requested to get a man to beat the
drum on the Sabbath, and for other meetings of the village,
as reasonably as they could." This was also the practice in
some of the other villages, for many years.

" At a village meeting 15th Feb. 1709, agreed to sell all
the undivided lands on the pond Rock to the upper end.
Thence South of a line from the south corner of Robert Dawson's home lot, a strait line to the northeast corner of Davenport's farme, except the parsonage lands, 30 acres near
the Cove, 12 near John Luddington's home lot, 12 under
the Indian grave hill: by the road leading to Southend 16.
—30 acres more under the Indian hill: and a 100 rods in
breadth from the path that leads to Capt. Alling Ball's.
The rest to be sequestered for building the minister's
house."

" 25th Feb. 1709. Another half division of land was made
at the rate of five acres on the £100 estate and one acre on
the Poll." Eliphalet Pardee drew the lots.

Name	Polls	£ s. d.	acres
Joseph Holt,	Polls 4	£46 10 00	$6\frac{1}{2}$ acres
Joshua Austin,	1	63 10 00	$4\frac{1}{2}$
Samuel Moulthrop,	4	50 00 00	$6\frac{1}{3}$
Thomas Goodsell,	10	157 00 00	18
Ebenezer Chedsey,	8	152 00 00	11
Eliphalet Pardee,	3	60 00 00	6
Joseph Abbot,	4	39 00 00	6
John Auger,	1	21 00 00	$2\frac{1}{4}$
Caleb Chedsey,	5	69 00 00	$8\frac{1}{2}$
John Potter,	7	64 10 00	$10\frac{1}{2}$
Robert Dawson,	2	22 10 00	$3\frac{1}{2}$
John Howe,	8	55 00 00	11
Abraham Heminway,	3	81 10 00	$7\frac{1}{4}$
John Heminway,	6	61 10 00	$9\frac{1}{4}$
Thomas Roberts,	1	22 00 00	$2\frac{1}{4}$
Samuel Hotchkiss,	2	39 00 00	4
Thomas Pinion,	2	68 00 00	$5\frac{1}{2}$
Joseph Tuttle,	8	46 10 00	$10\frac{1}{2}$
William Luddington,	8	70 00 00	$11\frac{1}{2}$
John Miles,	1	23 00 00	$2\frac{1}{4}$
John Russel,	9	66 00 00	$12\frac{1}{2}$
Thomas Smith,	7	46 10 00	$9\frac{1}{2}$
Matthew Moulthrop,	8	52 00 00	11
Daniel Collins,	6	37 10 00	8
Henry Luddington,	8	27 00 00	$9\frac{1}{2}$
Isaac Bradley,	7	67 00 00	$10\frac{1}{3}$
David Austin,	6	70 10 00	$9\frac{1}{2}$
Joseph Grannis,	6	40 10 00	8
Alling Ball,	6	95 00 00	11
John Thompson,	9	122 00 00	$11\frac{1}{4}$
Joseph Mallory,	8	30 10 00	$9\frac{1}{2}$
George Pardee,	9	130 00 00	$15\frac{1}{2}$
William Roberts,	7	30 10 00	9
Samuel Bradley,	1	20 00 00	$2\frac{1}{2}$
Samuel Russel,	5	87 10 00	$9\frac{1}{2}$
John Dawson,	2	28 00 00	$3\frac{1}{2}$
Jacob Robinson,	1	18 00 00	5
William Bradley,	1	20 00 00	2
John Moulthrop,	8	71 00 00	$10\frac{3}{4}$
Thomas Dawson,	1	25 00 00	$2\frac{1}{4}$
Samuel Thompson,	5	92 10 00	10
Mary Potter,	1	7 10 00	$1\frac{1}{2}$
James Denison,	1	100 00 00	6

Polls,   210   £2497 00 00 $328\frac{1}{2}$

The Southend men are not in this list.

In December 1713, the village laid a rate for the poor, of 1¼d. At that period wheat sold at 5s6. rye at 3s6. corn 2s2. as good as money.

In 1720, wheat sold at 5s. rye 3s. corn 2s. per bushel, and wood 2s6. per load.

The Mechanics were at this time, Joseph Tuttle, John Auger and Ebenezer Chedsey, shoemakers ; Samuel Bradley, lock-smith ; Daniel Bradley, black-smith ; Joseph Abbot and Jacob Robinson, weavers ; John Miles, clothier; Thomas Robinson and William Bradley, tailors ; Thomas Smith, cooper ; Isaac Bradley and Henry Luddington, carpenters.

" The Village meetings to be warned by beating a drum on Monday, from Chedsey's hill to Goodsell's hill, and also to call at some places to give notice of the meeting, to be given the same day morning before the meeting is held."

" 28th March 1715, Voted to lay lots from Capt. John Russel's, at the end of the hill and across it, sixty rods in length, up to Piper's brook, as broken land."—Some of the way the lots were forty rods long,—and they also divided other broken lands. In the same month they drew lots for the Pond Rock, and the other two half divisions, beginning at the end of the Rock. Forty-eight men drew their lots. They were the same as in the preceding list—

" And as the Southend men have not had their share, voted to make up the deficiency in the same manner, as for themselves." The men were Nathaniel Hitchcock, Eleazar Morris, John Denison, Samuel Smith, Thomas Hitchcock. This was the last division of land, it being now all taken up. The Indian Reservation was sold about the year 1730.

In March, 1717, Matthew Moulthrop, the third, sold his homestead to Thomas Shepard of Branford, and removed on to the hill west of Foxon.—Samuel Thompson, jun. built north of him. Next were Benjamin and Ashur Moulthrop. Israel Moulthrop bought the house which Eleazar Morris had begun to build just before his death—Henry Luddington was west of him. Robert Dawson, Samuel Smith and his son Isaac, Russel Grannis, —— Bracket and Edward Russel, north of Samuel Thompson. Isaac and Samuel Chedsey were south of M. Moulthrop.

From Mullen Hill on the Foxon Road, were James Denison, John Howel, Joseph Holt, succeeded by Timothy Andrews, then Isaac Holt, Samuel Holt, succeeded by his son Joseph. Eliphalet and William Luddington, succeeded by

Isaac Luddington—then Ebenezer Bradley, succeeded by Ezra Fields—then John Smith, Stephen Pardee, succeeded by Edward Russel, jun.—Isaac Goodsel—Daniel Holt and his son Dan—Jesse Denison, succeeded by John Denison and Joseph Grannis—then Thomas Grannis, —— Potter, Joseph, jun. and Isaac Grannis, Caleb Chedsey, jun. Samuel Russel, jun. Thomas Dawson, Israel Potter, Nathaniel Jocelin, Caleb Chedsey and his son Isaac—Isaac Penfield on the hill. Caleb Parmerly where the late Deacon S. Smith lived—and Joel Tuttle, succeeded by his son Christopher.

On the road west of Mullen Hill, were Samuel Hotch-kiss, succeeded by Dan Bradley—then Isaac Bradley, John Chedsey, John Russel, and the Davenport house.

West of Foxon road were Nathaniel Luddington, Jesse Luddington, Stephen Pardee, jun. and Levi Bradley.

On the Post road near Stoney River, were Daniel Bradley and his sons Stephen, Timothy and Jacob—Ebenezer Chedsey bought Isaac Bradley's house north of D. Bradley --Daniel Hitchcock succeeded John Potter--Abraham Ched-sey on Chedsey hill—Jared and Samuel east side of the Green, the latter succeeded by Zebulon Bradley—Gideon Potter on the west side of the Green—next south were John and Samuel Heminway, Stephen Thompson—Moses Thomp-son, succeeded by Mr. Street—Abraham Heminway, Jo-seph Potter—then James Way, David Potter and —— Mal-lory.—Samuel Bradley was opposite the Austin place, suc-ceeded by Simeon his son—then Caleb Bradley, Thomas Barns, Samuel Forbes, jun. and Nathaniel Barnes on the hill, and Daniel Auger opposite. Then Samuel Goodsell, succeeded by his son Jacob—then Daniel Collins and Abel his son—Thomas Robinson, jun.—On the back road north of Tuttle's bridge were Benjamin Robinson and Dan Goodsel and his son Edward. In Dragon woods were Job Smith, William Bradley, Henry O'Neal and James A. Broten.

Daniel Morris was on the Indian land, succeeded by Jo-seph Tuttle. Near the Bridge were Noah Tuttle, his son Timothy, Elam Luddington, Jehiel Forbes and the Hughes family.

The Rowe, Brown, Pardee, Woodward, Morris, and the Smith and Thompson families at southend, remain on the land of their ancestors. Abel and James Smith, Caleb and Nathaniel Hitchcock, Joseph Moulthrop, and some of the Robinson family, settled on the half-mile, now chiefly within the bounds of North-Haven. Jacob Robinson and son John, lived north of Foxon.

After the year 1716, for a long time, very little appears on record, concerning the civil concerns of the Village. The General Assembly having explained away all their privileges, rights and duties as a Town, they had nothing to do, nor any thing to enjoy, but under the jurisdiction of New-Haven, excepting the duties and privileges of a mere Parish.

Being silenced by the terror of law-suits and "the powers that be," they yielded; until another generation arose that had not known a Saltonstal, and which began to think again that the act of 1707, really meant something according to the natural import of words. And accordingly, on the 18th December, 1752, "Voted, That we will take up the privileges that the General Assembly and the Town of New-Haven have formerly granted for the time being; and in order to do this, do send our Memorial forthwith to the Town meeting now sitting."

"6th December, 1753. We the subscribers, Selectmen of the Town of East-Haven, hereby beg leave to inform the inhabitants of the Town of New-Haven in Town meeting assembled, that whereas the General Assembly of the Colony of Connecticut, at their session at Hartford, on the 8th May, 1707, on the humble petition of the then East Village of New-Haven, were pleased to order, "That the said Village, should be a Village distinct from the Town of New-Haven, and invested and priviledged with all immunities and privileges, proper and necessary for a Village, for the upholding the worship of God, as also their own civil concerns;" and did also grant them liberty of all such officers as are proper and necessary for a Town, to be chosen by themselves, in order and form as all Towns by law, for each or any Town, and that all such officers so chosen as aforesaid and sworn as the law directs, should be enabled with power and authority as fully and effectually for their limits and bounds as any such officers of any Town whatsoever, and should be freed from paying any taxes to the Town of New-Haven, and be called by the name of East-Haven. And whereas the Town of East-Haven, in pursuance of the said grant of the said General Assembly, did on the 6th December inst. in Town meeting regularly convened, proceed to choose the officers by law directed in Town meetings to be chosen, and to make such rules, orders and regulations, as were necessary for the welfare and due regulation of said

5*

Town, and are determined hereafter to continue to take
benefit of the said grant of the General Assembly, and therein conduct according to the laws of this Colony, respecting
the ˉregulation and due Government of Towns, we have
thought it our duty, and accordingly do in behalf of said
Town of East-Haven and by direction from them, hereby
notify the Town of New-Haven of such their resolutions
and conduct, in order that the said Town of New-Haven
may hereafter exempt themselves from any further care or
trouble respecting the affairs of the said Town of East-
Haven, the regulation thereof, or the appointment of officers therein, whereof we doubt not your favourable acceptance and approbation, and are with gratitude for your past
assistance, kindness and care :—
Gentlemen, your humble servants.

ROSEWELL WOODWARD,⎫
ISAAC BLAKESLEE,   ⎬ *Selectmen of the*
SAMUEL HEMINWAY,   ⎪   *Town of*
DANIEL HOLT,   ⎭   *East Haven.*

East-Haven, 6th Dec. 1753."
At the next meeting, 13th December, " Voted to defray
the expenses of the Selectmen in defending us from the
Town of New-Haven."
These proceedings, however, brought upon them, once
more, the broad hand of the General Assembly, as follows:
" *New-Haven, October,* 1754. Whereas by the law of
this Colony respecting the office and duty of listers, pro-
vision is made for the sum total of the list of the several
Towns in this Colony, to be sent in to this Assembly, and
whereas the Village, or Society of East-Haven, in the Town
of New-Haven, have sent the sum total of their list into
this Assembly, distinct from the Town of New-Haven,
which this Assembly judging to be contrary to the law aforesaid, for that Towns only are to send in their list, do reject
the same, it not being the list of any Town—But forasmuch
as it appears to this Assembly, that the said Society in
sending said list, acted through mistake and misapprehen-
sion, do thereupon order, that the sum total of the list sent
in by said Society, be added to the sum total of the list of
the Town of New-Haven, to make one sum, and that the
same be entered on the records as the list of said Town accordingly. It is also further ordered that the listers of
New-Haven inspect the list of the inhabitants of said Society, with the rest of the inhabitants of said Town, according to law. And the several persons who received and

made up the list of said Society, as listers, are hereby ordered to deliver the several lists of the inhabitants of said
Society to the listers of the Town of New Haven, that they
may make up one general list, to be delivered to the Town
Clerk as the law directs ; and the Secretary of the Colony
is directed to deliver two copies of this act to the Sheriff of
New-Haven County, one by him to be delivered to the listers of said Town of New-Haven, and the other to the person or persons who received and made up the lists of said
Society, for their direction respectively in the premises."—
[*Col. Records.*]

Thus another fatal blow was given to the act of 1707.
The Village, however, was very obstinate, and was determined not to yield. But in order to remove and prevent
any further objections to what they apprehended to be their
rights, on the 3d February, 1755, " They appointed a
Committee to apply to the General Court for Town privileges according to a former Grant, and to refuse to pay the
two last rates of the Town ; and to make an agreement with
New-Haven about it, if they could."

But this plan failed. They then resumed their old
ground, and on the 16th June, " Voted, that we will proceed
further with respect to our privileges granted formerly to
us by the General Assembly, and will try it in the common
law with the Town of New-Haven, if they strain for our
Town rates." And a Committee was appointed to manage
this business.

They persisted in choosing officers annually, and yet appear to have acted with New-Haven in Town business.
Nothing more appears on record respecting this controversy, until May, 1780, when the Village " Voted to apply to
the General Assembly, to ratify and confirm our Town
privileges, granted to this Village in 1707, and that a Committee go to New-Haven, and let them know that we are
determined to act in defence of said privileges."

In December, 1781, This business was again introduced,
and it was " Voted that a Committee be appointed to go to
New-Haven to the next Town meeting, to petition them to
give their assent and approbation to our taking up our Village grant of 1707, and to act upon the same."

" January 1, 1782. Voted, That Levi Pardee go round
to the people, to know whether they are willing to be a
Town, or not."

" 3d January, Voted, That we will petition the General Assembly, that they make us a distinct Town from New-Haven." In the prosecution of this object they persevered. And at length, after about 80 years of labour and controversy, obtained their object. In 1785, New-Haven consented that they should become a Town. They presented a petition to the General Assembly, and obtained the following grant.

" At a General Assembly holden at Hartford, on the second Tuesday of May, 1785 ; upon the Memorial of the inhabitants of the parish of East-Haven, in the Town of New-Haven, representing to this Assembly the many inconveniences they are subject to by reason of their being connected with, and being a part of the Town of New-Haven, praying that they may be constituted a distinct and separate Town by themselves, as per memorial ;

" Resolved by this Assembly, That the said inhabitants of said parish of East-Haven be, and they are hereby constituted a Town by the name of East-Haven. And the bounds of the said Town of East-Haven, shall be the same as the bounds of the said Parish now are, and the said Town of East-Haven shall be entitled to, and have and enjoy all the rights, privileges, and immunities that the other Towns in this State enjoy ; and shall have liberty to elect and appoint all officers necessary and proper for a Town, to lay taxes and collect them as Towns in this State are allowed by law, and to do and transact all matters necessary and proper for a Town. And the said Town of East-Haven shall be entitled to receive of the said Town of New-Haven, their part and proportion of all the Town Stock of said Town of New-Haven ; and said Town of East-Haven, shall pay their part and proportion of all the debts of said Town of New-Haven already incurred, in proportion to the sum of their list, in the list of the Town of New-Haven, and shall take upon them the charge and support of their part of the Town poor of said Town of New-Haven, in proportion as aforesaid. And the taxes of said Town of New-Haven, already laid, shall and may be collected and applied for the payment of the debts and expences of said Town of New-Haven, already incurred, and the same being paid and discharged, said Town of East-Haven shall be entitled to their part and proportion of the overplus, if any be, to be ascertained as aforesaid. And the said Town of East-Haven shall bear their part and proportion of supporting the bridges and highways within the bounds of the Town of New-Haven and East-Haven, in such part and proportion as shall be judged just and reasonable, by William S. Johnson, Jonathan Sturgis and John Chester, Esq. who are appointed a Committee for that purpose, all the circumstances of the Town being duly considered ; and said Committee shall appoint and set off to said Town of East-Haven their part and proportion of the poor of the said Town of New-Haven, and the stock and debts in proportion to their lists as aforesaid.

"And the said Town of East-Haven shall hold their first Town meeting, at the meeting-house in said East-Haven, on the first Tuesday of July next, at 10 o'clock A. M. when they may choose such Town Officers as by law are required, who shall remain in office until another meeting shall be held in and for said Town, in the month of December next. And said meeting shall have power and authority to transact all matters necessary for a Town, and to adjourn to a future period if necessary, said inhabitants, legal voters, being warned three days before said meeting by Isaac Chedsey, Stephen Smith and Joshua Austin of said Town of East-Haven, or any of them, to meet as aforesaid, and Stephen Smith shall preside at said meeting until a Moderator of said meeting shall be chosen, and shall take and count the votes of said Town for their Moderator ; provided nothing shall be construed to hinder the inhabitants of the Town of New-Haven from catching fish, oysters and clams within the bounds of said Town of East-Haven, under the same restrictions and regulations that the said inhabitants of said East-Haven shall be. Provided also, that the said Town of East-Haven shall have liberty to send one representative to the General Assembly of this State."—[*State and Town Records.*]

The first Town Meeting under this act was held in the Meeting-house on the first Tuesday of July, 1785. The meeting was opened with prayer by the Rev. Mr. Street, and a sermon adapted to the occasion from Psalm cxxii. 3, 7, 8, 9—And the necessary Town Officers were appointed.

Previous to these transactions, New-Haven confirmed the doings of the Village respecting the divisions of land in East-Haven, which had been the subject of so much controversy ; and the people of East-Haven on their part, relinquished their claim to all the common lands in the other

parts of the Town of New-Haven. Thus all their controversies, which had agitated the Town for about eighty years,
were brought to a happy issue.

Rev. John Woodward was admitted an inhabitant of
New-Haven, 1716, and obtained liberty of the Town to
buy of the Indians one acre of land, to accommodate his
house. He bought various pieces of land around him, and
thus became possessed of a convenient farm. In 1738, he
was chosen Moderator of Society meeting. This is his first
appearance on the Village records.

Deodate Davenport came from Stamford, and appears
first on Record, 1729. Samuel Forbes is mentioned, 1728,
and was employed in ship-building, on the point below the
mill. Joseph Bishop appears on record, 1751.

Samuel Heminway was the first Clerk of the Village. Then
Ebenezer Chedsey, from 1702, to his death in 1726. Then
Samuel Hotchkiss one year, and then Gideon Potter until
1757. Then Isaac Holt and Timothy Andrews a short
time. Then Simeon Bradley from 1763 to 1778, excepting
the year '68, when Abraham Heminway served. Joshua
Austin was chosen in 1779—and Josiah Bradley, 1787.

Joseph Potter was appointed Sexton in 1742. The price
for 3 winter months, all above 10 years, eleven shillings;
all under 10, ten shillings,—and the other 9 months,
six shillings. In 1747, Ebenezer Darrow was appointed
Sexton, and had one shilling more than J. Potter had.
Then in 1763, James Way—and in 1765 was succeeded by
Samuel Shepard, and he was succeeded by his son Thomas
Shepard.

A list of the Freemen in East-Haven was made up and
recorded in the year 1754—as follows :

Rev. Jacob Heminway	Samuel Thompson, Jun.
Capt. Thomas Smith	Eliakim Robinson
Joseph Tuttle	Thomas Robinson
Capt. Theophilus Alling	Dan Moulthrop
Capt. Samuel Smith	Ens. Daniel Holt
Capt. Deodate Davenport	Lieut. Isaac Blakeslee
Deacon Joshua Austin	Daniel Granger
Capt. Joseph Tuttle	Caleb Chedsey
Gideon Potter	Isaac Holt
Daniel Finch	Thomas Robinson, Jun.
Eliphalet Luddington	Patterson Smith
Samuel Bradley	Caleb Hitchcock
Isaac Penfield	James Smith

Zabulon Bradley
Samuel Forbes
John Woodward
Rosewell Woodward
John Moulthrop
Lieut. John Russell
Daniel Bradley
Moses Page
Amos Morris
John Shepard
Nathaniel Luddington
Abraham Heminway
Isaac Goodsell
Abraham Chedsey
Samuel Heminway, Esq.
Daniel Hitchcock
Joseph Bishop
John Heminway

Daniel Finch, Jun.
Jonathan Barnes
Stephen Thompson
William Rogers
Nathaniel Barnes
Benjamin Smith
James Denison
Daniel Auger
Abel Smith
Stephen Morris
Isaac Bradley
Daniel Smith
Stephen Bradley
Dan Bradley
John Chedsey
Joel Tuttle
Stephen Hitchcock.

61 Freemen.

In 1782 the General Assembly, by a special act, secured the right of the Ferry at Ferry Point, to the Parish of East-Haven. The water bounds between New-Haven and East-Haven were settled 1789. The line is in the middle of the Quinipiack River, and along the channel of the Harbour to the sea.

The same year the town granted the owners of the salt meadow the privilege of building a dam across the Stoney River at the lower narrows.

It being in contemplation to build a bridge at Dragon Point, a committee was appointed to oppose it; but without effect, for it was built in 1790—1. Samuel Davenport was then appointed to show cause why the people of East-Haven should not pay toll to Dragon Bridge; but after much altercation, the remonstrance came to nothing. In 1792, new roads were laid out to favour the bridge. In 1796, a grant was made by the General Assembly, for a bridge at the new Ferry, to Enos Heminway, Stephen Woodward and others. Thus the Harbour bridge was built.

" 16th Feb. 1797. At a Proprietors' meeting, granted to Enos Heminway, Stephen Woodward and company, of the bridge, the flats, 187 feet in width, from the landing where the lower Ferry hath lately been kept, running westward to the channel, on which a bridge of 27 feet in width is to be built on the centre, and the remainder for the perpetual use of the company for wharves, stores, &c. so long as the said bridge shall be built and be kept in good repair." They then voted to grant all the Flats to the town of East-Haven.

"March 13, 1797—Voted an enlargement of the burying ground. The north line to run straight from the northwest corner of Moses Thompson's house, running westward in a straight line and course, leaving Nehemiah Smith's house 57 feet to the south of said line." Then—" Voted that we do give up to the Town of East-Haven all the propriety right which we now have to the common and undivided lands and highways within said Town."

CHAP. V.

ON ECCLESIASTICAL AFFAIRS.

Society formed ; Church gathered ; Ministers ordained ; Meeting-houses built ; Glebe property laid out and sold.

THE inhabitants on the east side of the Quinipiack, from their first settlement, attended public worship at New-Haven ; but with great inconvenience, labour, and danger. They were obliged to leave home early in the morning, travel through the woods, on unmade roads, and then cross the Ferry, which was often dangerous. During the Indian wars and commotions, the women and children, on the Sabbath, were collected together at one house in the neighbourhood, under the protection of a guard, while some part of the families attended public worship at New-Haven. And for many years, the men were required by law, under the penalty of a fine, to appear at meeting, with their arms, ready for battle. Similar inconveniences attended the transaction of their business at New-Haven. It was natural for them, therefore, to anticipate advantages from being organized as a distinct parish from New-Haven. With zeal they prosecuted this object. In the year 1678, they petitioned New-Haven for their consent to become a distinct village, and for some other privileges. Not succeeding that year, on the 18th Aug. 1679, they renewed their application, which resulted as follows :

" At a town meeting held in New-Haven, 29th Dec. 1679 —and for the village on the East side, those inhabitants gave in their propositions to the Committee, which they desired might be granted, which were—

1. That they might have liberty to get a Minister amongst them for their meeting, and keep the Sabbath in a way as they ought.

2. That boundary might be granted them as high as Muddy River.

3. That they have liberty of admitting inhabitants among them, for their help in the work and maintenance of a Minister.

4. Thåt they may have liberty to purchase some lands of the Indians, near Mr. Gregson's, if the Indians are willing to part with it.

5. That what land of the Quinipiack is within Branford stated bounds, the right of the purchase may be given them.

6. Lastly, that they may be freed from rates to the Towne when they shall have procured a Minister."

This business was referred to a committee, to report at next meeting.

" At a Town Meeting, held in New-Haven, 29th Decr. 1679—the inhabitants of Stoney River, Southend, and some others, on the East side of the River, having formerly made a motion, and for several reasons therein expressed, to have liberty among themselves, to procure a minister to preach the Word and administer ordinances among them, and several other particulars, as in their petition more fully appears; the'Towne at their request appointed a Committee to examine and prepare matters against some other meeting; and after some consideration of the business, did prepare an answer, and made return to the Towne at the aforesaid meeting which is as followeth.

" 1. That they be encouraged and have liberty granted to get a Minister to settle amongst them as soon as it doth appear they are in a capacity to maintaine a Minister and uphold the ordinances of Christ.

" 2. That when they are settled in a village way with Ministry, they have liberty to admit their own inhabitants for the future, but to attend to such cautions and considerations for the regulation of their settlement, as may consist with the interest of religion, and the Congregational way of the Churches, provided for, to be upheld.

" 3. As to the purchase of land of the Indians near Mr. Gregson's farme; New-Haven being bound in covenant to supply the Indians with land for planting when they need,

6

how far liberty to purchase lands of them may consist with
that engagement, unless with due caution, is to be consider·
ed."

[The 4th article has been already quoted—see page 31.]

" 5. For the payment of rates to New-Haven, that they
be freed from it when they are settled in a Village way
with Ministry.

" 6. For Commonage, that the stated Commonage be at
liberty on that side of the River within their limits, for the
use of New-Haven as hitherto, and what shall remain for
commonage within be agreed upon.

" 7. That the inhabitants of New-Haven, that live in the
Towne, and have propriety in land on the Indian side,
whilst they so continue, pay their rates to New-Haven as
hitherto.

" 8. That their bounds shall be the north side of Alling
Ball's farme, by a line from the River as his line runs untill it meets with Branford line, above Foxon's ; and that
the farmers above that line be left at liberty to contribute to
the Ministry with them, and such not to pay to the Ministry at New-Haven, whilst they so do, untill further orders."

After the Towne had heard the considerations of the
Committee in answer to the inhabitants on the East side
respecting the Village ; the Town approved and confirmed it
to be their order by Vote.

Agreeable to this grant, the Village applied to the General Court for a law to locate and incorporate them as a Society. That transaction will appear from the following
documents. So early as May, 1667, they had requested
this privilege of the General Assembly, when they Resolved, " Upon the Motion of the Deputies of New-Haven, this
Court grants the Towne liberty to make a Village on the
East side of the East River, if they see it capable for such a
thing, provided they settle a Village there within four years
from May next."

" A General Court of Election held at Hartford, 13th
May, 1680. In answer to the petition of John Potter,
Samuel Heminway and Eliakim Hitchcock, that they might
have liberty (they having obtayned consent of New-Haven)
to become a Village and to set up a distinct Congregation
there, with liberty to invite and settle an orthodox Minister amongst them.

" This Court considering the great difficulties they have met withall in their passage to attend the publique worship of God hitherto, and upon hopes that they may be capable to set up and mayntaine the publique worship of God in that place, as a particular Society of themselves, doe grant them free liberty, if they do find themselves able, to proceed and carry on the worke in the best way they can, and for their encouragement therein and towards erecting a place for publique worship, this Court will free them from country rates for three yeares; the time to commence when they have a Minister amongst them, and then they are also to be free from the payment of rates to New-Haven, and not before ; and this Court doe desire Mr. Jones, Mr. Bishop and Capt. Nash, to treat with their neighbours of Branford to grant the said Village what enlargement they can upon the account of good neighbourhood, and the necessity of the case, and New-Haven purchase ; and this Court shall be ready to grant them what encouragement they may, as it shall be desired of them for the future ; and it is also ordered that if upon tryall they shall find themselves able to goe thorow such a worke as mayntayning a settled Ministry amongst them, and are destitute of one, they shall return to their first station to New-Haven till they shall be able to goe thorow the worke."—[*Col. Rec.*]

According to this grant the Village immediately proceeded in making arrangements to obtain a preacher.

" 17th January, 1681, They appointed John Thompson and Samuel Heminway to speak with Mr. James Alling to know his mind in reference to his settling with us in the worke of the ministry."

" At the same meeting the Village granted 100 acres of land to the encouragement of the Ministry amongst them. The one half of which they give to the first minister that shall settle with them in that worke. And the other half for the standing use of the Ministry here forever. And that this last fifty acres, given to the Ministry, shall not be given away to any, either by major vote or otherwise."

The Committee applied to Mr. Alling, who served them several months. but contemplating a long journey, he declined their invitation to stay longer with them. The Committee reported this to the Village meeting, and " they then agreed to look out some other meet person, to carry on the worke of the ministry here. They directed their Committee to renew their application to Mr. Alling, and if unsuccessful, then goe to Mr. Harriman, and treat with him, and desire his help in the Ministry amongst us, and further, to give him an invitation to a settlement in the worke of the ministry amongst us. It was also ordered that Matthew Moulthrop, and John Potter doe set out five acres of the land upon the Green, formerly granted, the one half for the Ministry, and one half for the first Minister that shall settle with us, and they are to leave the spring clear, for a watering place for cattle. It is also agreed that the 95 acres to the Ministry, and the minister that shall settle with us, the one half of it shall be laid as near home as may be, and the other half upon Stoney River."

This land was laid out as follows : " Five acres on the South-east corner of the Green, on which Mr. Heminway's house was built. 12 ½ acres beyond the bridge swamp. 31 acres lying at the Solitary Cove—this lot lies between the paths that goe to the Cove Meadow. 12 acres near John Luddington's home lot—16 acres by the road leading to Southend—48 acres under Indian Grave hill. And a 100 rods in breadth from the path that leads from Foxon's to Capt. Alling Ball's—and 30 acres on the half mile when that was divided."

A part of this land was sold to Rev. J. Heminway, to pay up the arrears of his salary. And some of it was sold to defray the expenses incurred for building the first meeting-house. And 50 acres was given to Mr. Heminway as the first minister. In 1739, the parsonage lands were all re-surveyed, and another piece was added, south of Samuel Hotchkiss's farm. " And all the above parcels of land, were by vote, sequestered and set apart to be improved for upholding the Presbyterian Ministry in this Society forever."—And entered on New-Haven records.

Mr. Harriman was employed, and the Village raised by tax £50 for his support—" current money with the merchant." And they gave him a formal call in November, 1683.

" They also voted to proceed immediately to build a house for the minister, and to finish it in a year." This they attempted to accomplish by a subscription, which is a specimen of the public spirit of the Village at that period.

" A Catalogue of the persons, together with the several sums they (this day) promise freely to contribute towards building the minister's house and fencing the home lot, which are as follows :"—

James Denison	£20	00	00
John Thompson,	20	00	00
Samuel Heminway,	20	00	00
Nathaniel Hitchcock,	10	00	00
Thomas Smith,	10	00	00
Eliakim Hitchcock,	6	00	00
George Pardee,	5	00	00
William Luddington,	5	00	00
Thomas Pinion,	2	10	00
James Tailor,	1	10	00
William Roberts,	1	10	00
Robert Dawson,	2	00	00
Isaac Bradley,	1	00	00

£104 10 00

" Matthew Moulthrop will do what he can. John Potter also. Joseph Abbot, 25 rods of rail fence about the home lot."

" The house is to be 36 feet long and two stories high. And to be set on the side of the Green, west of Matthew Moulthrop's." The house, however, was not built at that time, and it is probable that Mr. Harriman did not continue long with them ; as they seem not to have proceeded in their Society plans after 1684 or 5. For in 1686, they are mentioned in a land affair, as having returned to their former connection with New-Haven.—Unhappily, there is a chasm in the Village Records from April, 1685, to 23d December, 1703.

At a meeting held at the last mentioned date, " The Inhabitants voted to take up their Village grant ; and appointed a Committee to manage the concerns of the Village in order to a settlement, according to the General Court grant, and informed New-Haven of their design." They pursued that object, and in September the next year, appointed a Committee to prefer a petition to the General Assembly, to meet in October, at New Haven. A petition was presented and met with success.

" At a General Assembly at Hartford, May 1704. This assembly having considered the petition of Capt. Alling Ball and John Potter, inhabitants on the east side of the East River, in the Township of New Haven, moving, that whereas this Assembly did formerly grant that they should be a distinct society, and have liberty to call and settle a Minister amongst them, when they should find themselves able to

6 *

maintain the ordinances of God in a suitable manner, and that they doe apprehend that they are able so to doe, that, therefore, this Assembly would please to grant them certain privileges, and other matters and things for their encouragement, and enabling them to goe forward with that worke; this Assembly for divers weighty reasons doe see cause to referre the further consideration of their petition to their General Assembly in Oct. next. And if the inhabitants of New-Haven doe not appear, at the said General Assembly, and there make their pleas, then the petition shall be granted, with this restriction, that the propriety of lands shall not be concerned with."

" General Assembly, holden at New-Haven, 11th Oct. 1705, Samuel Heminway, Thomas Goodsell, Alling Ball, John Potter Jun. John Moulthrop, Samuel Thompson, and Abraham Heminway, presenting a petition on the behalf of the inhabitants, or Village on the East side of New-Haven East River, wherein they pray for the reestablishment of a former grant (excepting their freedom from countrie rates for three years, which privelege they have formerly enjoyed) and also empower them from time to time to make rates upon the inhabitants within the bounds of the said Village, as exprest and stated in the grant of New-Haven, Nov. 29, 1679—for the maintenance of their minister and building a meeting house, and to choose collectors, for collecting said rates, and a Constable and Societie Recorder to record the orders of the said Village, respecting the ministrie and meeting house."

[*Col. Rec.*]

While these matters were pending, they were making preparation, and looking about them, for a minister. Jacob, the youngest son of Samuel Heminway, and born in the Village, graduated at the college at Saybrook, under the Presidency of the Rev. Abraham Pierson, 1703, and was then about 20 years of age.—To him the people turned their attention.

"At a meeting of the Village, 20th Nov. 1704, Voted to look out for a minister to carry on the publick worship of God amongst us; and it was voted—

1. To seek to Sir Heminway that he would give them a taste of his gifts in order to settlement in the worke of the ministry. And—

2. Voted to desire John Potter, Sen. Caleb Chedsey, and Ebenezer Chedsey, to treat with Sir Heminway, to get him, if they could, to give them a taste of his gifts in preaching the Word."

At another meeting of the Village, 19th Dec. following—
" They having had some taste of Sir Heminway in preaching the Word, did declare their desire to have him go on in
the worke of the Ministry amongst us, in order to settlement ; and towards his encouragement they engage to allow
him after the rate of £40 by the year in pay. And, Voted
that George Pardee and Caleb Chedsey signify our desires
and propositions to Sir Heminway, and take his answer and
make returne."

The Committee immediately consulted Mr. Heminway,
and reported at the same meeting, " That Sir Heminway
does comply with their motion, God's grace assisting, and
does accept the proposition, and desires some consideration
with respect to wood."

The next month they voted to give him £50 a year. They
continued in this state until the close of the year 1706, when,
at a meeting, the village appointed " William Luddington
and John Potter to treat with Sir Jacob Heminway, to see
whether he will goe on in the worke of the Ministry amongst
us." And the same day reported Mr. Heminway's answer
in writing.

" Gentlemen, Whereas you have given me notice by two
men, that you desire me to carry on the work of the Ministry in order to settlement among you. I do, therefore, hereby give you notice that so far as God shall enable me thereunto, I am heartily ready and willing to gratify these your
desires upon these conditions—1. That you give me £50
yearly, and my wood. 2. That you build me a good convenient dwelling house, within 2 years time, or give me
money sufficient to do the same, one half this year ensuing,
and one half the next. 3. That when it is in your power,
you give me a good and sufficient portion of land.

From my study, 2d Decr. 1706. Yours to serve.

JACOB HEMINWAY."

On the 26th of the same month, the Village met and voted, " We do promise Mr. Heminway, if he will carry on the
work of the Ministry in said Village, to build him a house,
if we can, in two years after this date, and give him £50
pay, and his wood. And in the mean time, if he wants a
house, to hire him one." To accomplish these objects they
laid a tax of four-pence farthing.

In the year 1707, the village built a house for Mr. Heminway, 40 feet long and 20 feet wide, on a five acre lot, on
the south-east corner of the Green. One half acre was al-

lowed to set the house upon, adjoining to Mr. Heminway's
home lot. The wages in working at the house were three
shillings a day for a man, and six for a team.
The terms proposed were adjusted and ratified in
1709. They gave to him the house and lot it stood
on—also twelve acres on the cove road, twelve acres in
the bridge swamp, 30 acres in the half mile, £50 per annum, and sufficient wood, " if he performs the worke
of the Ministry so long as he is able ; or if it be our fault
that he is forced to leave us, it shall be his. But if it be his
fault, or he leaves the place, or is hindered in the worke,
then the property is to return to the Village. And he is to
have the use of the Parsonage land."
The same year, " 3d May, 1709, voted to petition the
General Assembly that we may embody into a Church
state."
" May 12, this Assembly do grant their consent and full
liberty to the inhabitants of the village of East-Haven, in
this colony, to embody themselves into a Church state, with
the approbation of their neighbouring churches."
The care and solemnity with which they proceeded in
preparing for that transaction is worthy of notice.
April 25th, 1710. " Upon some considerations about setting up the worship and ordinances of Christ in this place,
and in order to a suitable attendance upon so great and
weighty a worke, the village made choice of, and desired
sundry persons, whose names are underwritten, as a Committee, to take advice and search for the right way, as near
as may be ascertained, to prosecute the aforesaid worke,
under hopes of the blessing of God to accompany and suc-
ceed such a worke for soul good to us, and ours after us, to
many generations." The persons chosen for this object
were, William Luddington, Thomas Goodsell, Lieut. John
Russell, George Pardee, Caleb Chedsey, Sergt. John Potter,
and Daniel Collins.
With such views the Church was gathered and constituted a Congregational Church; and became a member of
the Consociation of New-Haven county ; that body having
been organized, according to Saybrook Platform, in 1709.
The Church was gathered on the 8th Oct. 1711, and Mr.
Heminway was ordained Pastor of the Church the same day.
But unhappily no Church Record can be found of the transactions of that day, nor of the affairs of the Church until
1755. It however appears, that Caleb Chedsey was one of
the first Deacons ; he died in 1713. Joshua Austin was

Deacon in 1718. And he and Thomas Smith were both Deacons at the time of Mr. Street's ordination, but were then very aged. To them succeeded Deodate Davenport and Daniel Hitchcock—then Samuel and Abraham Heminway—then Amos Morris, Stephen Smith, Samuel Davenport, John Morris, and Levi Pardee.

When Mr. Heminway commenced his labours, the village had no meeting-house. But at a meeting, June 10th, 1706, "The Village agreed to build, 20 feet long, 16 feet wide, and 17 feet between joints, and set it across the east end of the School House." William Luddington and John Russell were overseers of the work, and were allowed 3s. 6d. per day, other men 3s. and team 6s. This house served them until the year 1719, when they erected another house on the hill, or "*Nole*," the northwest corner of the Green, where the road is now laid. So early as the year 1714, the Village "voted to build a meeting-house 30 by 40 feet, 20 feet high, and jutted one foot at each end, with a strait roof." And the next year, they voted a sixpenny rate for the expense. In 1718 they began the house. Capt. John Russell, Nathaniel Hitchcock, Abraham Heminway and Samuel Hotchkiss, were the building Committee. And the next year they were charged " to hurry the work." The form of the seats and the pulpit were to be like those of Branford meeting-house : and a pew was to be built for the Ministry. Wages from the 10th Sept. to the 10th March, to be 2s. 6d. ; and the rest of the year 3s. team 5s. Indian corn 2s. 6d.

The house being sufficiently advanced to occupy, the 19th Oct. 1719, the Village met and " voted that the new Meeting-house should be seated :—that the first short seat should be reckoned equal with the second long seat and so on :— that Mr. Shepard, Mr. Tuttle, and William Luddington, should sit in the first short seat. And old Mrs. Heminway, Mrs. Bradley, Mrs. Denison and Mrs. Smith, shall sit in the first seat of the square body. Mr. Pardee, Mr. Morris, Capt. Russell, Sergt. John Thompson, Samuel Russell, and Samuel Clark, shall sit in the fore seat of the square body. And these six men are chosen to seat the rest of the meeting-house, or the major part of them to do it, according to their rates in 1717, and that by Monday next ensuing."

About 30 years afterwards, the meeting-house wanting repairs, it was motioned to build a new house ; but they continued to repair the old one for about fifty years, when they began the erection of the stone house. In the mean time the people growing remiss concerning the wood with which they had stipulated to supply Mr. Heminway, they voted to give him £50 in lieu of wood, provided it was not delivered in a specified time, for which they would be allow- ed 3s. per load.

20th Feb. 1722. " Voted, that Mr. Heminway shall have a piece of land for pasturing, adjoining to the west end of his home lot, as it is set out by Deacon Austin, Thomas Alcock and William Bradley. He to have the use of said land, so long as he shall continue in the worke of the Ministry amongst us in this place, he paying to the Village one shilling per year, yearly, so long as he improves said land for pasturing. The bounds of the land set out by the aforesaid three men, is about 13 rods on the Southend, on the westerly side 17 rods, and northerly 10 rods."

In Jan. 1737, they voted to sell the Parsonage, and con- stitute a permanent fund with the avails. This measure, however, was opposed, and John Heminway, Joseph Gran- nis, Samuel Russell, Matthew Rowe, John Dawson, Moses Thompson, James Denison, Isaac Penfield, Samuel Smith, and Isaac Howe, entered their protest against selling the Parsonage land.

In 1752. " Voted that Mr. Heminway shall name the Psalm in public, Nathaniel Barnes shall tune the Psalm, and in his absence Jacob or Isaac Goodsell."

Mr. Heminway continued in the Ministry 50 years, and died 7th Oct. 1754, in the 71st year of his age.

In March, 1755, Mr. Nicholas Street was invited to preach for the Society on probation, with the consent of the Rev. Association.

" At a Society meeting, 5th July, 1755, voted unanimous- ly to give Mr. Street a call to settle in the worke of the Gos- pel ministry with us, and appointed a Committee to treat with him on the subject." And in Aug. " Voted, that we will give Mr. Street for his settlement amongst us, £1500 money, Old Tenor; to pay £500 in one year; £500 in two years, and £500 in three years. And if he changes his prin- ciples from what he was settled upon, then he shall return the £1500 in money, to the Society." This was equal to about £126 proclamation money.

" Voted to give Mr. Street for his yearly salary £60, in New-York money, dollars at 8s. or any other money equiv- alent thereunto, for the first year; sixty-five in the same money for the second year, and seventy in the same money for the third year, and so to continue yearly so long as the said Mr. Street shall preach with us."

"Voted, also, that Mr. Street shall have the use of that piece of parsonage land by the two springs, three years after he is ordained." "Voted, also, that Mr. Street shall have the use of the two bigest pieces of land, so long as he shall continue in the work of the Ministry amongst us." At the same meeting Mr. Street personally appeared, and accepted of the aforesaid proposal. And was ordained by the Consociation of New-Haven County, 8th Oct. 1755.

In 1768, the Society again voted to sell all the Parsonage lands and give Mr. Street £80 salary. The next year, 30th Jan. 1769, "Voted to sell all the parsonage lands. The monies arising and accruing to the said Society from the sale of said lands shall be kept as a fund for the support of a regular Calvinistic Ministry, upon Saybrook Platform, especially as to the doctrines thereof, in East Haven; and that the interest of said fund shall annually be paid to such a ministry and no other, according to the original intention in the sequestration of said lands." The sales amounted to £390 9s. 9d. In 1779, it became convenient for some of the purchasers to make payment in the depreciated Continental Bills, when they were already reduced four to one, i. e. one dollar was worth only 25 cents in silver. A vote of the Society was obtained to call in the money; and thus all that fund sunk in their hands to about $300!! For the sake of this fund, Mr. Street had previously relinquished the parsonage and his wood, and accepted of £80 salary.

The same year the Society voted to build a new meeting-house. And in voting where it should stand, 37 votes appeared for the Green, and 27 for the end of Mullen Hill. A large Committee was then appointed to fix upon the place; but they could not agree. The next year, they chose Capt. Eliakim Hall, Col. Chauncey, and James Wadsworth, a Committee for that purpose, who met, and their doings were reported to the Court. But the people were not yet satisfied. The same result attended another Committee in March 1771. In Dec. of the same year, they tried another vote: when 20 votes appeared for the Green, 2 for Thompson's corner, and 29 for the end of the hill. Being convinced that they should not agree, in Feb. 1772, they voted to apply to the County Court, and request that two of the Judges and another man be of the Committee. They met and fixed the stake on Thompson's corner. In this decision the Society acquiesced, and began to make preparations to build.

The end of the hill was the centre of the Society, and nearly in the centre of the population, north and south. The Green would be more convenient for the south and east part of the society. The Southend people had to go round by the Cove and come out on the Green. The road was crooked, long, and some part of the way very uncomfortable. The present road from the meeting-house to Southend was laid out after that period.

John Woodward, Amos Morris and Stephen Morris, and afterwards Stephen Thompson, Joel Tuttle, and Stephen Smith, were of the building Committee. Isaac Chedsey and Dan Bradley were chosen in 1774. "27th April, 1772, Voted to build a stone house 60 feet long, and to lay a sixpenny rate for it." The Committee were authorized to purchase the land of John Thompson, and pay for it out of that rate. The house was begun without a steeple, but a few enterprizing men were determined to have one, and finally obtained a Society vote for it, and also to add eight feet to the length. The outside of the walls now measure 70 feet by 50, exclusive of the steeple. In 1773 and 4, the walls were raised and covered. The seats were then removed from the old house into the new, and public worship commenced in it in Sept. 1774. The finishing of the house was suspended for several years.

It was a great and honorable work, and there stands as a lasting monument of the enterprize, public spirit, wisdom and perseverance of the undertakers, and especially of the leaders. It was a cheaper building than one of wood :— They had stone and lime, and teams and laborers enough to do the work. A stone house saved them money.—The papers containing the accounts of the building are lost, and the expense of it cannot now be ascertained. But it is supposed that when they began to meet in it, it had cost ten or eleven thousand dollars. The steeple and inside of the house were finished several years afterwards. For the war coming on, nothing could be done. Indeed, the society has never seen a more favorable period for this great work. They were then united as one people. And the society, probably, never contained a company of men of more enterprize or greater resolution and public spirit, than that generation contained. The Revolutionary war commenced the next year. And when that war was terminated, divisions began to appear, and have considerably diminished the active ability of the society to perform such a work again—and in a few years a number of those influential and enterprizing men were removed by death. And though there is yet a considerable portion of wealth in the society, it is not accompanied with the same resolution and enter- prize which the Fathers possessed.—But it ought to be con- sidered, that the hand of the Lord was in the work. The time had come when the "Lord's house should be built," and then men and means were prepared to execute the work of the Lord, and fulfil the divine purpose. *"Except the Lord build the house, they labour in vain that build it."* And when the work was done, the people had occasion to say, *"the Lord hath done great things for us, whereof we are glad."*

A serious calamity, however, befel the builders. The workmen were raising the last window cap, on the back side, when the scaffold gave way, and three men with the stone in their arms fell to the ground. Toney was considerably in- jured, but in two weeks was so much recovered that he ran away. Mr. Stephen Thompson had his skull fractured, was trepanned, and after much suffering, recovered. Mr. Joseph Hotchkiss had one leg crushed by the stone, passed through ten months of suffering, but was finally raised to comfortable health, and is yet alive.

The society resumed the work of finishing the house in 1791, for which they laid a tax of one penny half penny. The work was accomplished, and the house was put into good order; but was greatly damaged by a dreadful torna- do, Oct. 8th, 1797, between 6 and 7 o'clock on the evening of the Lord's day. The repairs of the house cost the socie- ty about one thousand dollars.

Mr. Street having a large family, and a small salary, and having gone through the distresses of the war on a depre- ciated currency; in 1787, petitioned the society for relief. After some debate about it, twenty pounds, by vote, were added to his salary. With this grant a few men were ex- tremely displeased, and some having been displeased on some other account, they united with a few Episcopalians then in the town, and formed an Episcopal society. The following document will exhibit the date and form of that transaction :—

"East-Haven, 31st March, 1788. At a meeting of the Episcopal Society of the Church of England, so called, le- gally warned, at the house of Mr. Samuel Tuttle, in said East-Haven, at 2 o'clock P. M. on Monday, 31st March,

7

1788; the subscribers, members of said Church or Society, under the kind patronage of the Rev. Bela Hubbard, Rector of Trinity Church, of New-Haven, being present, who willingly and cheerfully accepted us under his care and patronage, proceeded to the usual and necessary business of choosing the needful and customary parish officers in said Society of East-Haven. Accordingly, voted John Bird to be Clerk of said Society; and being duly sworn, upon the oath of fidelity and oath of office, according to law—also voted, Capt. Samuel Barnes, Moderator, John Bird, Clerk, Samuel Tuttle, James Pardee, Church Wardens;—Jehiel Forbes, Capt. Samuel Barnes, Samuel Thompson, Capt. Stephen Thompson, Jun. Ichabod Bishop, Vestrymen. At the same time voted for five Vestrymen, but that only three shall be a quorum, with full power and authority, as the five by vote elected."

"Let this certify all whom it may concern, that I was present at the above-mentioned meeting, and that the above-mentioned persons were approved of in their several respective offices to which they were appointed.

Witness my hand, 31st day of March, 1788.

BELA HUBBARD,
Rector of Trinity Church, New-Haven."

The next year they erected their Church house; at the raising of which, through some injudicious management, the frame fell, and killed Jeremiah Bradley, and several others were much injured.

The Rev. Mr. Street died 8th Oct. 1806, in the 77th year of his age, having just completed the 51st year of his Ministry. He and Mr. Heminway served the Congregation 101 years.

CHAP. VI.

SCHOOLS AND EDUCATION.

THERE is no account of Schools on record, until the beginning of the last century. Their deficiency, in regard to even a common education, was very great. Some of their public men,—men who sustained various offices and appointments of trust, were unable to write their names.— Their mark is made at the bottom of several instruments on record. Experience taught them the necessity of paying more attention to the education of their children.

13th Jan. 1707, a Committee was appointed at a Village meeting, "to see after the schools, and agree with a man to keep school in East-Haven, to teach children to read and write." The Committee accordingly agreed with Mr. Heminway to take charge of the school.

In 1728 the Village was divided into four Districts, and the public money into as many parts, according to the number of children over 5 and under 15 years of age. The next year they agreed to employ a school-master, as near the middle of the village as was convenient. Some part of the time at South-end, and some part at Foxon's, according to the number of children from 8 to 18 years of age. In 1732, it was fixed between 6 and 16—At that time Foxon district included all the families north of the Bloomary brook, and a line running west to Claypit brook. A school was begun in Dragon district, 1730.

The first school-house was on the "Green, or Market place." And afterwards east of the present meeting-house. One stood on the hill near Matthew Moulthrop's house, west of Foxon: and in 1767, one was built a little north of Bloomary brook.

In 1742 the school-money was divided thus: Two thirds for the schools below the Bloomary brook, and one third north of that line, and so west, over to Nanny Capel's brook. Foxon district was then very thrifty and populous, but has since declined in wealth and population.

In 1743, "It was voted that the Southend children shall have their proportion of the school money, from the age of 4 to 18." In 1769, the Village was divided into six school districts. The public school money was derived from the sale of the public lands in Litchfield County.

Though the people of this town have been favoured for more than a century with a College at their door, they have not availed themselves of that advantage, to give their sons a public education. Only six have enjoyed that privilege— viz:

Jacob Heminway, graduated		1704
Thomas Goodsell,	in	1724
John Goodsell,	in	1724
Jared Potter,	in	1760
Asahel Morris,	in	1789
Amos Pardee,	in	1793

Agreeable to the new law respecting the school fund of

this State, a census of the children between the ages of 4 and 16 has been taken every year in the month of August, and is as follows:

	In 1820	1821	1822	1823
Middle District,	166	165	160	165
Southend Do.	33	36	35	44
West Do.	54	54	61	47
Dragon Do.	68	74	78	79
Foxon Do.	55	56	58	53
Total,	376	393	392	388

A few years since, a Library Company was formed, and gathered about 75 or 80 volumes; but for seven years past no regard has been paid to it, by the appointment of the proper officers. Several attempts have been made to obtain a meeting of the company, but have failed!

—◦◦◦—

CHAPTER VII.

Population—Taxable Property and Taxes.

THE only data on which we can ascertain the population of East-Haven, for about one hundred and fifty years after its first settlement, is the scale by which the division of land was made; and this, so far as it goes, may be considered generally accurate.

In 1683, there were 20 families within the bounds of the Village, and 121 polls, which is six to a family, and one over. Besides these, there were five unmarried men, and one widow, which makes the population of that year 127.

In 1702, there were 32 families, and 192 polls, which gives the proportion of six to a family; besides eight unmarried persons who drew lots for themselves;—whole number 200: which makes an increase of 73 in 19 years.

In 1709, there were 33 families, and 200 polls, exclusive of 10 single persons who drew lots for themselves;—making 210. Beside these there were five families at Southend, who did not at this time draw lots of land. If we allow six to a family for them, the population will be 240. There were a few tenants and servants who are not included in this number; and with that addition, the population might amount to 270 persons.

In 1754, there were 61 freemen. Some of these were old men, and had small families ; and doubtless there were some men who had families, and who were not freemen.— If we reckon the number of families at 70, and allow six persons to a family, the souls will be 420. The population in 1754 did not, probably, exceed 500 souls ; for in the years 1736, '42, '43, 73 children died, and 29 adult persons, some of whom were heads of young families.

In 1769, there were 64 voters in a society meeting, respecting the place where the new Meeting-House should stand. On that occasion, doubtless nearly all the voters in the society attended.

The regular census of the United States affords an accurate view of the population of the town at four equi-distant periods. The official returns stand thus :

1790, 1025 persons. | 1810, 1209 persons.
1800, 1004 | 1820, 1237

There are at this time, 1824, about 200 families in the town, which, according to the census of 1820, contain upon an average more than six to a family.

Taxes.—The amount of the Grand List in East-Haven,

In 1683, was £1794 00 00
1702, 2550 00 00
1709, 2397 00 00

The valuation amount of property for the United States direct tax, in 1815, was $351,225 : property in other towns, $2426. 1504 dollars were deducted. The amount of tax was $1006 22. In 1816, the amount of valuation was $375,703 : Property of non-residents deducted, $22,918 : leaving $353,785. The tax on this sum was 133½ mills pr. cent. which raised $470 95.

The state of property will further appear, from the annexed list for the year 1785, when East-Haven became a Town :

140 Polls between 21 and 70,	£2520 00
38 Polls between 16 and 21,	342 00
581 Cattle above two years old,	1172 00
97 Horses do.	284 00
5809 Acres of Land,	1331 00
12 Tons Shipping,	9 00
3 Chaises,	11 00
8 Watches,	12 00
7 Clocks,	9 00
247 Smokes,	117 15
Assessments,	217 00
	£ 6025 15

[7*]

In 1790, the List was $19,922 58
In 1795,   21,106 20
In 180?,   21,946 21
In 1818,   21,747 32

Under the new Assessment law of 1819, the list stood thus :

185 Houses,	$103,310	at	2 per ct.	$2066 20
7993 acres of land,	223,178	at	3	6695 34
88 horses,	2,847	at	8	227 76
584 cattle,	11,460	at	6	687 60
3 mills,	3,200	at	3	96
1 store,	100	at	3	30
19 carriages,	605	at 40		242
55 clocks,	229	at 50		114 50
7 watches,	65	at 50		32 50
Bank Stock,	4,500	at	6	270
Money loaned,	3,828	at	6	229 68
Assessment,	210	at		210
119 Polls,	4,760	at $40 each,		4,760
	$358,292			$15,661 58

1822.

186 Houses,	$102,776	at	2 per ct.	$2055 32
8392 acres of land,	213,770	at	3	6413 10
82 horses,	3,013	at 10		301 30
749 cattle,	11,002	at	6	660 12
1 store,	300	at	3	9
3 mills,	2,700	at	3	81
7 chaises,	245	at 25		61 25
3 waggons,	120	at 15		18
62 clocks and watches,	251	at 50		125 50
Bank Stock,	6,200	at	6	372
Money loaned,	2,590	at	6	155 40
139 Polls,	4,170	at 30		4170
Assessments,	220			220
	$347,347			$14,641 99

The Town has, for several years, voted from 3 to 3 ¼ cents tax to defray the current expenses of the Town—and from 1 to 2 cents for the repair of the roads.

CHAP. VIII.

Losses by War.

IN the French war of 1755, a number of men were drafted from East-Haven for the English army near the Lakes, and the greater part of them were lost by sickness and battle. Of these I have obtained the following names, viz. Jacob Moulthrop, David Moulthrop, Adonijah Moulthrop, Jacob Robinson, Benjamin Robinson, Thomas Robinson, jun. David Potter, John Mallory, Abraham Jocelin, Samuel Hotchkiss, James Smith, Samuel Russel and Stephen Russel, brothers, and Asa Luddington. Benjamin Russel was captured at sea.

In the war of Independence, which began 19th April, 1775, the following persons were lost.—In 1776, Elijah Smith was killed in battle upon Long-Island ; Thomas Smith conducted a fire ship to the enemy, but was badly burnt, and the attending boat having left him too soon, he had to swim ashore, where he was found three days after, in a helpless state ; he was brought over to Rye, and there he died.—Nathan Andrews died a prisoner. In 1777, Isaac Potter perished in the prison-ship. The 5th July, 1779, Isaac Pardee was killed on Grave or Fort hill, by a cannon shot. In October, on board a privateer, Zabulon Bradley was killed ; Richard Paul, Jacob Pardee, jun. Asa Bradley, Abijah Bradley, and Elijah Bradley, were made prisoners, and all, except the last, perished in the prison ship at New-York, the following winter. In 1780, Medad Slaughter died in the prison-ship. In 1781, John Howe was killed by the Tories when they surprised Fort Hale. John Walker was killed upon Long-Island.

Thus twelve young men were lost ; and several men returned from captivity so injured by hard usage, that they pined away and died, particularly Edward Goodsell, Isaac Luddington and Jared Heminway.

On the 4th July, 1779, the enemy intending to capture New-Haven, landed a covering force on Morris' Neck and Southend, and marched directly to Tuttle's hill, where they encamped that night, and the next day re-embarked. They were led by the Tories. In this invasion they burnt most of the buildings within their reach, and made the *rebel Whigs* feel the effects of Royal British vengeance.

To meet these losses, and those of other Towns of a similar

nature, in May, 1792, the General Assembly of Connecticut passed an act appropriating " 500,000 acres of land
west of Pennsylvania, for the relief of the sufferers by fire."
The damage in each Town was assessed, and the amount of
each person's loss in East-Haven was as follows:

Amos Morris,	£1235	15	4
John Woodward,	838	17	3
John Woodward, jun.	740	19	11
Elam Luddington,	408	6	7
Joseph Tuttle,	79	9	5
Jacob and Abijah Pardee,	402	8	2
Jehiel Forbes,	173	13	1
Mary Pardee,	134	14	0
Mary and Lydia Pardee,	40	8	4
Noah Tucker,	99	17	4
	£4154	9	5

Equal to $13,848 24.
They burnt eleven dwelling houses, nine barns and some
other out buildings. Gurdon Bradley lost £66 00 00 in a
sloop that was burnt. The enemy and the militia plundered
the inhabitants of all they could carry off. The whole of
this loss was collected by the Commissioners appointed for
this purpose, and the amount was £421 1 4. The entire
loss of East-Haven by this invasion, in property, was $15,-
251 79.

—⚬∞⚬—

CHAP. IX.

Natural History—Tornado and Curiosities.

THE Town of East-Haven contains about nine thousand
acres of land. The soil is generally light and sandy; but
capable of yielding good crops when properly cultivated. It
is congenial to Indian Corn and Barley. In favourable
seasons, potatoes do well. In some parts of the Town
Rye succeeds, but is very subject to blast and rust. By
good husbandry the lands may be made more productive;
though unhappily there is very little good pasturage in the
Town. There is very little clay, and some parts of the
Town are encumbered and disfigured with rocks and ragged
barren hills.

About the first Spring, or the head of Bloomary Brook, and the head of Clay-pit Brook, and along the intervale of Stoney River, good brick clay may be obtained. Some of the best land lies in the Fresh Meadows and Cove Swamp, which are now uncultivated and unproductive. Were those low lands drained, as they probably will be at some future period, they would be the most productive lands in the Town.

Along the sea-shore, there is a range of Granite rock of the purest kind, but it is not found in any other part of the Town. The Pond Rock and the ridge west of it are Green or Whinstone. The same kind of Rock appears in detached eminences and ridges, in some other parts of the Town. Sand-stone of the secondary formation, commences on the Indian land north-east from the Cove, and running north, spreads through Dragon woods, and terminates on the Davenport farm. Another mass lies on the east side of the Fresh Meadows, and runs in a north-east direction to the north line of the town, on the half mile. The Green-stone, generally, on the surface, is in such a state of fracture, as to be nearly useless, except the smaller fragments, which make excellent gravel for roads. In some places the sand stone is in a state of decomposition. In the ridge north of Mullen Hill, Agates are found in abundance.

The plains appear to be composed of sand, coarse and fine, washed from the lands and vallies on the north, and accumulating gradually by some powerful operating cause. The salt marshes are founded upon a bottom of sand like that of the plains adjacent.

The Town is well supplied with water of an excellent quality. There are numerous Springs and some fine Rivulets ; while Stoney River and the Furnace Pond afford an inexhaustible supply of water of the best kind.

The Pond is about three miles long, and from one hundred yards to three hundred broad, and very deep.

The fisheries in the waters of East-Haven are excellent and valuable. In Quinipiack River, oysters are taken in vast quantities, and those of a superior quality are taken in the Cove and Stoney River.

Clams, black and white fish, abound in their season. White fish are used, in vast quantities, for manure.

The trade in oysters is carried to a great extent. From sixty to an hundred thousand bushels, are annually imported. These are opened, put up into small kegs, and dispersed all over the northern and western country, quite into

Canada. The amount of sales for this Town and vicinity is estimated at twenty-five thousand dollars during the fall and winter season. And it sometimes probably exceeds that sum.

A considerable number of the men are employed in the coasting, packet, and oyster trade. But this town has suffered exceedingly by the loss of active men at sea. Farming business occupies the attention of the principal part of the male population.

On the 8th October, 1797, great damage was done by a Tornado, which passed over the centre of the Town. The same week, the following account of it was published in a New-Haven paper.

"On Sunday evening last, between six and seven o'clock, we experienced a violent gale of wind from the westward, attended with heavy rain and thunder. The damage done in this town was not great, compared with that done at East-Haven and Branford.

"The roofs of some buildings were injured, the tops of chimneys blown off, and windows blown in, some trees and fences blown down, and a barn in the New Township removed from its foundation. At East-Haven the steeple of the meeting-house was blown down, which falling on the roof, broke through the side, where it fell, leaving only one rafter standing, and penetrating the floor, greatly damaged the seats. A large new house was removed from its foundation ; several dwelling houses were partly and others entirely unroofed. A number of barns met the same fate. Three large barns were entirely demolished : the materials of which they were built were scattered in every direction. The town of Branford experienced nearly the same fate. Part of the roof of the meeting-house was blown off, and all the windows on the western side destroyed ; six or seven houses, a new store and several barns, unroofed, other barns blown down, the trees in several fine orchards laid prostrate. The height of the tornado continued but a few minutes. We have not learnt all the particulars of this disastrous gale, nor how far the storm extended."

The same Tornado is described in Dwight's Travels, with the addition of several particulars to the above account.

"On Lord's day, October 8, 1797, in the afternoon, a Tornado, the commencement of which, so far as I was able to learn, was at Upper Salem in the County of Westchester and State of New-York, passed over Ridgefield, in Connecticut, and thence over Redding, Newtown, Huntington, Derby, Woodbridge, New-Haven, East-Haven, Branford, Guilford, and Killingworth; whence it directed its course over the Sound. At times it rose from the earth, and held its most furious career in a higher region of the atmosphere. Such was the fact at New-Haven, where, although its force was great, it did not blow with sufficient strength to do any material damage. At Upper Salem, it destroyed orchards, groves, and buildings. At East-Haven it blew down the steeple of the Presbyterian Church, and ruined several other buildings. It left many marks of its violence also at Branford, and some other places; while in others it did little or no mischief. This alternate rise and fall of a Tornado, I have not seen mentioned; nor do I remember a storm of this kind, at so late a season, in any other instance."

Another violent gale, called by some the *Salt Storm,* occurred on the 3d Sept. 1821. Light showers passed in the morning; it was somewhat misty through the day, with a light rain about 5 o'clock P. M. the wind rising about that hour, it having been all day about south and south-east.— At 6 o'clock it became a gale, still increasing and blowing with dreadful violence until 11 o'clock, when it broke, and a calm succeeded. In this town very little rain fell; but in the region about New-York, a vast quantity poured down. The sand and gravel, however, were scooped from the earth and dashed against every opposing object. A salt spray covered every thing within its reach, and mingling with the dirt then afloat, rendered the glass windows quite opaque, and formed a coat so firm, that it was not easily washed off.

The morning light disclosed a scene of mournful devastation, among the vegetable kingdom. Trees of every kind were stripped of their foliage, and also of their fruit. The small limbs upon the windward side were killed, and still exhibit the deadly properties of the storm; and along the coast the fruit trees are rendered barren. Many small trees were destroyed. The shrubbery and the vegetation of the garden and the field, appeared as is common after a severe and early frost. The atmosphere was loaded with a very nauseous fetor. The buckwheat was completely destroyed; the corn lay prostrate, the leaves of which were whipped into small strings. The weather afterwards being very warm, the trees and living shrubbery put forth new leaves, and the fruit trees and the lilac were adorned with flowers.

The deadly effects of the salt on vegetation might be traced twelve or fifteen miles inland; but gradually diminishing according, to the distance from the shore. It having been a very dry season in this town, and the ground being very hard, but few trees were overturned, compared with what took place a few miles north, where the ground was softer, and there great havoc was made among the tall timber.

A singular phenomenon of frequent occurrence is noticeable in this town, respecting the motion of thunder clouds proceeding from the west. The cloud advances over the harbour, and approaches Fort Hill, presenting a great, and in a dry season, a hopeful appearance of a refreshing rain. But presently it breaks, and then separates to the right and left; one part passing to the north of the village, and the other part passing down the harbour and across the south end of the town, pours down its refreshing streams upon the Sound. And sometimes no rain at all falls upon the plains east of the hill, and at other times only a sprinkling from the skirts of the cloud. Whether the hill possesses a repulsive, or the water an attractive quality, that operates upon the cloud, is a question left to the wisdom of the reader to solve.

The town affords a few curiosities. On an island in Stoney River, there is a regular cavity cut into the Granite Rock, and called the *Indian Well.* It is from twenty-six to thirty-three inches diameter, and very smooth, especially the bottom of it. It is now about five feet in depth, but formerly it was deeper. When the dam below was built, some part of the rock was removed, and much injured its natural appearance. The water on both sides of the island passes through a narrow channel of Granite Rock. I have seen similar excavations in the beds of the Mohawk River below the Cohoes falls, which were evidently formed by sand and pebbles, set into action by the rotatory motion of the water. Such cavities are common near the falls of Rivers. The Indian well was, doubtless, produced by the attrition of the sand and pebbles which passed over this rock, it being then in or near the bed of the River. The bottom of the River was then from eight to twelve feet above the present high water mark, the valley on the north being once a considerable lake, and connected with the Furnace pond. A great change has evidently passed over the land and marsh in that vicinity. Stumps and the fragments of trees lie in the bed and banks of the River. The marsh has but a small depth, and lies on a bed of sand. Some fragments of Indian manufacture, and other articles, have been thrown up in ditching the marsh.

On the land of William Woodward, and a few rods west of his barn, is a rock of Greenstone, resting in a few places, over a cavity, upon a ridge of Sandstone. The under side of the rock is very smooth. Its mean height is about five feet and a half, and its length and breadth is about eight feet. The top of it is flat. There is no other rock of the kind in that neighborhood. Is this rock of Celtic origin?— Its size and peculiar position resembles that of other rocks in this country which have been the subjects of scientific speculation.

Another rock, of Sandstone, somewhat similar to the other, not so high, but having a longer table, is on a hill of considerable elevation, west of Bridge Swamp. It originally rested on the apex, like an inverted cone, but now reclines towards the South. From this situation there is a charming view of the Sound and the surrounding country.

The great burying place of the Indian Tribes in this Town and vicinity, is on the north end of the hill on which the Fort stands, which, anciently, in allusion to this place, was called *Grave Hill.* Some of the graves have been levelled by the plow, but many of them are yet visible. In the year 1822, I examined three of these graves. At the depth of about three feet and a half the sand stone appears, on which the bodies were laid, without any appearance of a wrapper or enclosure. They all lay in the direction of south-west and north-east—the head towards the west. Of two of them, the arms lay by the side; the other had the arms across the body, after the manner of the white people. The large bones and teeth were in a sound state. The thigh bones of one measured 19 inches in length, the leg bone 18, and the arm from the elbow to the shoulder 13. By measuring the skeleton as it lay, it was concluded to be that of a man of six and a half feet high. No article of any description appeared with the bones. It is said, that about 50 or 60 years ago some of these graves were opened, and a number of Indian implements, of the kitchen and of war, were found in them. Few Indians have been buried there within a century past.

The Indians had a Fort on the hill in the burying ground, and from that circumstance it was called Fort Hill. It is

also a tradition that they had another on the hill north of
Daniel Hughes' house, and near the old ferry road. The
appearance of shells shows that they had a village on that
spot. The same indications appear in the woods of Southend Neck, west of the sluice. Great quantities of oyster shells
are collected among the rocks and in the little vallies, and
on the banks of the River, showing the places where their
weekwams stood.

It was stated in the first chapter of this history that Thomas Gregson, who settled at Solitary Cove, and several others, on a voyage to England, were lost at sea. That affair
is noticed by Dr. Mather, in his Magnalia, with an account
of the apparition of a ship, contained in a letter to him from
the Rev. James Pierpont, Pastor of the Church at New-Haven, successor to Mr. Street, and who was settled there 2d
July, 1685. As the loss of Mr. Gregson was a calamity to
the early settlement of East-Haven, I conclude that this
account may be introduced into this work with propriety.
It is a singular affair, and will be amusing to most of the
readers. I insert it without any comment, leaving every
reader to make what speculations he pleases concerning it.

"Behold, a fourth colony of *New-English* Christians, in
a manner *stolen* into the world, and a colony, indeed, *con-
stellated* with many stars of the *first magnitude*. The colony was under the conduct of as holy, and as prudent and as
genteel men, as most that ever visited these *nooks* of *America:* and yet *these* too were tried with very humbling circumstances.

"Being *Londoners,* or merchants and men of traffic and
business, their design was in a manner wholly to apply
themselves unto trade; but the design failing, they found
their great estates sink so fast, that they must quickly *do
something.* Whereupon, in the year 1646, gathering together almost all the strength which was left them, they
built one ship more, which they freighted for *England,* with
the best part of their tradeable estates: and sundry of their
eminent persons embarked themselves in her for the voyage.
But, alas, the ship was never after heard of!—She founder-
ed at sea; and in her were lost, not only the *hopes* of their
future trade, but also the *lives* of several excellent persons,
as well as divers *manuscripts* of some great men in the
country, sent over for the service of the Church, which were
now buried in the ocean. The *fuller story* of that *grievous
matter,* let the reader with a just astonishment accept from

the pen of the Reverend person, who is now the Pastor of *New-Haven*. I wrote unto him for it, and was thus answered.

" Reverend and Dear Sir—

" In compliance with your desires, I now give you the relation of that *apparition* of *a ship in the air*, which I have received from the most credible, judicious, and curious surviving observers of it.

" In the year 1647, besides much other lading, a far more rich treasure of passengers (five or six of which were persons of chief note and worth in *New-Haven*,) put themselves on board a *new ship*, built at Rhode-Island, of about 150 tons; but so watty, [crank,] that the master (Lamberton) often said she would prove their grave. In the month of January, cutting their way through much ice, on which they were accompanied with the Rev. Mr. *Davenport*, besides many other friends, with many fears, as well as prayers and tears, they set sail. Mr. *Davenport*, in prayer, with an observable *emphasis*, used these words, *Lord, if it be thy pleasure to bury these dear friends in the bottom of the sea, they are thine, save them!*" The spring following, no tidings of these friends arrived with the ships from *England;* New-Haven's heart began to fail her; this put the godly people on much *prayer,* both public and private, *that the Lord would (if it was his pleasure) let them hear what he had done with their our friends, and prepare them with a suitable submission to his Holy Will.* In *June* next ensuing, a great *thunder storm* arose out of the *north-west;* after which, (the hemisphere being serene) about an hour before sun-set, a SHIP, of like dimensions with the aforesaid, with her canvass and colours abroad, (though the wind northerly,) appeared in the air, coming up from our harbour's mouth, which lyes southward of the Towne, seemingly with her sails filled under a fresh gale, holding her course north, and continuing under observation, sailing against the wind, for the space of half an hour.

" *Many* were drawn to behold this great work of God; yea, the very children cryed out, *There's a brave ship!*— At length, crouding up as far as there is usually water sufficient for such a vessel, and so near some of the spectators as that they imagined a man might hurl a stone on board her, her *main top* seemed to be blown off, but left hanging in the shrouds; then her *missen top;* then all her *masting* seemed blown away by the board; quickly after the hulk brought unto a careen, she overset, and so vanished into a smoaky cloud, which in some time dissipated, leaving, as every where else, a clear air. The admiring spectators could distinguish the several colours of each part, the principal rigging, and such proportions, as caused not only the generality of persons to say, *This was the mould of their ship, and thus was her tragic end;* but Mr. *Davenport* also in public declared to this effect, *That God had condescended, for the quieting of their afflicted spirits, this extraordinary account of his sovereign disposal of those for whom so many fervent prayers were made continually.*

Thus I am, Sir, Your humble servant,
JAMES PIERPONT."

CHAP. X.

Roads and Public Lands.

WHEN Thomas Morris, in 1671, bought the little Neck, a four rod road was reserved, in his deed, " from the Cove to Fowler's Creek, in the way to Southend."

In 1673, the Southend men and George Pardee, paid the Indian George, Sagamore, twelve shillings for a road of one rod from the Cove to the country road.

In 1692, " On Motion made by the Southend men in reference to the highway through the Indian land, it was voted, that Thomas Trowbridge, sergt. Winstone, John Potter and sergt. Cooper, or any three of them, be a Committee to state out and settle the way formerly used, as described by the Town's former order. And they are to inform themselves by such as know how the way went in times past, or ought to go, and make return to the Town of what they do ; also that they treat with the Indians, to settle matters lovingly with them." This vote was executed as follows :

"NEW-HAVEN, 10th June, 1692.

" Whereas there was a former agreement between New-Haven Towne and the Indians, for a highway through the Indian field to George Pardee's land, yet for peace sake with the Inhabitants of Southend, and George Pardee have given to George the Sagamore, twelve shillings in money, for which, I the underwritten do ratify and confirm the same and do grant the same highway to be on record, beginning at the dirty Swamp by the Iron worke path, which was Mr. Gregson's land, for which I do further engage that there shall be but two pare of barrs or gates throughout my land to George Pardee's, which I the foresaid Sagamore George will make and maintaine forever, and do further engage myself, my heirs, to secure the same highway to them, their heirs and assigns forever from me, my assigns, or any from or under me. As witness my hand and seal—dated as above.

his

INDIAN ✕ GEORGE.

mark.

Testors—UMBESA,
    HASOMAUG,
    JOHN POTTER,
    JOHN COOPER."

In December, 1727, "It was voted that the two rod high way laid out through the new Indian field on the east side, and running through the same, and established by the Committee to dispose of said land, one rod whereof was purchased by the Southend people of the Indians, be and remain an highway forever."—[*Pro. Records.*]

27th December, 1686. "And the road or way to the Ferry through the Neck to continue where it now is, and from the Ferry on the East side, the way to be continued where it is, four rods wide to Stoney River, and the end of our bounds Branfordward."—[*Pro. Record.*]

"And the Highway to be continued where it was, and that is from Old Ferry Point at the place called the Stables, four rods wide. And from the way that leadeth to Stoney River Farmes the highway to be continued where or near where it is as may be, leading to the sea at Solitary Cove, lying between the sea and the proprietors there, and so to go on where it doth over the little or Morris' Neck unto Southend Farmes."

"And also a road or highway from Stoney River Farmes to the Bogmine plaine, where it is, or lately was, when Bogmine was carted to the Iron workes, and from the said Bogmine plain, onwards upon the plaines, near where it lieth to the end of our Town Bounds towards Wallingford."

"Also a highway from the last mentioned highway beginning at the Southernmost run of water that runs into Mr. Davenport's Cove, to be continued unto the River near the

8*

Ferry below Dragon point, and upon the bank by the River side, between the lots that are or may be."

" And also a highway at first laid out from Stoney River home lots and houses, of a good breadth, to be continued between the fields or lots and the meadows or swamp leading to Solitary Cove; not to be encroached upon. The above ordered to be recorded."—[*Pro. Record.*]

" Here followeth the record of the highway in the third division according as the Sizers and Surveyor gave a description of them in writing.

" Also upon the east side of the East River a highway is allowed from the bridge on the East River to the commons in Widow Howe's lot."

" Also a highway at the rear of those lots that come up unto Branford line that was, beginning at Hercules' meadow, to run into Wharton's brook."

" Also a highway at the West end of those lots that come to Branford line that was, and is a division of lots that are on Hercules' plaine."

" All which ways are allowed four rods wide, only that in Widow Howe's lot from the bridge is six rods wide. Also those highways are to be where the ground will allow, and not to be compelled to run strait. Also a high-way allowed to run from the bridge on the East River, by the River to Joseph Ford's land. And one highway from the Bogmine Wharffe up to the Country road."—[*Pro. Record.*]

Roads on and near the Pond Rock.

" 23d March, 1715—The Pond Rock shall be laid out to the Proprietors which carried on the building of the Minister's house, and a highway to be laid out on the top of said Rock as shall be most convenient for that use, from the hither end, so to the end of our bounds, three rods wide. And there shall be a sufficient highway left between the said Rock and the River lots, so called, for the use of the Proprietors of the Rock and the River lots."—[*E. H. Rec.*]

" East-Haven, 18th April, 1710. We William Luddington, John Russel and Caleb Chedsey the Selectmen, considering the necessity of stating highways, do order, that the way between John Heminway's and John Miles', their home lot, shall be four rods wide, and along the like breadth, until you come to the Pumpkin lot. And so from the Southeast Corner of Joseph Tuttle's land on the one side and the Pumpkin lot on the other side, four rods wide untill you come to sergt. John Moulthrop's land, commonly called *plains lot,* on the northeast side, and a like breadth between the forementioned plains lot and John Luddington's lot and John Auger's land on the south west side, and so to continue as the road now is, untill you come to the Indian field."

" As also a highway from the northwest corner of Mr. Thomas Goodsell's home lot on the one side, and on the northeast corner of Samuel Russel's land on the other side, four rods wide while you come to the South corner of Samuel Goodsell's land, and then all the undivided land between Samuel Goodsell's and John Howe's land, and so along untill you come to the east side of John Heminway's land, and from thence as that land runs untill you come to that land laid out for parsonage land, and from thence turn to the west between said parsonage and aforesaid Heminway's land untill you come to the Indian land, and from thence southward till you come to George Pardee's land.

" As also a highway beginning at the Northeast corner of Lieut. John Russel's home lot, four rods wide between said home lot and other land of said Russel's, on the north side of it, and turning to the north-west, untill you come to the said Russel's pasture. Samuel Russel's being on the southwest side of said highway, and from said pasture forementioned, turning southward and south-west along the undivided land untill you come to the country road.—[*E. H. Record.*]

" 20th December, 1710, Caleb Chedsey and Samuel Russel and Samuel Thompson, Selectmen, added as follows. As also from Matthew Moulthrop's home lot Westward of the River lots until you come to John Dawson's home lot of four rods wide."

" As also from Hall's Cartway on the west side of the bridge swamp to the country road four rods wide, between land of John and Abraham Heminway and land of John Howe's on the west, and land belonging to Daniel Collins and Samuel Goodsell's on the East."

" As also a highway of two rods wide on the west side of Moulthrop's plains lot, the whole length of said lot, till it comes to the road that leads to Southend."—*E. H. Record.*

" December 21, 1724. Voted that there be a continuance of a highway from Jonathan's Point through Mr. Davenport's farme and a corner of Capt. Ball's farme to the Country road as formerly, with a pare of bars, which such as have occasion, shall pass and re-pass, they having so done shall shut the said barrs."—*Pro. Record.*

April, 1726. " Resolved, that a highway be continued
from the highway already purchased of Mr. Pierpont
through the half mile to the highway at Hitchcock's lot at
Muddy River, the said highway to be four rods wide and to
run as the land will allow to accommodate the same;
through a highway from Wallingford line to the Southward,
at the east end of the third division, till it intersect
the highway abovementioned."—[*Pro. Record.*]

" At a Proprietors' Meeting held in East-Haven, 12th
May, 1720, Mr. Jacob Heminway petitioned for a part of
the Green next to the spring where the burying place is.
Sergt. John Heminway protested against any part of the
Green being taken up or disposed of for any other use than
to lye common as it now lies. Voted that Mr. Heminway
shall not have any part of the land.—Voted that the Green
shall not be disposed of except it be for some public use,
that it may be beneficial to the whole of the Proprietors."—
[*E. H. and N. H. Record.*]

" March 22, 1728. Then laid out a highway beginn in
at the South-east corner of the Orchard belonging to John
Shepard, and north-east of the Country road that runs over
the Bridge Swamp. Said Orchard is near the fresh meadow, four rods wide; and by land of Nathaniel Barnes, till
it comes over Luddington's brook : then up the hill as the
path runs, four rods wide untill it comes over the Vineyard
brook ; then up the hill as the path runs, four rods by Nathaniel Barnes' untill it comes to the said Barnes' East
Corner. Then runs westerly eight rods; then down the
hill to Isaac Howe's lot.

THOMAS ALCOCK and } *Com.*"
JOHN RUSSEL,   }

[*E. H. Record.*]

5th Jan. 1731. " We set off (between Mr. Davenport's
and the Ferry to East-Haven) four rods westerly from the
south-west corner of William Greenough's lot a little above
the Cove, above the Ferry, run south 18 degrees east, 23
rods and 3 feet, to a large white oak; thence south 11 degrees and 30 minutes west, 13 rods, to a heap of stones."

" Then we set off another highway of 3 rods wide, to the
line of the Indian land, to meet with a highway laid between
the Ferry field and the said Indian land; then south 28°
30″ east, 15 rods, to a heap of stones on the point of a rock;
thence east 3° south, 39 rods and 5½ feet, to a heap of stones
four rods west of Peter Woodward's land."

" Then we laid out another highway out of this, west 35°
south, 19 rods, to Joseph Tuttle's land, of four rods wide.—
Then we run from the aforesaid heap of stones east 15° 30''
24 rods, to a heap of stones in a wall, 6¼ rods from said
Woodward's land, Then south 43° east, 18 rods, to a heap
of stones on a point of rocks, 4 rods from said Woodward's
land. Thence east 22° north, 24 rods. Thence east 30½°
north, 20 rods, to a heap of stones on a rock. Thence south
21° north, 12 rods. Thence south 34° north, 21½ rods, to
a white oak with stones at the root. Thence north 21° east,
50 rods, to a heap of stones. Thence north 30° east, 18½
rods, to a red oak tree with stones at the root. Thence east
32° north, 23½ rods, to a heap of stones. Thence 40½° east,
29 rods, to a walnut pole with stones at the root. Thence
north 34° east, 33 rods, to John Rowe's south-east corner.
Thence north 30° east, 51 rods, to said Rowe's northeast
corner.

"Furthermore, we laid another highway, which comes
across by and adjoining to the aforesaid highway, beginning
at the country road which leads from East-Haven to New-
Haven, where we measured for the highway four rods wide,
out of the south side or end of Eleazar Brown's land, running westward 32 rods, and until we come to the aforesaid
Rowe's north-east corner, where we measured for highway
8½ rods in breadth, still running westward until we come
over the swamp, and partly up the hill, to a point of rocks.
Then beginning at 5⅛ rods in width, and running southerly,
continuing so until we come to the top of the hill; and from
thence four rods in breadth until we come six rods southerly
of Matthew Rowe's south-east corner of his Dragon lot;
and two rods in Eleazar Brown's Dragon lot;—then turning westerly, beginning the highway six rods wide, running
down hill 13 rods, narrowing gradually until said way be
but four rods wide, so continuing the highway four rods
wide between the said Rowe's and the said Brown's lot,
until we come to the top of the hill, from where is the de-
scent down to the bank of the river, where we set off for
highway, besides the four rods out of said Brown's land,
5¾ rods, and continued to four rods westerly; thence 12
rods, to a point until the said way be but four rods wide, so
continuing the highway four rods wide to said bank, between
said Rowe's and said Brown's land. And for a recompense
to Eleazar Brown, for what we took from his lot to accommodate the highway, we agreed, and laid out to him a corner

of land, joining to the south east part of his land at Dragon, bounded northerly 11¾ rods by his own land, westerly 37½ rods by his land at the south, and 8 rods in breadth, and easterly by common or undivided land, being in quantity two acres and fifty rods of land.

JOSEPH MIX,
CALEB HOTCHKISS, } *Com.*"
JOHN HITCHCOCK,

" Proprietors voted acceptance."—[*Pro. Record.*]

" New-Haven, 1731. Then laid out a highway of two rods wide for the use of the Town and proprietors of said New-Haven, on the east side of the Ferry River, within said Town, between the Ferry Farme, so called, and the land commonly called Indian land. Said highway running from the country road, leading from the Ferry to East-Haven, eastwardly, so far as to the eastward line of said Indian land.   ISAAC DICKERMAN, } Townsmen."
                     JOSEPH MIX,

[*Pro. Record.*]

" At a meeting of the Village of East-Haven, 2d September, 1707, the Village made choice of Lieut. Russell, Samuel Thompson, and Thomas Smith, to see upon what terms they may agree with persons concerned for a cart highway through some of the River lots, and make report at the next meeting."

No report of this Committee appeared at the next meeting, nor have I been able to find any proceedings on this subject untill 12th January, 1747, on which day the Village meeting " Voted, that Moses Thompson, Matthew Rowe, and Isaac Penfield, be a Committee to clear the highway by Isaac Holt's house, and others that needed."

" A highway, laid out by us, whose names are underwritten, meeting with a highway in Branford, laid out to East-Haven line, near Caleb Parmerly's land, 4 rods in breadth, running westerly, by said Parmerly's land, to a white-oak stump, and from thence to a dog-wood stump by said Parmerly's land, and from thence to a white-oak stump by said Parmerly's land, and from thence to a white-oak tree at the corner of Thomas Dawson's land, and from thence to a walnut pole in said Dawson's fence, and from thence to a white-oak stump near Samuel Russell's corner of his lot, and from thence to a white stump and stones, and from thence to a Walnut pole with stones, and from thence to a heap of stones, as are all the forementioned stations, meeting with the highway that leadeth from Joseph Tuttle's to the Pond Rock. March 24th, 1734.

ALLING BALL, ⎱ *Com.*"
JOHN RUSSELL, ⎰

Proprietors confirmed the report.

" Beginning at the highway next to the Pond Rock and so running northward till it comes to or near the hill, northward of Caleb Chedsey's dwelling-house. Said highway is 3 rods wide, and is laid out to be 2 rods in width in Parmerly's land, and one rod in width in Thomas Dawson's land till it comes to the River, and 14 rods in Caleb Parmerly's and Caleb Chedsey's land in the half mile, and 1½ rods in Nathaniel Jocelin's land ; to or near the valley northward of said Chedsey's house two rods wide in said Jocelin's land, and 1½ rods in said Chedsey's land ; and from thence turning a little eastward through a corner of said Chedsey's and Isaac Penfield's land 4 rods wide till it comes to the top of the hill, and then turneth westward thro' land of the heirs of George Pardee. Thence along said Dawson's land and Samuel Russel's on the west, and John Smith's on the east, untill it comes to *James' Run*, so called, then 4 rods till it comes to Bull swamp bridge."

" Also, another highway beginning a little northward of said Chedsey's dwelling house, and so running thro' Foxon's as the road now runs, 2¼ rods wide, till it comes to Joseph Grannis' dwelling house ; and from thence 4 rods to Piper's brook." *[E. H. Records.]*

28th April 1732.—Laid out a highway from Samuel Bradley's lot, called *Mount Harry*, 4 rods from a white oak pole, west running south by the widow Chedsey's—thence south by Joseph Holt's lot 4 rods—thence by Jonathan Austin's, south, 4 rods west—thence southerly to John Rowe's south corner, 4 rods wide—east to a heap of stones and black oak pole, southerly to Daniel Russel's lot to a white oak stump, 4 rods to a black oak pole West, then running East by said Russel's lot 4 rods south to a white oak pole, running east and south by Russel's lot to James Dennison's Northwest corner to a Walnut tree, continuing by said Denison's Southeast Corner, then running Southwesterly by said Denison's lot to his Southwest corner—then running west southwest by Joseph Holt, Joseph Tuttle, Samuel Hotchkiss, till it meets with the country road that leads to Muddy River, which road is 4 rods wide.

[Pro. Record, E. H.]

ALLING BALL, ⎱ *Com.*"
JOHN RUSSELL, ⎰

Proprietors' meeting.—" It is proper that Samuel Russel should have a conveniency to go to his land near Bull swamp, and there being a piece of land which Capt. Theophilus Alling hath in his possession between said Russel's land and the highway that is called Bull swamp road, which is common land ; and we Joseph Holt, Thomas Alcock and John Thompson being appointed to lay out a highway across said common land from said road, to said Russel's land, and in the most convenient place, and is bounded by heaps of stones by the road ; the highway we laid out two rods wide, a heap of stones each side, and runs Southwesterly to said Russel's land, containing two rods wide through, and is bounded by heaps of stones, each side said highway by Russel's line, the bounds were appointed and settled, March, 1733."

" 13th Feb. 1734. A highway laid out near where Nathaniel Luddington lives, from said Luddington's land 6 rods wide at the north end, running Southerly by land of Daniel Russel's till it meets with the highway; and said highway to be 3 rods wide where it meets with the highway at the Southeast corner of said Daniel Russel's land."

[*E. H. Record.*]

" 28th May, 1739. Joseph Holt and Thomas Alcock being called to lay out a highway, (being chosen thereto by the proprietors in East Haven,) of 4 rods wide, leading from East Haven up by the Bloomary, and running Northerly till it comes to a lot belonging to Samuel Bradley's line on the north, and stakes and stones south, and extends 4 rods wide along by said Bradley's line, till it comes to land belonging to John Moulthrop.—[*E. H. Records.*]

JOSEPH HOLT,   ⎰
THOMAS ALCOCK, ⎱ *Surveyors.*"

" We the Subscribers being appointed to lay out needful highways by the Proprietors of East-Haven, and within said Parish of East-Haven, and being called to lay out a highway from the country road by the west side of the fresh meadows within said Parish, and said highway extends along the said meadow as the path runs, till it comes to land in the improvement of Joseph Holt, and then turns up west by said Holt's land, and runs round northward till it comes to Peter Woodward's lot, called Sperry's lot, and so by said lot till it comes to a highway that goes down to the country road that leads to the Ferry.   And we began at the country road Southwest of said meadow, and the breadth of said highway is 4 rods wide, and the east side of said highway is bounded with heaps of stones, running with a line from a heap of stones between the parsonage land and the country road, to a stump and a heap of stones, and so continues below the hill 4 rods, till it comes over the brook or spring, and all the upland between the swamp and fence as it now stands, by Chedsey's land, and so between said Holt and Chedsey to the fence on the east side the said Highway, and so along between said Holt and Joseph Tuttle's land to the fence on each side, and so up between said J. Tuttle's land and Peter Woodward's to the fence, and each side, till it comes to the corner of said Woodward's lot, and then turns round to the highway, 4 rods. Laid out by us, 5th April, 1737.

THOMAS ALCOCK,
JOHN RUSSEL, and } *Surveyors.*"
JOSEPH HOLT,

[*E. H. Record.*]

" We the subscribers being appointed by the proprietors of East-Haven to lay out highways in East Haven, where it may be judged needful, we have, therefore, now laid out these highways upon the Green or Common in East-Haven, following, viz.: One road from the house of Gideon Potter, 10 rods wide, eastward, untill it comes to the upper end of the New-Lane and Samuel Bradley's house lot. Another from that, Northward, 10 rods wide, until it comes to the country road. And another 10 rod road from the meeting-house, running about Southeast, untill it comes to the head of the said New-Lane. And another road, 10 rods wide, from the house of Abraham Chedsey, Southward, down to the swamp of John Heminway: And another road from the said Chedsey's house, down to John Heminway's swamp, by John Heminway's and Moses Thompson's house lot, 10 rods wide. Also, another road from Moses Thompson's Barn eastward down to the Spring from Thompson's home lot to the swamp of John Heminway about 8 rods. [*E. H. Record*]

ALLING BALL, } *Surveyors.*"
JOSEPH HOLT,

"Feb. 9, 1744. We the Subscribers, being called to lay out a highway near the head of the Mill pond, to the line between New-Haven and Branford, and we did as follows, viz.: We began at the said pond, and for conveniency of landing we laid out the highway 25 rods by the pond, and on the west of the highway we ran northeast and by north 30 rods by the end of the rock lots, and on the east we run northwest 11 rods, and then we laid out a two rod high-

9

way, north bearing to the east, along by the end of the rock
lots, till we come to John Swayne's land, and then North-
east to the line between New-Haven and Branford.

JOHN RUSSEL,   } *Com."*
MATTHEW ROWE, }

[*E. H. Record.*]

" A highway laid at the Gap of the Rock."

" We began by Abraham Heminway's land near the Gap,
and run 10 rods to the said pond, and 9 rods by the said
Pond, and 12 rods by the rock and across to the first station ;
and a 4 rod highway from said land thro' the Gap at the
most convenient place, and so to extend till it comes over
the River up to the country road between Daniel Bradley's
homested, and the homested belonging to the heirs of Ebenezer Chedsey deceased. Laid out by us.
16th July, 1744.

ISAAC PENFIELD,   ⎫
DANIEL HITCHCOCK, ⎬
SAMUEL HEMINWAY. ⎭

[*E. H. Record.*]

" We the Subscribers being appointed by the Inhabitants
of East-Haven to run the line for, and lay out a road thro' a
farm now in the possession of William Rogers, in the half
mile, did as follows :

" Begun at Abel Smith's southeast corner, at the east side
of the highway, and run to the east of South 23 rods to a
small stump ; and then running south 17 rods to a large
white oak stump, and then southeast 21 rods to a white oak
pole ; and then set off 6 rods to the west side of said highway
to a sumach bush ; and then southeast and by east 13 rods,
to a stake ; and then south bearing to the west 45 rods, to an
heap of stones, and then southwest 39 rods, to Isaac Blakeslee's corner, and then running 5 rods south bearing to the
west to a white oak bush, and then 13 rods south to an ash
stump, and then 31 rods southwest to John Howe's to a former highway.—As witness our hands.

" The above is 6 rods wide.

MOSES THOMPSON, ⎫
DANIEL HITCHCOCK, ⎬ *Com.*"
JOHN RUSSEL,   ⎭

" 12th March, 1733. Voted, That the land between Stoney-River and Mill-River, on the south side of the Country
road, between said Rivers and the Road, be and remain for

the use of the proprietors forever, and not to be inclosed or taken up by any person under any pretence whatever."

[*E. H. Records.*]

Capt. Amos Morris bought the land, and at his own expense made a causey and road across the Cove Meadow, and by perseverance prevailed to get a road through the woods up to the old South-end road. This was an expensive enterprize, and is of great public utility. Yet when the Town assumed the road, they voted to allow him nothing for it. However, after much altercation, and the appointment of several Committees, the Town voted to allow him $40!! The road was then got through to Mew's Lane, in 1787. In 1792, another attempt was made to lay the road through up to the Meeting-house. And the report of the selectmen respecting it was accepted. But it was not executed untill 1797, when the Town "Voted to open the road from the Meeting-House to Capt. Morris's Causey three rods wide."

"5th Jan. 1795. We laid out a highway through the Old plains ; beginning at a Button Ball Tree about 24 rods south of the causey in the line of the Old highway ; then running southeasterly thro' the lands belonging to the heirs of Jacob Smith dec'd, 53 rods and 19 links, in a strait line from said Button Tree to the Northeasterly corner of the stone wall lately belonging to James Thompson, dec'd. Said highway, as by the subscribers surveyed and laid out, $2\frac{1}{2}$ rods in width north of the said Tree, and said corner of said stone wall, which makes the northerly line through the land of the said Smith's heirs, 54 rods and 24 links. Thence through the lands lately belonging to Stephen Thompson $19\frac{1}{2}$ rods on the south line, which reaches said corner of said stone wall and $2\frac{1}{2}$ in width, to metes and bounds northernly from said corner, which makes the northernly line through said land 23 rods, and 2 rods in length.

" We then began at the northwesterly corner of said new highway, and laid, in addition to the old highway that led from the said causey to Southend, one rod in width off from the lands belonging to said heirs, 24 rods in length, which reaches the meadow at the northeasterly end of said Causey. All which lands by said survey from the heirs of said Smith, is $\frac{3}{4}$ of an acre and 38 rods. Damages for which were assessed at £18.   [Stephen Thompson gave his land for the road.]

DAN HOLT,
JOHN WOODWARD, } *Selectmen.*"

[*É. H. Record.*]

This is the only road the Town owns on Southend Neck. The roads there were laid out by the Proprietors of the neck, according to agreement among themselves.

The road that leads to the New Ferry was surveyed 30th May, 1787, and £15 damage was awarded to Henry F. Hughes, with liberty to have his house remain where it stands, "so long as he shall improve it." Nothing was a-warded to the other men through whose land it was laid, either because they were specially benefitted by it, or had in possession the old four rod highway that was laid out to the old Stable or Ferry Point, 1686.

The road was laid out by Amos Morris, jun. Dan Holt, Selectmen.

[*E. H. Record.*]

A road was laid out on the half mile at the north end of the Town as follows :

" Beginning at a brook near Ebenezer Holt's house, and running easterly to Branford line, where it meets a highway this day laid out by the Selectmen of the Town of Branford, two rods wide ; running through the land belonging to Eliphalet Rogers and others, to us unknown, 78¼ rods, which makes 157 rods of land.   Damages assessed at £10 19 6 lawful money.   10th June, 1796.

JAMES CHEDSEY,
ENOS HEMINWAY, } *Selectmen.*"

[*É. H. Record.*]

Road on Dragon Bank.

" Beginning at the highway that leads to the Old Ferry, called Pardee's Ferry, and running northeasterly, on the west side of Samuel Tuttle's Hill, through said Tuttle's land 81 rods, and 3 rods in width, 1½ acres and 3 rods. Damages £4 6 8.   Said road still runs said course through Henry F. Hughes' land 27 rods and 9 links, 3 rods wide. Damages £0 12 0.   Said road still runs said course from said Hughes' land, through the Widow Mary Pardee's land, 69 rods of land.   Said road is still 3 rods wide, and leads into the highway a little westward and northward of said Mary Pardee's house—still running with said highway northward, taking a small corner off from said Widow Pardee's land in the pasture lying north of said house. Damages £4 10 0. Then laid 22 rods of land for said highway through Jared Pardee's land, which takes a small piece at the first mentioned place where said road left the Old Ferry highway, and a small piece of about two rods off from his land that lies north of where the Old barn stood. Damages 12s. Said road still keeps its course from said Widow Pardee's pasture lot, taking a small corner off from John Woodward's land at the southwest corner. Then taking the Old highway running northward, taking a small piece of land from the northwest corner of Stephen Woodward's land. No damage. From said Woodward's land, said highway runs northward through the land that belongs to the heirs of Daniel Brown, adjoining to the Old highway, and running northward to the highway that leads by Ezra Rowe's house about 3 rods in width, makes $3\frac{1}{4}$ acres ;— Damage £12 10. Said road crosses the Old highway and runs through Ezra Rowe's home lot, 10 rods, 3 rods wide. Damage £2 12 6. Running northward through John Rowe's home lot 9 rods, 3 rods wide. Damage £2 0 6. Still keeping said course through Matthew Rowe's old house lot 8 rods, 3 rods wide. Damage £1 16. Said road keeps said course through Stephen Rowe's land, 20 rods, 3 rods wide. Damage £4 10. Still keeping said course through Ezra Rowe's land, 30 rods, 3 rods wide. Damage £2 00. Said highway still runs, nearly northeasterly from the last mentioned Rowe's land, through Samuel Davenport's land 87 rods, 3 rods wide—which leads into the country road that leads by Samuel Davenport's house, a little northward of the brook that crosses said country road, south of said Davenport's house. Damage £8 00. Surveyed 29th August, 1791, by

JOHN WOODWARD,
ENOS HEMINWAY,
ISAAC CHEDSEY,
AZARIAH BRADLEY,
} *Com.*

" Whole cost, £43 9 8."

" In Town meeting, 22d Sept. 1791, this report was accepted and approved."

In 1824, the Selectmen agreed with Reuel Pardee and John Mitchel, for land for a two rod highway on the south side of their lots, being formerly called the Indian field. The road runs east and west, between the two roads that go

to the Cove. For the land and fence, the Selectmen allowed Reuel Pardee sixty dollars, and John Mitchel thirty-six
dollars.

The State road from North-Branford to Dragon Bridge,
being now principally taken up for a Turnpike, is omitted.

PART II.

CONTAINING

AN ACCOUNT

OF THE

Names, Marriages, and Births,

OF THE

FAMILIES WHICH FIRST SETTLED, OR WHICH HAVE RE-
SIDED IN EAST-HAVEN,

From its settlement in 1644, to the year 1800.

THE following account was collected from the public and family records, from tradition, and from the monuments of the dead. Of some, no dates could be found. The families are traced as far back as there are any authentic memorials of them. Those which have removed from the town, are also noticed, where records or other correct information respecting them came in the way of the compiler. They are arranged in alphabetical order. The name of each family is stated in large capitals: the branches or descendants of the original family, are designated by small capitals.

Note.—*This mark* [†] *added to the names, signifies that the persons died young.*

Names, Marriages, and Births.

ABBOT,

JOSEPH, had Abigail, Aug. 15, 1700, who married Nathaniel Jocelin, 1720 ; Mary, Nov. 14, 1704, died unmarried.

ALCOCK,

THOMAS, married Mary Gedney, April 17, 1706. They had Martha, 1707 ; Lydia, who married Isaac Blakely ; Philip, March 3, 1714. His 2d wife, Widow Abigail Austin, Jan. 11, 1716, and had Anna, Oct. 20, 1717 ; Thomas, Sept. 6, 1720.

ALLEN,

THOMAS, married Dorothy Mallory, Dec. 7, 1769. They had Thomas,† Infant,† Roger, Mary, who married Amos Broton, 1791 ; Thomas, Philemon, Betsey. Roger married Rhoda Tuttle, 1789.

ALLING,

THEOPHILUS, son of SAMUEL, was born, Feb. 17, 1679, and married Elizabeth Smith, June 17, 1708. They had Titus, Timothy.—2d wife, Widow Elizabeth Bradley.

TITUS, married Deborah Page. They had Titus, Lydia, Abigail, Nathaniel,† Deborah, Theophilus, Jonathan, Phebe, Nathaniel, Mary, Justus.

TITUS, JUN. married Widow Lucinda Hickox, Jan. 27, 1789. They had Sylvia.

ANDREWS,

JEDEDIAH, married Hannah Thomas, 1731. They came from Woodbridge, and had John, May 17, 1731 ; Mary, June 15, 1733 ; Lydia, Jan. 16, 1735 ; Gideon, March 2, 1737.—2d wife, Elizabeth Baldwin, 1740, had Jedediah,† May 1, 1741 ; Hannah, Oct. 17, 1743 ; Jedediah, Feb. 3, 1751 ; Timothy, May, 1753 ; Nathan.

JEDEDIAH, JUN. married Ame Bradley. They had Infant.†—2d wife, Abigail Barnes, Feb. 15, 1778, had Infant,† Infant, 1779 ;† Jedediah, April 3, 1781 ; Hannah, Jan. 25, 1783 ; Elizabeth, June 26, 1786 ; Abigail, Infant,† Saltrue.

TIMOTHY, married Dorcas Smith, 1776. They had Nathan.

ANDREWS,

TIMOTHY, married Rachel Adkins. They came from Wallingford, and had Elisha, Dec. 12, 1746 ; Timothy, April 27, 1749 ; Rachel, Dec. 25, 1751, who married Samuel Crumb, 1772 ; Phineas, Nov. 25, 1752 ; Benjamin, Dec. 18, 1755.—2d wife, Widow Anna Holt, Jan. 25, 1758, had Samuel, Nov. 1758 ; Temperance, Nov. 28, 1760, who married Joseph Hotchkiss, jun.

ELISHA, married Sarah Moulthrop, 1769. They had Jared, March 25, 1770 ;† Timothy, Oct. 10, 1772 ;† Jared, March 28, 1774 ; Lydia, Oct. 10, 1776 ;† Nathan, Nov. 9, 1778 ; Sarah, Nov. 30, 1780 ; Lydia, Oct. 21, 1782; Rachel, Oct. 16, 1784 ; Mabel, April 13, 1787 ; Lue, Oct. 27, 1792.

JARED, married Dorothy Phelps, 1792. They had Eliza, Mary, Sylvia, Samuel, Susan.

NATHAN, married Mehitabel Pardee. They had Reuel, Betsey, Almira, Mabel, Harriet, Mary, Nathan, Sarah.

AUGER,

NICHOLAS, *was a learned Physician of New-Haven. He made his will in* 1638, *in which he mentions his sister* Esther Coster, *and his brothers* JOHN *and* ROBERT, *and* Nicholas, *the son of* JOHN, *and the youngest of* JOHN'S *sons. His will was executed in* 1669.

ROBERT, married Mary Gilbert, Nov. 20, 1673. They had Esther, Oct. 19, 1677 ; John, Nov. 26, 1678†; Ann, Nov. 14, 1682; John, Nov. 16, 1686.

JOHN, married Elizabeth Bradley, July 1, 1710. They had Mary, Aug. 28, 1711, who married John Higgins ; John, Isaac, Abraham ; Elizabeth, who married Ives ; Lydia, who married Charles Thomas, 1742 ; Daniel.

JOHN, jun. married Rachel Barnes, 1744. They had Rachel, Oct. 27, 1744; Keturah, June 17, 1746 ; John, June 11, 1748†; Peter, June 12, 1750 ; John, June 19, 1753 ; Puah, May 1, 1755.

DANIEL, married Elizabeth Hitchcock. They had Philemon, May 20, 1754 ; Lois†; Elizabeth, who married Rosewell Bradley, 1779, and Samuel Forbes, 1782.—2d wife, Mabel Brown.

PHILEMON, married Tabitha Perkins. They had Rosewell, Oct. 20, 1780 ; Lois, Sept. 20, 1782.—2d wife, Mary Shepard, Jan. 1, 1790, had Elizabeth, Jan. 10, 1793 ; Daniel, July 16, 1795; Abraham, Dec. 26, 1798†.

AUSTIN,

JOHN,* married Mary Atwater, 1667. They had John, April 23, 1668†; David, Feb. 23, 1670; Joshua, Sept. 3, 1673; Mary†; John, Oct. 14, 1677;† Mary, April 17, 1680†; a son, 1683.†—His wife died 1683, and he married Elizabeth Bracket, Jan. 21, 1684, and had Sarah, Jan. 23, 1685.

DAVID, married Abigail ——, and had Abigail, April 5, 1699; David, Oct. 2., 1703; Stephen, Jan. 1, 1705; Jonathan, April 27, 1708; Mercy, 1710, who married Samuel Holt, 1737, and Caleb Hitchcock; Lydia, who married Ebenezer Darrow.

DAVID, JUN. married Rebekah Thompson, Feb. 11, 1731. They had, David, May 6, 1732; Samuel, April 3, 1734; John, Sept. 23, 1736; Sarah, Aug. 13, 1737; Rebekah, Feb. 26, 1739.—2d wife, Hannah Punderson, had Hannah, Aug. 21, 1741, who married Rev. Nicholas Street, 1766; Punderson, Jan. 18, 1743† ; Punderson, Feb. 10, 1744; Jonathan, July 31, 1745.

DAVID, 3d, married Mary Mix, Dec. 14, 1752. They had Rebekah, Dec. 16, 1753; Mary, Oct. 24, 1755†; David, March 19, 1759; Ebenezer, June 18, 1761; Sarah, July 24, 1763; Elizabeth, June 1, 1765; Hannah, Oct. 26, 1767; Elisha, March 23, 1770; John; Mary, 1776, who married Rev. Andrew Yates.

SAMUEL, married Lydia Woolcot, Dec. 6, 1759. They had Samuel, Oct. 7, 1760; William, Sept. 8, 1762; Lydia, Dec. 9, 1764.

JOHN, married Anna Mix. They had Anna, who married Rev. Daniel Crocker.

JONATHAN, maried Sarah Beecher. They had Thaddeus, John, Sarah, Nancy, Eli Beecher.

STEPHEN, married Martha Thompson, April 19, 1732. They had Tryphena, May 10, 1733; Stephen, June 17, 1735†; Mary, Jan. 25, 1740; Stephen, May 7, 1743; Abraham, May 25, 1749; Martha, Feb. 13, 1751.

JONATHAN, of DAVID, sen. had Abigail 1738†; Lydia, Sept. 17, 1740.

JOSHUA, married Mehitabel Hitchcock. They had Silence, Feb. 28, 1714; Joshua, Sept. 17, 1733.

---

* A petition dated Oct. 6, 1656, was presented to New-Haven Government, from the inhabitants of Greenwich, to be received under their care. John Austin was one of the petitioners.

JOSHUA, JUN. married Abagail Hitchcock, May 6, 1756. They had Lois, Feb. 16,1759†; Daniel, June 5, 1762; Lois, May 11, 1764.—2d wife, Susunna Page.

DANIEL, married Sarah Pardee, Sept. 5, 1787. They had Wyllys, 1790†; Mary, June 18, 1792; John Pardee, April 3, 1794; Stephen, March 31, 1796; Sarah, Feb. 9, 1805.

BALL,

ALLING, married Dorothy. They had John, April 15, 1649 ; Eliphalet, Feb. 11, 1651 ; Alling, June 27,1656.

JOHN, had Eliphalet, May 29, 1680 : John, Sept. 30, 1685 : Sarah, Sept. 26, 1687, who married John Miles, 1710 : Hannan, Jan. 12, 1690 ; Mercy, April, 1692, who married Joseph Mix, 1709 ; Mary, Oct. 21, 1694; Caleb, June 6, 1697.

JOHN, JUN. married Mary Tuttle, 1716. They had John, Nov. 21, 1716 : Mary, Aug. 11, 1718 : Eliphalet, Sept. 18, 1721†; Eliphalet, July 29, 1723 ; Timothy, Nov. 10, 1724 ; Stephen ; Hannah.

CALEB, married Abigail Osborne, 1720. They had Joseph, Sept. 9, 1721 ; Sarah, Nov. 25, 1723 ; Abigail, Oct. 12, 1727; Caleb, Dec. 2, 1729 ; Moses, Aug. 22, 1732.

ELIPHALET, married Hannah Nash, Feb. 13, 1672, and died July 16, 1673.

ALLING, JUN. married Sarah Thompson, Nov. 27, 1678. They had Sarah, Aug. 26, 1679, who married Joseph Ives, 1700 ; Lydia, Jan. 30, 1681, who married Rev. Jacob Heminway, 1712 ; Alling†; Mercy, who married Eleazar Morris, jun. ; Mabel, who married Abraham Chedsey, 1722 ; Alling.

ALLING, 3d, married —— Griswold. They had Lydia, Oct. 29, 1725, who married Abel Smith, 1737 ; Lucy, who married Ephraim Brush ; Alling, Eliphalet, Wait, Daniel, Oliver.

BARNES,

THOMAS, *signed the Colony Constitution,* 1644. *He and his brother Daniel, settled on the plain south of Muddy River.* He had Elisabeth, May 28, 1650 ; Thomas, Aug. 26, 1653 ; Abigail, Jan. 11, 1656 ; Daniel, 1659 ; Maybee, Jan. 25, 1663.

THOMAS, JUN.—*North-Haven*—Had Mary, 1682 ; Thomas, July 21, 1684†; Thomas, July 26, 1687 ; Sarah, 1689, who married Samuel Moulthrop ; Rebekah, March 12,

1691; Abigail, June 10, 1693 ; Elisabeth, Nov. 10, 1695 ; Deborah, Feb. 1, 1698 ; Hannah, May 31, 1702 ; Samuel, April 11, 1705 ; Nathaniel, Jan. 11, 1707 ; Abraham, 1711.

SAMUEL, *North-Haven,* married Rebekah Parker. They had Justus, Jan. 3, 1730† ; Rebekah, April 28, 1733†; Hannah, Sept. 5, 1735 ; Titus, Dec. 21, 1739†.—2d wife, Elisabeth Tuttle, had Rebekah, July 27, 1741† ; Samuel, April 24, 1743 ; Elisabeth, March 1, 1745 ; Isaiah, Jan. 2, 1748.—3d wife, Dorcas Turner, had Dorcas, Dec. 26, 1753† ; Justus, March 6, 1756†.

SAMUEL, JUN. married Hepzibah Collins, 1764. They had Samuel, Jan. 3, 1765 ; Jeremiah, March 9, 1767†; Elisabeth, March 18, 1769† ; Chauncey, Feb. 1, 1771 ; Elisabeth, March 7, 1773; Sarah, Nov. 4, 1775†; Polly, Jan. 29, 1777 ; Amos, Oct. 14, 1779† ; Bela Collins, Dec. 18, 1781.

CHAUNCEY, married Huldah Smith, May 29, 1794. They had William, Maria, Samuel, Melinda, Jeremiah, Almira, Chauncey.—*And by a second marriage this mother had three more.*

NATHANIEL, married Mary Russel. They had Nathaniel†, Abraham†, Abraham†; Mary, who married Daniel Holt, *Wallingford;* Eunice, who married Samuel Brittin. —2d wife, Abigail Hotchkiss, had Ichabod.—3d wife, widow Abigail Howel, March 22, 1745. Had John, Jan. 28, 1746; Abraham, Nov. 18, 1747 ; Isaac, Dec. 21, 1749; Nathaniel, Aug. 28, 1751 ; Abigail, Feb. 4, 1753, who married Jedediah Andrews, 1778 ; Desire, Feb. 20, 1755, who married Samuel Luddington, 1787 ; Hannah, Oct. 2, 1757, who married Ephraim Chedsey, 1786 ; Jacob, Nov. 11, 1759 ; Levi, May 9, 1762.

ICHABOD, married Esther Tamadge, Aug. 12, 1756. They had Erastus, Hezekiah†, Thomas†, Esther, Abigail, Anna.

JOHN, married Abigail Collins, Oct. 10, 1763. They had Obedience, Abel, John† and Elihu.

ABRAHAM, married Hannah Grannis, Jan. 1, 1776. They had Thomas, Sept. 22, 1782 ; Mehitabel.

ISAAC, married Lois Pardee, Feb. 12, 1776. They had Mehitabel, March 30, 1777 ; Abraham Jared, August 4, 1778† ; Mary, Aug. 2, 1780 ; Isaac, Dec. 12, 1782† ; Jacob, Nov. 19, 1785 ; Huldah, June 9, 1788 ; Reuel, April 21, 1793 ; Julia, Nov. 7, 1796.

NATHANIEL, married Abigail Heminway, March 16, 1777.
10

They had Abraham, Sarah, Abiudt, Nathaniel, Drusilia, Anson, Heminwayt.

LEVI, married Huldah Grannis, 1791. They had Levi, Asenath, Lydia, Nancy.

JACOB, married Hannah Chedsey, July 30, 1789. They had Silas, Harriet, Hannah, Sarah.

ABRAHAM, (of THOMAS, JUN.) had Dimon, and three daughters.

JONATHAN, married Martha Frost. They had Jonathan, Aug. 26, 1750; Martha, Oct. 28, 1751, who married Jonathan Finch ; Solomon, 1753.

SOLOMON, married Lydia Smith. They had Lydiat, Lydiat, Martha, James, Lydia, and three infantst.

BLAKESLEY,
ISAAC, married Lydia Alcock. They had Amos, Philemon, and Maryt; Abraham, Lydia; Mary, who married Eliphalet Pardee, 1756; Isaac ; Hannah, Aug. 29, 1741, who married Joseph Holt, jun.

BRAY,
ASA, married Lydia ——. They had John, Flora, Lydia, Abigail.—2d wife, Hannah Hull, had Mary ; Hoadley.

BRADLEY,
ISAAC, married Elisabeth ——. *He appears first on Branford Records in* 1674. *He is then noticed as a " sojourner at New-Haven," and the Town granted him a home lot of two acres at Canoe brook. He removed to East-Haven,* 1683. They had Isaac, William, Samuel ; Daniel, Dec. 20, 1696 ; Sarah, who married George Parde, 3d, 1703 ; Elisabeth, who married John Auger, 1710.

WILLIAM, married Elisabeth Chedsey, Jan. 7, 1713. They had Caleb, Oct. 17, 1714 ; Ebenezer, March 25, 1716, who married Mabel Grannis, and *removed to Northbury ;* Joseph, July 13, 1718 ; Elisabeth, who married John Thompson, *New-Haven ;* Desire, who married Eliphalet Tuttle ; James, June 15, 1726.

CALEB, married Sarah Russel. They had Elisabeth, May 3, 1737, who married John Shepard, 1765 ; James, Nov. 9, 1739 ; William ; Tyrus, Rosewell, *these two were lost at sea;* Ame, who married Jedediah Andrews, jun. 1776 ; Huldah, who married Joel Northrop, 1773 ; Sa-

vah, who married Isaac Page, 1770 ; Lucretia, who married Joseph Moulthrop ; Lydia.

WILLIAM, married Rebekah Ives. They had Lucretiat ;
Joelt ; William, May 18, 1763 ; Abigail, who married
Nathaniel Yale, 1791 ; infantt.

WILLIAM, JUN. married Mary Moulthrop, Oct. 6, 1785.
They had Pollyt, William, Solomont, Lucretia, Rosewell,
Tyrus, Polly, Elisabeth Rowe, Solomon.

ROSEWELL, married Elisabeth Augur, 1779. They had
Ame.

SAMUEL, married Sarah Robinson, Jan. 7, 1715. They
had Zebulon, Oct. 6, 1715 ; Isaac, Nov. 30, 1717 ; Dan ;
Levi ; Sarah, 1728, who married Isaac Chedsey, 1752 ;
Simeon, 1731 ; Azariah, 1734 ; Gurdon, 1738.

ZEBULON, married Elisabeth Heminway, July 10, 1740.
They had Abraham, June 13, 1741 ; Josiah, Sept. 17,
1743 ; Asa and Jared,† May 9, 1746 ; Jared, May 30, 1749;
Abijah, Oct. 31, 1751 ; Zebulon, Oct. 12, 1753 ; Elisabeth,
Dec. 15, 1756, who married Andrew Davidson, 1774 ; Eli-
jah, Oct. 10, 1759.

ABRAHAM, married Ame Heminway, Jan. 23, 1760.
They had Mary, Abiudt, Rachel, Abiudt, Abraham, Sydneyt, Nancy, Sarah, Jared, Sydneyt.

JOSIAH, married Comfort Hitchcock, Feb. 2, 1764.
They had Jeremiah, Aug. 11, 1766; Loruhamah, April 7,
1769, who married Jonathan Goodsell, 1791 ; Abigail, Jan.
19, 1773† ; Zebulon, Sept. 16, 1774 ; Abigail, Oct. 22,
1776, who married Samuel Holt, jun. 1796 ; Elisabeth,
Dec. 16, 1779, who married James Heminway, 1798.

ZEBULON, married Elisabeth Goodsell, May 11, 1794.
They had Infantt ; Tryphena, Dec. 19, 1796 ; Abigail,
Dec. 27, 1798 ; Jeremiah, June 6, 1800.

ASA, married Ame Morris, 1768. They had Amos ;
Jerusha, who married Benjamin Hutchins ; Abiud, Gurdon,
Elijah.

AMOS, married Elisabeth Bradley, May 5, 1793. They
had Betseyt, Jaredt, Jared, Amos, Betsey Morris, Asa,
Jane Adeline, Elijah, Luther, Elisabeth.

JARED, married Sarah Smith, April 8, 1768. They had
Sarah, March 16, 1769, who married Samuel Bradley ; E-
lisabeth, Oct. 28, 1770, who married Amos Bradley, 1793 ;
Lorinda, Oct. 9, 1772, who married Heminway Holt, 1795 ;
Asenath, Nov. 2, 1774, who married Hezekiah Wood-
ward, 1794 ; Jared, April 2, 1778; Asa, July 19, 1781 ;

Anson, Sept. 22, 1783; Elias, May 13, 1786; John Smith, Aug. 28, 1788.

ABIJAH, married Sarah Thompson, 1769. They had James; Esther, who married Stephen Heminway, 1791; Abijah; Desire, who married Eleazar Heminway.

ELIJAH, married Esther Thompson. They had William, Nancy†, Polly, Ame.

ISAAC, married Hannah Heminway. They had Eli, Oct. 6, 1747†; Anna, Dec. 26, 1749; Isaac, July 9, 1753; Eli, Elihu, Hannah, Enos, Desire, Asahel.

ELIHU, married Sibyl Grannis, May 22, 1780. They had Hannah, Sarah, Enos, Polly, Leura, Eli, Almont, Levi, Annat, Annat.

DAN, married Sarah Judd, 1751. They had Benjamin, Feb. 18, 1753; Uriel, Sept. 9, 1755; Edmond, Sept. 24, 1757; Sarah, Nov. 27, 1759, who married John Hungerford; Nehemiah, April 13, 1762; Ichabod, Nov. 10, 1764. —2d wife, Mehitabel Heminway, Feb. 12, 1767. Had Heminway, John, Major, Hezekiah, Samuel, Elihu, Polly, Reuel.

EDMOND, married Lydia Chedsey, 1781. They had Dan, March 27, 1784; Sarah, Feb. 11, 1786; Adah, July, 1788†; Adah, Anson, Twins, Triplets, Willard, Dana, Chester, and four more that died infants.

LEVI, married Hannah Chedsey, 1748. They had Samuel, April 5, 1750; Briant, Levi.

SAMUEL, married Abigail Thompson, Dec. 18, 1777. They had Elisabeth, Samuel.

SIMEON, married Abigail Denison, July 26, 1759. They had Irene, May 6, 1760, who married Nehemiah Smith, 1793; Abigail, Jan. 6, 1762, who married Collins Hughes, 1790; Mabel, Dec. 16, 1763, who married John Tyler, 1786; Jesse, July 31, 1766; Joel, Nov. 17, 1768; Sarah, July 8, 1771; Oliver, Feb. 15, 1774; Levi, Sept. 23, 1777; Abraham, Aug. 20, 1780.

JESSE, married Lydia Holt. They had Susan, Nov. 11, 1788; Lydia, Jan. 29, 1791; Heminway Holt, June 6, 1792; Jesse, Nov. 29, 1793; Oliver, Feb. 19, 1796.

JOEL married Lovisa Bradley, January 30, 1794. They had Abraham, June 15, 1795; Abigail, June 29, 1798; infant†; Mabel Tyler, May 26, 1802; Amos, July 11, 1804; Lovisa,† Joel Nelson, Jesse, Lovisa, Amanda.—2d wife, Mary Barnes, had Reuel Barnes.

AZARIAH married Elizabeth Thompson, Nov. 7, 1759.—
2d wife, Elizabeth Woodward, Jan. 18, 1764. They had
Elizabeth, July 12, 1765; Samuel, Jan. 6, 1767; Esther,
Aug. 15, 1770, who married Leverett Bradley, 1791; John,
April 9, 1774;† Lydia, July 8, 1776; Rosewell, Aug. 15,
1780.

SAMUEL married Sarah Bradley. They had Laura, William, George, Esther, Lue, Azariah, Adeline, Lydia, Samuel, Justin.

GURDON married Mary Woodward, Jan. 30, 1766. They
had Mary, May 6, 1767, who married Laban Smith, 1789;
Huldah, June 16, 1770, who married Jehiel Forbes, 1794;
John, April 30, 1777; Lue, Oct. 1, 1780; Willet and Susan,† 1784; Justin, May 20, 1787.

DANIEL married Mehitabel Heminway. They had Mary, April 2, 1720, who married Benjamin Pardee; Stephen,
Nov. 13, 1723; Abigail, June 26, 1725; Daniel, March 6,
1728; Timothy, May 6, 1731; Jacob, July 7, 1734.

STEPHEN married Thankful Smith. They had Anna,
Dec. 9, 1748; Sarah, March 3, 1751; Timothy, John, Mary,† Stephen, Mary, Leveret, Lois, who married Stephen
Thompson, Jun. 1779; Mehitabel, who married Ichabod
Bishop, 1775.

TIMOTHY married Sarah Goodsell, 1762. They had Lucinda, March 6, 1763; Lathrop, Dec. 14, 1764; Sarah,
March 2, 1766; Elizabeth, Sept. 24, 1768; Timothy,
Sept. 14, 1770; Levi, Jan. 14, 1772; John, Polly, Lorana.

STEPHEN, Jun. married Mehitabel Luddington. They
had Mary, April 2, 1782;† Justus, March 20, 1784;† Mary, April 12, 1786; Justus, March 31, 1788;† Thankful,
Dec. 13, 1790; Lucinda, April 28, 1793; Stephen, Aug. 6,
1795; Mehitabel, June 28, 1798.

LEVERET married Esther Bradley. They had Susan,
Sept. 2, 1791; Sarah, John Smith, Emeline, Maria,†
Elizabeth Maria.

JACOB married Elizabeth Goodsell. They had Daniel,
Jan. 16, 1756; Sibyl, May 3, 1758; Lydia, Oct. 12, 1760,
who married Levi Parker; Joseph, May 16, 1763;† Mary,
Nov. 24, 1765, who married Russel Grannis, 1789; Amma,
Nov. 21, 1769; Lovisa, March 28, 1772, who married Joel
Bradley, 1794; Hezekiah, July 21, 1774; Asahel, June 5,
1778.

DANIEL married Eunice Ives, Jan. 11, 1776. They had
Nathaniel Hitchcock, April 23, 1778;† Olive, July 11,

1780; Elizabeth, Oct. 27, 1782; Sibyl, Nov. 7, 1784; Joseph, Nov. 4, 1786 ;† Lydia, April 22, 1789 ; Eudocia, July 20, 1791 ;† Sarah, May 3, 1794 ;† Eunice, Feb. 18, 1797.

AMMA married Lydia Grannis, June 26, 1794. They had James, April 28, 1795 ;† Nancy Sylvina, Nov. 24, 1797; James, May 8, 1801 ;† Almira.

ASAHEL married Asenath Grannis. They had Betsey, Asenath,† Eben, Joseph, Mary, Jared,† Jared, Asahel, Lydia.

BRITTIN,

SAMUEL, married Eunice Barnes, 1773 ; had Mary, 1778.

BISHOP,

JOSEPH, married Hannah White. They had Charles, Joseph, Benjamin, Ichabod, Elisabeth, who married James Thompson ; Hannah, who married Silas Curtis, 1769 ; Ruth.—2d wife, Mehitabel Holbrook, Nov. 12, 1750, had Jared, April 2, 1752 ; Lois, June 27, 1754, who married Jacob Smith, 1778 ; Polly, Aug. 7, 1756, who married Joel Mulford, 1782; David, Oct. 17, 1758 ;† Rachel, April 23, 1761, who married Daniel Smith, 1781 ; Stephen, Aug. 21, 1763 ;† Stephen, April 13, 1767; Sarah, April 8, 1768, who married Enos Bradley.

CHARLES married Mary Forbes, Dec. 13, 1774. *No issue.*

BENJAMIN married Abigail Hotchkiss, 1769. They had Beni, Elizabeth,† Elizabeth, Silas.

ICHABOD married Mehitabel Bradley, March 9, 1775. They had Hannah, Joseph, Polly, James, John, Elias.

BROTON,

JAMES ADKINS, married Abigail O'Neal. They had Hannah, William, Martha, Abigail, Patience, Henry, Mehitabel, Sophia, Amos and Anna,† Mary.

AMOS married Mary Allen, Sept. 19, 1791. They had James,† Nancy,† James, Hartwell, William, Orin,† and by a second marriage with Amasa Mallory, she had six more.

BROWN.

FRANCIS, *New-Haven,* married Mary. He signed the Colony Constitution, 1639. They had Eleazar, Samuel, Ebenezer, John, Lydia.

ELEAZAR, *New-Haven,* had Eleazar, Jan. 6, 1663 ; Gershom, Oct. 9, 1665 ; Daniel, Jan. 16, 1668.

GERSHOM, *New-Haven,* had Eleazar, 1696 ; Hannah, Jan. 1, 1702; Olive, Feb. 22, 1708.

ELEAZAR married Sarah Rowe, Jan. 21, 1725. They had

Sarah, Feb. 3, 1726, who married Timothy Gorham; Gershom, March 29, 1728; Abigail, June 12, 1730, who married Enos Potter; Eleazar, 1732; Hannah, June 19, 1735; Olive, who married Nathaniel Brown; Sarah, who married —— Rockwell; one married —— Hall; Daniel, Nov. 3. 1743.

DANIEL married Hannah Ingliss, April 24, 1770. They had Isaac, Feb. 27, 1771; Hannah, Nov. 18, 1772; Daniel, Sept. 11, 1774 ;† Sarah, April 23, 1776; Rosewell, Oct. 6, 1778; Phila, Aug. 30, 1780; Clarissa, June 14, 1783; Daniel, Dec. 20, 1784; Aner, Oct. 13, 1786; Mary, Dec. 21, 1788.

DANIEL, *New-Haven*, had Daniel, April 26, 1698; Joseph, Dec. 1, 1701; Isaac, March 20, 1709; Mary, Dec. 16, 1716.

BURNHAM,

DAVID, married widow Rachel Luddington, 1792. They had James, Jan. 4, 1793; William, June 11, 1795; Martha, Oct. 5, 1797.

BUTLER,

JAMES, married Lucretia Foot. They had Samuel, James, Merit, William.

CAMP,

HEZEKIAH, married Lydia. *They came from Milford to Southend about* 1704, *and afterwards removed to Canaan, Litchfield County.* They had Hezekiah, Abiel, Joel, Lydia, who married Amos Morris, 1745; Rebekah, who married David Leavitt; Abigail, who married Joel Northrup; Sarah,† Samuel, *who was an eminent minister of the Gospel in the Town of Ridgefield, where he died;* John.

CARNES,

THOMAS, married Mary Brown. They had Elisabeth. Aug. 8, 1684; Alexander, Dec. 19, 1685; Joseph, Aug. 4, 1687.

CHEDSEY,

JOHN, *Deacon of the first Church in New-Haven, signed the Colony Constitution,* 1644, *being then about 23 years of age;—he removed to Stoney River,* 1681. *This name, in England, is spelled Chedsey, and is the name of a Town. And so it appears on the old records and monuments. It was so used by the sons of* JOHN CHEDSEY. *It has since been changed to* CHIDSEY. *But for the sake of uniformity, I have used* CHEDSEY *instead of* CHIDSEY, *through the book.*

He married Elisabeth ———. They had Mary, Sept. 22, 1650†; John, Oct. 21, 1651, *died without issue;* a daughter, 1653†; Joseph, Dec. 5, 1655; Daniel, July 30, 1657†; Mary, Nov. 21, 1659, who married William Wilmot, 1692; Caleb, Nov. 20, 1661; Hannah, Jan. 7, 1663, who married Caleb Mix; Ebenezer, Feb. 10, 1665; Elisabeth, Dec. 16, 1668†; Sarah, 1670, who married Samuel Alling.

JOSEPH, married Sarah ———. They had Hannah, Jan. 28, 1696; Joseph, Aug. 15, 1698†; Sarah, May 13, 1700; Abigail, April 28, 1702; Rachel, March 17, 1704; Dinah, May 14, 1707; Abel, March 7, 1709†; Joseph, Aug. 8, 1710; *and he removed to North-Guilford,*

Deacon CALEB, married Anna Thompson, May 10, 1688, and Hannah Dickerman, July 6, 1693. They had Daniel, March 25, 1695; Caleb, May 9, 1697; Abraham, March 31, 1699; Mary, Oct. 30, 1701, who married Jona. Gilbert, 1725.

CALEB, JUN. married Widow Abigail Smith. They had Isaac, Nov. 8, 1731; Caleb, Sept. 1, 1738.

ISAAC, married Sarah Bradley, 1752. They had Sarah, Jan. 28, 1753, who married Levi Pardee, 1771; Samuel, Aug. 28, 1754†; Abigail, Oct. 5, 1758, who married John Goodsell, 1776; Lydia, May 8, 1761, who married Edmond Bradley, 1784; Caleb, July 25, 1763; Lois, Sept. 25, 1765, who married Joel Thompson, 1782; Deborah, Jan. 3, 1768, who married Nathan Godard; Ame, July 25, 1771, who married William Smith, 1795; Samuel, April 24, 1773; Isaac, 1776†.

CALEB, married Rebekah Page. They had Isaac, April 27, 1793; Laura, Eliza, Luther, Solomon, Jared Goodsell, Lucretia.

SAMUEL, married Betsey Holt. They had Sarah, Russel, Harriet, Lorinda, Anna, Samuel, Almira, Betsey, Lydia Bradley, Abigail Holt, Hannah.

CALEB, 3d, married Mehitabel Moulthrop, Sept. 3, 1759. They had Thankful, who married Jesse Luddington, Jun. 1779.

ABRAHAM, married Mabel Ball. They had Mabel, May 31, 1723, who married William Woodward; Hannah, July 4, 1725, who married Levi Bradley, 1748; Mary, Oct. 8, 1727†; Daniel†, Daniel†, Twins†.—2d wife, Mary Todd, had Mary, 1735†; Infant†.—3d wife, Widow Bathsheba Grannis. Had Abraham, Sept. 23, 1741; Daniel, May 22, 1743; Joseph, Desire, Mary.

ABRAHAM, JUN. married Hannah Goodsell, March 27,

1766. They had Danielt, Saraht, Azelt, Lydiat, Abraham; Lydia, who married James Thompson; Jacob, Azel, Malachit, Clorinda, Desiret.

ABRAHAM, 3d, married Abigail Beach. They had John Harrington Beach, Harriet.

JACOB, married Abigail Ann Benham. They had Daniel Manderville, Emmeline Parinda, Matildat, Matilda Ann, Charles Benham.

JOSEPH, married Sarah Goodrich, 1769. They had Timothy, Feb. 26, 1770; Bartholomew, June 19, 1771; Abraham, Sarah, Isaac, Jacob, Daniel, Mabel, Fanny, Naomi, Zacheus.

EBENEZER, married Priscilla Thompson. They had Sarah, Dec. 8, 1689, who married John Dawson, 1708; John, Nov. 6, 1691†; Elisabeth, Feb. 6, 1693, who married William Bradley; John, March 4, 1695; Samuel, June 6, 1699; Ebenezer, Dec. 6, 1701; James, Aug. 23, 1704†; Abigail, April 1, 1707, who married Daniel Hitchcock; Isaac, June 3, 1710.

JOHN, married Mary Foot, Feb. 8, 1715. They had Sarah, Dec. 6, 1716; John, Sept. 15, 1720; Eunice, March 31, 1723, who married Moses Luddington.

JOHN, JUN. married Sarah Shepard, Dec. 21, 1745. They had Abigail, May 6, 1747, who married John Goodsell, 1773; John, Dec. 16, 1749; Ephraim, March 19, 1752; Rosewell, July 17, 1754; Street, Nov. 15, 1756; Sarah, Oct. 1758, who married Richard Barret, 1780; Rhoda, 1760; Samuel, 1762†; Mary, Sept. 26, 1765, who married Phineas Curtiss, 1787; Eunice, 1768, who married William Walker; Ezekiel, Oct. 8, 1770.

JOHN, 3d, married Anna Luddington, March 8, 1770. They had Hannah, Jan. 18, 1771, who married Jacob Barnes, 1789; Abigail, Nov. 19, 1773, who married Noah Welton, 1792; Anna, May 5, 1775, who married Levi Baldwin, 1796; Street, Sept. 8, 1778·; Sarah, Aug. 5, 1780; John, Jan. 22, 1783†; Samuel, Hervey, Charlottet; Horace.

EPHRAIM, married Desire Denison, Feb. 26, 1778. They had Desire, March 5, 1783.—2d wife, Hannah Barnes, 1786.

ROSEWELL, married Hannah Lanfear. They had Reuel, Sept. 5, 1776; Ralph, Feb. 2, 1779; Polly, Feb. 22, 1781†; Polly, July 11, 1783; Rosewell, March 24, 1786; Frederic, Rutherford, Nancy.

Ezekiel, married Lydia Gorham. They had William, Susan, Frederick, John, Edward, Sarah, Charles.

Samuel married Deborah Goodsell. They had Samuel, Oct. 14, 1722 ; Deborah, Nov. 28, 1725.

Samuel, jun. married Hannah Grannis. They had Levy, Feb. 1, 1745; Sarah, Dec. 1, 1747, who married George Stanclift, 1780, and Gideon Allen ; Hannah, May 6, 1749, who married Asa Mallory, 1778 ; Huldah, Nov. 24, 1751, who married Ezra Rowe, 1773.

Levy married Hannah Potter, Sept. 10, 1770. They had Huldah, Oct. 27, 1773 ; Samuel, April 14, 1775 ;† Sarah, March 1, 1778 ; Hannah, Nov. 14, 1780 ; Samuel, April 12, 1783 ; Deborah Goodsell, Sept. 7, 1785.

Isaac, (of Ebenezer,) married Mary Pardee. They had Sarah, who married Ezra Fields ; Mary,† Ebenezer, James.

Ebenezer married Elizabeth Grannis, June 26, 1761.. They had Isaac, who married Lydia Smith, 1791; Mary, who married Asher Moulthrop, 1783 ; Jacob ; Sarah, who married Samuel Grannis ; Elizabeth, who married Caleb Smith, 1794 ; Desire,† Abigail, who married Levi Moulthrop.

James married Mehitabel Grannis. *No issue.*

COLLINS,

DANIEL, married Abigail Thompson, Sept. 8, 1698. They had Daniel, July, 1699 ;† Abel, Aug. 4, 1702 ; Amos, Oct. 1704 ;† Lydia, Feb. 1707 ;† Priscilla, who married Daniel Holbrook ; Lydia, Dec. 1710 ;† Daniel, March 1, 1713 ; Abigail, Sept. 14, 1717 ; Rebekah, Feb. 29, 1720.

Abel married Rebekah Bartholomew. They had Mercy, who married Bordwell Hughes ; Hepzibah, July 14, 1743, who married Samuel Barnes, 1764 ; Abigail, Aug. 15, 1744, who married John Barnes, 1764.

COLT,

Truman, married widow Anna Pardee. They had Wyllys Forbes, Anson Truman.

COOPER,

JOHN, *removed from New-Haven to Stoney River, about the time the Ironworks were established, of which he was an agent.* He had John ; Sarah, who married Samuel Heminway, 1662 ; Hannah, who married John Potter, 1661.

John, jun. married Mary Thompson. They had Rebekah ;† a daughter, 1668 ; Mary, 1669 ;† John, Feb. 23, 1770; Samuel, June 2, 1675 ; Abigail, Oct. 3, 1679.

LEVI married Thankful Dayton, Dec. 6, 1775. They had Patty, Nov. 24, 1776; David, Nov. 13, 1778; Sarah, Feb. 26, 1781; Zeruah, Jan. 20, 1783; Levi, Jan. 20, 1788.

CURTISS,

PHINEAS, married Hannah Russell, May 28, 1759. They had Benjamin, Abigail, Phineas.

PHINEAS, JUN. married Mary Chedsey, July 4, 1787. They had Polly, June 12, 1788; Hannah, March 17, 1790; Russel, March 16, 1792; Loly, Feb. 12, 1794; Asenath, Feb. 28, 1796; Benjamin, March 19, 1798; Major, Dec. 20, 1800; John, April 26, 1802; Susan, Feb. 11, 1804; Street, 1806.†

CRUMB,

SAMUEL, married Rachel Andrews, Dec. 15, 1772. They had Anna, Elisabeth, Rachel, Samuel.

DAWSON,

ROBERT, *settled at Foxon's Farms in* 1683. He then had John, born in 1677. After this he married widow Hannah Russel, and had Thomas, 1693.

JOHN married Sarah Chedsey, July 1, 1708, and Mercy Luddington, 1715. They had Timothy, April 27, 1716 ;† Robert, March 2, 1718; Anna, 1720 ;† Titus,† John.

ROBERT, married widow Thankful Grannis. They had Desire ;† Mary, wife of Samuel Smith, Jun.; Abigail, who married Timothy Way, 1765; Susan, who married David Downs, 1768; Huldah; Joel, who married Sibyl Luddington, 1787.

JOHN, JUN. married Mary Moulthrop. They had Mary, Timothy, Titus, Sarah.

TIMOTHY married Anna Holt, Jan. 2, 1772. They had Holt, Thomas, Mary.

HOLT married Irene Shepard, 1793. They had Anna, Eliza, Polly Jennet, William, Henry.

THOMAS, married Hannah Robinson. They had Sarah, 1723, who married Stephen Smith, 1760; Mary ;† Hannah, who married Stephen Grannis; Lydia, who married Samuel Grannis; Mary,† Joseph.†

DAY,

WILLIAM, married Abigail Woodward, Nov. 14, 1771. They had Samuel, May 20, 1773; Mary, May 25, 1775.

who married George Landcraft; Joseph, Dec. 31, 1777 ; William Thomas, March 27, 1780; Abigail, 1782.

DARROW,

RICHARD, married Sarah Shepard. They had Richard, May, 1711 ;† John, June, 1713 ;† John, Oct. 24, 1716; Ebenezer, 1719.

EBENEZER, married Lydia Austin. They had Ebenezer, March, 1743 ;† Abigail, July 29, 1745 ; Jemima, Feb. 9, 1748 ; Asa, May 22, 1750 ; Eunice, Jan. 23, 1755 ; Ebenezer, Sept. 18, 1757 ; Titus, Sept. 15, 1753 ; Lydia, 1759.†

DAVIDSON,

ANDREW, married Elizabeth Bradley, Dec. 15, 1774. They had Elizabeth, Oct. 7, 1775, who married Truman Russel ; John, Oct. 31, 1778 ; James, Sept 11, 1781 ; Abijah, April 23, 1784 ; Nancy, June 15, 1788; Jeremiah, Jan. 5, 1791 ; Leuramah, July 28, 1793 ; Rachel, Sept. 5, 1795 ;† Fanny, Oct. 22, 1797 ; Sarah, Sept. 22, 1800.

DAVENPORT,

REV. JOHN, *was a son of the Mayor of Coventry, in England, was born 1797, and was sent to Brazennose College, Oxford, 1613. He began to preach when he was 19 years of age. Being persecuted by Archbishop Laud, and other furious spirits, he came over with the Colony that settled at New-Haven, 1638, being about 41 years of age. He was the first Pastor of the first Church in New-Haven, and having continued about 30 years, he removed to Boston. He was an eminent preacher of the Gospel about 54 years. He died of an apoplexy, 15th March, 1670, in the 73d year of his age; he left one son, John.*

JOHN, married Abigail, *a daughter of the Rev. Abraham Pierson, the first minister of Branford,* Nov. 27, 1663. They had John, June 7, 1665 ;† Elisabeth, Oct. 7, 1666, who married Warham Mather, 1700; Abigail, who married Rev. James Pierpont; John, 1670 ; Mary, who married Nathaniel Weed, 1694.

Rev. JOHN, 3d, *was graduated at Cambridge College, 1687, and was the third Pastor of the Church at Stamford, and died Feb. 5, 1731, in the 36th year of his ministry.* He married Martha, the widow of John Selleck, April 8, 1693 : *her maiden name was Gould.* They had John, Jan. 21, 1695 ; Sarah, who married William Maltbie, 1724, and

Rev. Eleazar Whelock, 1735 ; Martha, July 17, 1700, who ma ried Thomas Goodsell, jun. ; Theodora, Nov. 2, 1703 ; Deodate, Oct. 23, 1706 ; Elisabeth, Aug. 28, 1709.—2d wife, widow Elisabeth Maltbie, daughter of John Morris, had Abraham, James.

DEODATE, married Lydia Woodward, 1730. They had Sarah, July 7, 1731, who married John Mix ; Martha, May 26, 1733, who married Gould S. Silliman ; William, 1734†; John, 1738 ; Samuel, 1740 ; Rosewell, 1742† ; Lydia, 1746, who married Samuel Holt.

JOHN, married widow Anna Pierpont, 1780, and widow Phebe Todd—but had no issue.

SAMUEL, married Mary Street. They had Sarah, Jan. 31, 1767, who married Ira Smith, 1784 ; Rosewell, April 28, 1768 ; Hezekiah, Dec. 11, 1769 ; Mary and Martha, Dec. 16, 1771—Mary married John Woodward, 1794 ; Martha married Eli Potter, 1793 ; Street, Jan. 28, 1775.

ROSEWELL, married Esther Heminway, 1793. They had John, April 5, 1794 ; William, Nov. 28, 1796 ; Mary, Nancy.

DENISON,

JAMES, *appears first on Record in* 1663, *when he bought the shore of William Andrews, in Southend Neck.* He married Bethiah Boykim, Nov. 25, 1662. They had James, Aug. 1664†; John, Nov. 1665† ; Mary, July 26, 1668 ; Sarah, April 12, 1671, who married Joseph Sacket, 1710; James† and John, Feb. 6, 1677 ; Elisabeth, Nov. 24, 1681, who married Samuel Harrison, 1707 ; James, Jan. 5, 1683.

JOHN, married Grace Brown, *daughter of John, and grand daughter of Francis Brown.* They had Abigail, Nov. 13, 1705, who married Daniel Granger ; Sarah and John†, May 10, 1708, who married Joseph Trowbridge ; Elisabeth, Aug. 28, 1710, who married Samuel Thompson ; Mehitabel, Oct. 2, 1713, who married Samuel Heminway ; Mary, March 29, 1716, who married John Woodward.

JAMES, JUN. —— had Jesse, James, Desire, who married Benjamin Smith ; Lydia, who married Jacob Goodsell, 1755 ; Sibyl, Abigail ; Sarah, who married Samuel Moulthrop ; John.

JESSE, married Abigail Heminway, Aug. 25, 1740. They had Abigail, who married Simeon Bradley, 1759.

JAMES, married Sarah Smith. They had Sibyl†, Sarah,

11

Desire, who married Ephraim Chedsey ; Jesse, who married
Mabel Woodward—*but had no issue ;* Dorothyt, Abigail,
Lydia, Jamest.
 John, married Sarah Hough, 1761. They had Chauncey, who married Sarah Grannis, 1782 ; Obedience, Samuel, Leveret, Hannah, Lois, James, Sarah, John, Jesse
and Desire, Ephraim Hough, Zina, Ezekiel Rice.

EGGLESTON,
 DAVID, married Elisabeth Higgins, Dec. 1,1765. They
had Zebra, John, Abraham.
 John, married Olive Page. They had Betsey.

EVERTON,
 WILLIAM, married Isabel Holbrook, Nov. 14, 1755.
They had Daniel, March 17, 1757 ; Esther, Sept. 8, 1759,
who married Addereno Forbes ; Mary, April 23, 1762, who
married William Merriam; William, Dec. 18, 1764; Jared, May 21, 1767 ; Isabel, April 20, 1769, who married
Enos Tamadge ; Holbrook, Feb. 5, 1772.

FARNHAM,
 Bela, married Anna Morris, Nov. 13, 1797. They had
Emmeline, Amos Wilcoxt, and Joseph Camp.

FARREN,
 ZEBULON, married Desire Heminway, March 3, 1768.
They had Jacob, Sarah, Mehitabel, who married Lot Sizer ;
Lorinda, who married Phineas Clark; Abraham, Eli, John,
Samuel, Major, Oct. 10, 1790.
 Jacob, married Lydia Dunham. They had James, Jo-
sepht, Sarah, John, Lue, Sydneyt, Belinda, Sydney, Jo-
seph Dunham, Lydia Almira.
 Abraham, married widow Hannah Barnes. They had
Eli, Anna, Zebulon.

FIELDS,
 Ezra, married Sarah Chedsey. They had Mary, who
married Isaac Bradley, jun. 1778; Lydia, who married
Isaac Hotchkiss, 1775, and Chandler Pardee, 1790 ; Sarah, who married Joseph Pardee, 1783 ; John, Mercy, who
married John Bray ; James, Samuel, Ezra.

FINCH,
 DANIEL, had Daniel, April 10, 1719 ; Gideon, Feb.

21, 1720 ; Ebenezer, Jan. 3, 1723 ; Elisabeth, who married Joshua Dudley, 1752 ; Avis, who married Aaron Blakesley, 1759 ; Anna, March 3, 1728, who married E-lam Luddington, 1748 ; Joseph, May 1, 1729 ; Damaris, who married Jared Foot ; Abigail, Lydia, April 1, 1736.

DANIEL, married Rebekah Bartholomew, Oct. 20, 1742. They had Gideon, Oct. 13, 1743 ; Rebekah, Feb. 27, 1746.

JOSEPH, married widow Chloe Tamadge, Sept. 16, 1755. They had Elam, Jonathan, Sarah, Mary, Joseph, Ichabod.

JONATHAN, married Hannah Hotchkiss. They had Milton, Reumah, Orton†.—2d wife, Martha Barnes.

FORD,
BENJAMIN, married Anna Slaughter. They had John-son, Feb. 6, 1783 ; Benjamin, May 1, 1785.

FORBES,
SAMUEL, married Mary Thompson. They had Samuel, Jehiel, Levi, Isaac, April 2, 1742 ; Sarah, who married Jared Potter, 1764 ; Mary, who married Charles Bishop, 1774.

SAMUEL, JUN. married widow Elisabeth Bradley, 1782. They had Huldah, Samuel.

JEHIEL, married Mabel Morris, 1757. They had Eli, Levi, Samuel, Jehiel, Eleazar, David.

ELI, married Rhoda Osborn.—2d wife, widow Lois Smith, had Morris.—3d wife, Eleanor Ottee ; had Betsey, Sarah, Almira, Eli.

JEHIEL, JUN. married Huldah Bradley, 1794. They had William, Julia, Adeline, Mary Ann, Jane and George†.

SAMUEL, married Sylvia Rogers. They had Anna†.—2d wife, Leah Whiting, had Betsey, David, Alford, Samuel.

LEVI, married Sarah Tuttle. They had Anna, March 23, 1770; Mary, Feb. 6, 1772; Sarah, May 20, 1774; Levins, July 8, 1776 ;† Timothy, 1778† ; Lydia, Sept. 10, 1780 ; Ame, Oct. 8, 1782 ; Levi, March 14, 1785 ; Bela.

ISAAC, married Hannah Heminway, May 1, 1766. They had Sarah, March 7, 1767, who married Jeremiah Beecher ; John, Dec. 19, 1770 ; Isaac, April 15, 1773 ; Amasa, March 19, 1778 ; Parson, March 19, 1783.

JOHN, married Anna Holt.—2d wife, Ame Holt. They had Anson, William, Horace†, Horace†, Justin, Jared.

ISAAC, JUN. married Anna Bradley, Dec. 8, 1794. They

had Harriet, 1796†; Mary†, Henry, Mary Ann, Huldah†, Willet, 1713†.

ELIAS, married Abigail Shepard, Nov. 26, 1755. They had Elias, Abigail, Aaron.

FROST,

ALLEN, married Mary Walker, 1791. They had Mary.

FULLER,

JOHN, married Lydia Moulthrop, March 13, 1766. They had Sarah†, John†, Lois†, Lydia, Sarah, Lois.

GOODSELL,

THOMAS, *appears on Branford records*, 1679. *He removed to Stoney River*, 1692, *and married* Sarah Heminway, June 4, 1684. They had Samuel, Feb. 28, 1685; Mary, Dec. 28, 1686, who married Henry Tolles, 1728; Sarah, Sept. 14, 1689; Lydia, May 3, 1692, who married Josiah Rogers; Deborah, Dec. 29, 1694, who married Samuel Chedsey; Abigail, Oct. 4, 1697† ; Abigail, Feb. 28, 1699, who married Thomas Smith, 3d, and Caleb Chedsey, jun. ; Thomas, Jan. 4, 1702; John, Dec. 21, 1705.

SAMUEL, married Mary Frisbe. They had Samuel, Oct. 30, 1710; Jonathan, June 22, 1712 ; Isaac, March 14, 1715; Isabel, Sept. 9, 1717, who married Caleb Hitchcock, 1739; Mary, Dec. 17, 1719, who married Samuel Hotchkiss ; Jacob, July 22, 1722 ; Dan, June 16, 1724.

SAMUEL, JUN. married Mary Hotchkiss. They had Samuel, Jan. 1738† ; Mary, Feb. 13, 1740, who married Isaac Luddington ; Deborah, Aug. 23, 1742, who married Thomas Frisbe ; Levi, June 17, 1745, died in 1768.—2d wife, widow Lydia Cooper ; had Lydia, who married Benjamin Baldwin, 1780 ; Martha.

JONATHAN, married Elisabeth Todd. They had Elisabeth, July 11, 1739, who married Jacob Bradley ; Jonathan, Feb. 21, 1741 ; Josiah, March 27, 1742† ; Josiah, Dec. 1743†; Sarah, Oct. 24, 1745, who married Timothy Bradley ; John, 1747 ; Josiah, Jan. 22, 1750 ; Samuel, March 10, 1756.

JONATHAN, JUN. *Branford*, married Hannah Tyler. They had Mary, Aug. 22, 1762; Jonathan, Feb. 21, 1764; Simeon, June 30, 1766 ; Hannah, Aug. 24, 1768 ; Josiah, Aug. 12, 1775 ; Sarah, March 17, 1778.

JONATHAN, 3d, *Branford*, married Loruhamah Bradley,

Oct. 17, 1791. They had Jeremiaht, Mary, Charles, Dennis and Danat, Dana, Grace.

JOHN, married Abigail Chedsey, 1773. They had Elisabeth, Aug. 21, 1774, who married Zebulon Bradley, 1794 ; John, Nov. 6, 1777.

ISAAC, married Elisabeth Penfield, 1737. They had Isaac, Jan 16, 1738 ; Hannah, Feb. 31, 1740, who married Matthew Man, 1763 ; Penfield, July 2, 1742 ; Abigail, Oct. 29, 1744 ; Thomas, Nov. 30, 1746 ; Samuel, April 4, 1749 ; Timothy, Feb. 25, 1752 ; Elisabeth, Sept. 15, 1754 ; Mary, Dec. 6, 1757 ; Saxto, July 5, 1760 ; Jacob, Feb. 17, 1763.

PENFIELD, married Hannah Thompson, April 19, 1765. They had Hannah, who married Caleb Todd, 1784; Elisabeth.

SAMUEL, married Abigail Goodrich, 1775. They had Ira, Abigail, Major, William, Penfield, Irene, Betsey, Elvirat.

JACOB, married Sarah Beckley, 1746. They had Hannah, Oct. 22, 1746, who married Abraham Chedsey, jun. 1766 ; John.—2d wife, Lydia Denison, 1755 ; had Sarah, who married Jared Bishop ; Lydia, who married Amos Rice ; Bethia, May 1, 1764, who married James Baldwin.

JOHN, married Abigail Chedsey, 1776. They had Sarah, who married Jared Luddington ; Jacob, Jared, Lydia, Irene, Hannah, John.

DAN, married Abigail Moulthrop, June 30, 1748. They had Edward, May 8, 1749 ; Amos, July 6, 1751 ; Dan, March 28, 1754 ; Isabel, Nov. 5, 1757, who married John Wise, 1781 ; Abigail, April 21, 1761, who married Benjamin Barnes, 1781 ; Levi, April 7, 1764 ; Anna, March 22, 1767, who married John Shepard, 1789 ; Amost, Dan married Desire Potter ; Levi married Eunice Gilbert.

EDWARD, married Lucy Luddington, 1770. They had Jesse, May 21, 1771 ; Mary, Sept. 6, 1772, who married Morris Scott, 1792 ; Mehitabel, March 20, 1774, who married Russel Lanfear ; Ame, Feb. 7, 1776, who married Joseph Holt, jun. 1797 ; Amos, Aug. 9, 1780.

THOMAS, married Martha Davenport, Oct. 6, 1731. They had Sarah, who married Jeremiah Woolcot.

GRANGER,

DANIEL, married Abigail Denison. They had Abigail, who married Daniel Whedon ; Sarah, who married Eli Tul-
11*

lar, 1760 ; Denison ; Mary, who married Joseph Tuttle, 1761 ; Thaddeus, Oct. 24, 1745.—2d wife, Sarah Perkins; had Daniel, Aug. 28, 1756 ; Thomas, Lemuel.

GRANNIS,

Joseph, was the son of Edward, *North-Haven, and was born* March 12, 1677, and married Hannah, *daughter of John Russel,* Nov. 3, 1702. They had Joseph, William, Russel, Thomas, Stephen, Isaac, Sarah, who married Matthew Moulthrop 4th ; Anna, who married Ashur Moulthrop ; Mabel, wife of Ebenezer Bradley ; Hannah, who married Samuel Chedsey, jun.

Joseph, jun. married Bathsheba Thompson, 1728. They had Desiret.—He was lost at sea.

William, married Thankful Allen. They had William, Thankful, who married Benjamin Moulthrop, 1761 ; Desire, who married Aaron Page.

William, jun. married Sarah Grannis. They had Sarah, who married Chauncey Denison, 1760 ; Sibyl, who married Elihu Bradley ; Anna, Robert, Levi, Aaron, Gurdon, Thomas, Mehitabel, Thankful.

Russel, married Lydia Forbes. They had Russel, Samuel, Stephen, died at sea ; David.

Russel, jun. married Lucy Luddington. They had Nathaniel, Mary, who married John Hughes, 1778 ; Lucy, who married Daniel Hughes ; Lois, who married Chandler Robinson, 1781 ; Russel, Abigail, Lydia, who married Charles Wedmore, 1786.

Nathaniel, married Martha Smith, 1777. They had Stephen, Abigail, Martha, Nathaniel, Russelt, Lydia, Lois, Elisabeth.

Russel, 3d, married Mary Bradley, May 28, 1789. They had Levi, Lucy, Alva, Mary, Russelt, Anson, Sylvia, Bradley, Davidt.

Samuel, married Lydia Dawson. They had Samuel, Lydia, who married Joseph Smith and Josiah Moulthrop ; Russel.

David, married Mary Shepard, Dec. 9, 1762. They had Mary, who married Giles Eaton ; Huldah, who married Levi Barnes ; Lydiat ; Lydia, who married Amma Bradley; Sarah, who married Elihu Webster; Mabel, who married Hiel Burr ; Asenath, who married Asahel Bradley, 2d ; Elisabeth, who married Francis Burrass ; Davidt.

Thomas, married Mehitabel Thompson. They had Sa-

rah, who married William Grannis, jun. ; Abigail, who
married Joseph Russel, 1764 ; Joseph, Jemima, who married
Isaac Moulthrop, 1761 ; Mehitabel, who married James
Chedsey, 1769 ; Thomas, died at sea ; Hannah, who married Abraham Barnes, 1776 ; Samuel, died at sea.

JOSEPH, married Olive Luddington. They had Elihu,
Samuel, Joseph, Thomas, Olive, who married Ebenezer
Holt ; Ame.

ELIHU, married Polly Bunnel. They had Polly†, Olive,
Polly, Eunice, Sarah, Ame, Wealthy.

SAMUEL, married Sarah Chedsey. They had Joseph,
July, 24, 1791 ; Nancy, Betsey, Olive, Harriet, Thomas.

STEPHEN, married Hannah Dawson. They had Joel,
Stephen, Jacob, Mabel, Lydia, Jerusha.

ISAAC, married Keziah Moulthrop. They had Elisabeth,
Oct. 22, 1741, who married Ebenezer Chedsey, 1761.
Ame, Aug. 11, 1744, who married Stephen Shepard, 1765 ;
Didamea, Jan. 30, 1748, who married Samuel Smith, jun.
1773 ; Isaac ; Jared, Aug. 1756 ; Loruhamah, who mar-
ried Joseph Moulthrop, 1774.

ISAAC, JUN. married Mary Luddington. They had Sarah, who married Stephen Shepard, jun. ; Mary.

JARED, married Martha Luddington. They had Isaac†,
Ame, Jared, 2 Infants†.—2d wife, Eunice Munson, had
Horace, Louisa, Mary Ann, John, Frederic, Isaac.

GREGSON,

THOMAS, *was a principal man in the Colony at New-
Haven, and the first white settler in East-Haven. His settlement was made at Solitary Cove ; he was lost at sea in
1647.*—Jane, *his widow, lived to a great age.* They had
Richard and Mary, *who resided in London ;* Anna, who
married Stephen Daniels ; Susan, who married —— Crit-
tenden ; Sarah, who married —— Whitehead ; Phebe, who
married Rev. John Whiting; and three more daughters.

HEMINWAY.

The name HEMINWAY, *in East-Haven, is* HEMENWAY,
and HEMMENWAY *in Massachusetts. But in England it is*
HEMMINGWAY, *which is the original and real name. It was
probably altered to make it shorter. English names of persons and places generally, have the consonant doubled at
the end and beginning of a syllable in the middle of the*

word. And IN—*is followed with* G, *as will appear from the following examples:*

Cottingham ; Collingham ; Corringham ; Coddington : Cossington ; Deddington ; Doddinghurst ; Nottingham ; Lullington ; Hemmingburgh ; Pennington ; Warrington ; Waddington ; Collingwood ; Harrington ; Luddington ; Birmingham ; Watlingstreet ; Darklington ; Walsingham ; Abingdon ; Eckingham ; Darking ; Epping ; Wiggington : Odingsell ; Edlinghall ; Bevington. *The same is true of a multitude of other words in the English language.*

SAMUEL, married Sarah Cooper, 1662. They had Sarah, July 26, 1663, who married Thomas Goodsell, 1684 ; Samuel, Dec. 13, 1665 ; Mary, July 5, 1668 ; Hannah, Sept. 14, 1670, who married John Howe, jun. ; Abigail, Feb. 16, 1672, who married Joseph Holt, 1706 ; John, May 29, 1675 ; Abraham, Dec. 3, 1677 ; Isaac† and Jacob, Dec. 6, 1683.

JOHN, married Mary Morris, 1703. They had Mehitabel, May 30, 1702, who married Daniel Bradley ; Mary, April 28, 1704, who married Samuel Russel and Samuel Smith ; Desire, March 2, 1707, who married Moses Thompson ; Hannah, Dec. 11, 1709, who married Samuel Thompson ; Samuel, March 12, 1713 ; John, Oct. 7, 1715.

SAMUEL, married Mehitabel Denison. They had Mary, May 13, 1734, who married Jacob Pardee ; Jacob, April 19, 1737 ; Samuel, Jan. 1739† ; Desire, who married Zebulon Farren, 1768 ; Mehitabel, March 18, 1745, who married Dan Bradley, 1767 ; Samuel, May 9, 1748 ; Eli, Sept. 2, 1753 ; Sarah, May 18, 1758, who married Enos Heminway, 1777.

SAMUEL, JUN. married Hannah Morris. They had Stephen, Eleazar, Esther, who married Rosewell Davenport, 1793 ; Samuel.—2d wife, widow Sarah Bradley, 1787 ; had Jacob, Augustus.

STEPHEN, married Esther Bradley, Feb. 21, 1791. They had Hannah, April 25, 1792 ; Morris, Sept. 2, 1796.—2d wife, Mary Andrews ; had Esther, John, Mary, Alford and Albert, Harriet, Erastus, Jennet, Almira.

ELEAZAR, married Mary Woodward, June 22, 1794.—2d wife, Desire Bradley ; had Polly, Sarah, Emily, Oscar Morris, Eliza, Samuel, Eleazar, Abijah, Mehitabel, Mary, Edward.

JOHN, JUN. married Mary Tuttle, Nov. 9, 1738. They had John, Aug. 6, 1739 ; Joseph, June 6, 1741† ; Ame,

May 25, 1743, who married Abraham Bradley ; Joseph, March 14, 1745 ; Hannah, Feb. 14, 1747, who married Isaac Forbes, 1766 ; Jared, May 17, 1749 ; Moses, Aug. 14, 1751 ; Joel, May 21, 1754 ; Mary, Sept. 1, 1755, who married Ezekiel Hayes ; Lydia, May 22, 1759, who married Jacob Pardee, jun. 1777.

JOHN, 3d, married Jemima Hitchcock, Aug. 25, 1761. They had John.

JOHN, 4th, married Hannah Thompson, 1797. They had Harriet, Laura†, Merit, John†, Maria.—2d wife, widow Abigail Holt, 1806 ; had John, Orilla, William.

JOSEPH, married Elisabeth Woodward, Dec. 21, 1769. They had Abiud, Rosewell†, Jared, Haynes, Ruel†, Elisabeth†.—2d wife, widow Abigail Thompson, April 19, 1786 ; had Thompson and Joseph†, Sarah.

JARED, married Huldah Woodward, June 9, 1774. *No issue.*

MOSES, married Martha Tyler, 1776. They had James, June 12, 1777 ; Mary, May, 1779† ; Chandler, Nov. 17, 1783 ; Eben Tyler, 1785† ; Harvey, June 1, 1788 ; Eben Tyler, Dec. 18, 1791 ; John, Joel†.

JAMES, married Elisabeth Bradley. They had Polly, Oct. 8, 1798 ; Josiah, June 10, 1801† ; Samuel, Sept. 6, 1803 ; Hiram, Dec. 5, 1805† ; James.

ABRAHAM, by his first wife had Sarah, who married Enos Potter.—2d wife, Sarah Tamadge, Nov. 11, 1713 ; had Abraham, Jan. 1715† ; Elisabeth, Oct. 3, 1716, who married Zebulon Bradley ; Abigail, March 17, 1719, who married Jesse Denison, 1740 ; Isaac, Feb. 1721† ; Anna, Feb. 1723† ; Hannah, Oct. 22, 1724, who married Isaac Bradley ; Abraham, April 1, 1727.

ABRAHAM, JUN. married Mercy Tuttle, April 24, 1746. They had Isaac, Feb. 1747† ; Sarah, Feb. 17, 1749, who married Jacob Eaton, 1769 ; Abraham, April 10, 1751 ; Abigail, May 17, 1753, who married Nathaniel Barnes, jun. 1777 ; Enos, Sept. 17, 1755 ; Mercy, July 5, 1757, who married Daniel Smith ; Elisabeth, May 1, 1760, who married Leavit Pardee, 1782 ; Isaac, May 3, 1762 ; Jacob, Nov. 1764.

ABRAHAM, 3d, married Anna Smith, Aug. 11, 1771. They had Sarah, Polly, Anna, Eliza, Abraham, Isaac, Jacob, Laban.

ENOS, married Sarah Heminway, April 23, 1777. They had Samuel, April 25, 1778 ; Sarah, Sept. 17, 1780 ; Bet-

sey, Oct. 25, 1782 ; Nancy, May 7, 1785† ; Anson, Oct,
10, 1787† ; Willet, 29th, and Wyllys, 30th Jan. 1791.
    Isaac, married Eunice Beecher. They had Charlotte†,
Susan, Eunice, Polly, Isaac, Twins, Charlotte, Abraham.
    Jacob, married Abigail Lindsley, Dec. 23, 1784. They
had Lucretia, Nancy, Jacob Street, Lavina, Mercy, Polly,
Eunecia, Abraham, Caroline.
    Rev. Jacob, married Lydia Ball, May 3, 1712. They
had Lydia, 1715, who married Hezekiah Pierpont, 1737.

HICKOX,
    Darius, married Lucinda Street, Sept. 3, 1779. They
had Darius.

HIGGINS,
    John, son of John Higgins *of Westchester, New-York,
was brought to East-Haven, when a boy, and put under the
care of Daniel Bradley.* He married Elisabeth Auger.
They had Timothy, Jan. 30, 1734 ; Isaac, Oct. 5, 1740;
John, March 10, 1743 ; Elisabeth, May 13, 1746, who
married David Eggleston, 1765 ; Abraham, Feb. 26, 1748.

HITCHCOCK,
    MATTHIAS, *signed the plantation Covenant at New-
Haven,* 1639, *and was one of the purchasers of Southend
Neck.* He had Eliakim, Nathaniel, John, Elisabeth, June
4, 1651.
    Eliakim, married Sarah Merrick, (of Springfield,) Nov.
4, 1667. They had John, Aug. 1668† ; Sarah, Oct. 16,
1669, who married Jacob Robinson ; Hannah, March 19,
1672 ; Thomas, 1674 ; Samuel, March 7, 1678 ; Eliakim,
Oct. 2, 1680 ; John, Nov. 1, 1683 ; Joseph, July 23, 1686.
    Samuel, had Thomas, Samuel.
    Eliakim, jun. had Eliakim, Thomas.
    Nathaniel, married Elisabeth Moss, Jan. 8, 1670. They
had Elisabeth, March 17, 1672 ; Nathaniel, July 28, 1678 ;
Abiah, Oct. 26, 1680, who married Samuel Peck, 1703 ;
John, Jan. 28, 1685 ; Ebenezer, April 9, 1689 ; Mary,
July 20, 1692, who married Samuel Clark, 1718.
    Nathaniel, jun. married Rebekah Morris. They had
James, Dec. 5, 1703 ; Nathaniel, Dec. 16, 1705 ; Daniel,
April 17, 1708 ; Caleb, Sept. 2, 1712 ; Benjamin, Aug.
22, 1715 ; Rebekah, March 28, 1718, who married Daniel
Leak ; Elisabeth, Aug. 10, 1721, who married Daniel Au-
ger ; Stephen, July 6, 1724.

James, married Elisabeth Ray. They had James.

James, jun. married Phebe Leak, Oct. 1753. They had Mary, Phebe, James†, Elisabeth.

Nathaniel, 3d, married Elisabeth Mansfield, Feb. 14, 1728. They had Nathaniel, Dec. 7, 1728 ; Lydia, Dec. 7, 1730 ; Lois, Aug. 28, 1732 ; Hannah, Dec. 6, 1733 ; Eunice, Mary, Sarah, Daniel, Amos, Joel, Zachariah.

Daniel, married Abigail Chedsey, March 12, 1729. They had Jemima, March 3, 1730† ; Abigail, April 25, 1734, who married Joshua Austin ; Levi, Jan. 1739† ; Comfort, Aug. 9, 1742, who married Josiah Bradley, 1764 ; Jemima, Dec. 17, 1744, who married John Heminway, 1761 ; Anna, Sept. 24, 1746, who married Dan Holt, 1765.

Caleb, married Isabel Goodsell. They had Jacob, July 4, 1739 ; Samuel, 1741 ; Caleb, March 3, 1749 ; Isabel, May 3, 1751.

Jacob, married Phebe Ives, Oct. 9, 1760. They had Abigail†, Jacob†, Enoch†, Phebe, Abigail, Jacob, Caleb.

Benjamin, married —— Rice. They had Benjamin, Abigail.

Stephen, married Sarah Leak, Feb. 9, 1749. They had Rebekah, Dec. 3, 1749 ; Levi, July 30, 1751† ; Sarah, Levi,Abigail, Rhoda, Daniel, Stephen, Deborah, Mary Amna.

John, *whether the son of Eliakim or Nathaniel I cannot determine,* married Mary Thompson, March 4, 1708.—2d wife, Abiah Basset, 1711 ; had Mary, March 6, 1712 ; Samuel, Nov. 5, 1713 ; Abiah, Aug. 6, 1715 ; Joseph, Feb. 13, 1717 ; Thankful, Feb. 9, 1719 ; Sarah, Feb. 13, 1721 ; Abigail, Sept. 2, 1722 ; Amos, June 12, 1724.

Ebenezer, married Anna Perkins, 1711. They had Timothy, Aug. 20, 1713.

EDWARD, married Frances ——. They had John, Samuel.

HOLT,

WILLIAM, *New-Haven,* married Sarah ——. They had John, 1645 ; Nathaniel, 1647 ; Mercy, 1649 ; Eleazar, April 5, 1651 ; Thomas, July 3, 1653 ; Joseph, April 2, 1655 ; Benjamin, Jan. 6, 1658.

John, married Elisabeth Thomas. They had Elisabeth, Sept. 23, 1674 ; John, March 23, 1679 ; Joseph, June 22, 1680 ; Daniel, March 30, 1689.

Joseph, married Abigail Heminway. They had John, Aug. 2, 1706 ; Joseph, Oct. 20, 1708, lost at sea ; Daniel, Sept. 6, 1711 ; Samuel, July 30, 1713 ; Abigail, Aug. 4,

1716, who married John Howel and Nathaniel Barnes ; Elisabeth, April 21, 1718 ; Isaac.

DANIEL, married Anna Smith. They had Abigail, Nov. 22, 1736, who married John Moulthrop and Samuel Shepard; Anna, March 27, 1741†; Dan, Oct. 18, 1744; David, Oct. 1751†; Anna, March 14, 1752, who married Timothy Dawson, 1772.

DAN, married Anna Hitchcock, Dec. 5, 1765. They had Daniel, July 5, 1767 ; Sarah, Nov. 25, 1769, who married Samuel Thompson, 1786 ; Lydia, Aug. 25, 1770, who married Jesse Bradley, 1788 ; Heminway, Feb. 26, 1772 ; Anna, May 16, 1773, who married John Forbes, 1793 ; Philemon, July '21, 1775; Ame, Feb. 26, 1778, who married John Forbes ; Lois, Feb. 19, 1780, who married Horatio G. Street ; Betsey, Oct. 2, 1781, who married Samuel Chedsey ; Jared, Feb. 3, 1783 ; Abi, Feb. 9, 1788, who married Jared Goodsell ; Abigail, Jan. 23, 1789.

DANIEL, married Hannah Holt, Jan. 12, 1789. They had Daniel, Jared, Hiram, Hannah, Belinda.

HEMINWAY, married Lorinda Bradley, Dec. 2, 1795. They had Merit, Sarah, Willet, Jared, Lorinda, Anna, Heminway.

SAMUEL, married Mercy Austin, Oct. 13, 1737. They had Joseph, Aug. 8, 1738 ; Samuel, March 24, 1741†; Samuel, Nov. 10, 1743 ; Thomas, March 12, 1748†.

JOSEPH, married Hannah Blakesley. They had Mercy, Jan. 6, 1760, who married Hezekiah Todd, 1783 ; Ebenezer, July 6, 1762 ; Hannah, Aug. 17, 1767, who married Daniel Holt, 1789 ; Joseph, June 5, 1773.

EBENEZER, married Olive Granniss. They had Philemon, Abigail, Joseph, Elisabeth.

JOSEPH, JUN. married Ame Goodsell. They had Laban, Lucretia, Nancy, Edward, Mary.

SAMUEL, JUN. married Mary Rowe, Oct. 10, 1765. They had Elisabeth†, Samuel, Mary, who married Joseph Bishop. —2d wife, Lydia Davenport.—3d wife, widow Ann Martin.

SAMUEL, 3d, married Abigail Bradley, May 12, 1796. They had Alford, Jeremiah, Mary.

ISAAC, married Mary Morris. They had Isaac, Jan. 1, 1743 ; Desire, Dec. 10, 1744 ; Mary, July 24, 1747 ; Jacob, Jan. 13, 1750 ; Eleazar, Aug. 1, 1752 ; Nicholas, Oct. 4, 1755 ; Lois, Jan. 14, 1758.

HOLBROOK,

DANIEL, married Priscilla Collins. They had Lydia, Dec. 25, 1729, who married Jonah Atwater; Mabel, Oct. 22, 1731, who married Joseph Bishop, 1750; Isabel, Sept. 10, 1734, who married William Everton, 1755; Abigail, June 3, 1737, who married Timothy Cooper, 1766; David, Dec. 15, 1739†; Daniel, Nov. 12, 1742†—*These two were drowned together.* Hannah, Jan. 23, 1745, who married Jonathan Woodin, 1764.

HOTCHKISS,

SAMUEL, married Sarah Tamadge, 1678. They had Mary, Jan. 1, 1679; Sarah, April 7, 1681; Samuel, March 6, 1683; James, Dec. 8, 1684; Abigail, Feb. 12, 1686.

SAMUEL, JUN. married Sarah Bradley, Jan. 10, 1705. They had James, Feb. 1707†.—2d wife, Hannah Russel, had James, March, 1711†; Sarah, March 12, 1712; Samuel, Jan. 5, 1715; Mary, March 5, 1718, who married Samuel Goodsell, jun.; Abigail, Feb. 27, 1721, who married Nathaniel Barnes; Joseph, Feb. 15, 1725; James, Jan. 1728†; Enos, May 13, 1731.

SAMUEL, 3d, married Mary Goodsell, 1744. They had Samuel†, Mary, Sarah, Samuel, Ebenezer, Hannah, Anna.

JOSEPH, married Esther Russel. They had Abigail, May 6, 1748, who married Benjamin Bishop, 1769; Mary, June 24, 1750, who married Elihu Moulthrop; Sarah, 1752†; Isaac, Dec. 30, 1754; Joseph, July 31, 1756; Esther, April 13, 1759, who married John Rowe, 1778; Samuel, Aug. 26, 1763; Heman, July 1, 1765; Asaph, Oct. 7, 1767; Gideon, Dec. 25, 1769.

ISAAC, married Lydia Fields, Dec. 4, 1775. They had Lydia, Dec. 12, 1776, who married Titus Sanford, 1795; Betsey, May 2, 1779, who married Samuel Tuttle, jun.; Sarah, March 19, 1781; Lois, Aug. 26, 1783.

JOSEPH, JUN. married Temperance Andrews. They had Anna, Sept. 22, 1780; Lyman, March 20, 1784; Esther, June 28, 1787; Orilla, April 14, 1791; Polly, May 15, 1793; Huldah, Oct. 11, 1798.

HEMAN, married Elisabeth Rowe, 1793. They had Harriet, Horace, Samuel Russel.

ASAPH, married Hannah Russel, 1788. They had Elisabeth, Gideon, Polly, Lorinda, Asaph, Esther.

ENOS, married Elisabeth Shepard. They had Enos, Jan.

25, 1757†; Enos, Stephen ; Hannah, who married Jonathan Finch ; Samuel, April 25, 1778.

HODGE,

THOMAS, married Jane Moulthrop. They had Lydia, Aug. 12, 1718 ; James, April 17, 1720 ; Hannah, Sept. 21, 1722; Job, April 24, 1726 ; Keziah, Aug. 12, 1729; Abel, March 8, 1731.

HOWEL,

JOHN, married Abigail Holt, 1732. They had Joseph, Nov. 7, 1734†; Henry, April 10, 1736 ; Desire, July 29, 1738†; Samuel, Nov. 29, 1741 ; Joseph, Jan 8, 1744.

HOWE,

JEREMIAH, *appears on record, New-Haven,* 1654, *and had a son John.*

ZACHARIAH, had John, Dec. 21, 1667.

JOHN, JUN. married Hannah Heminway. They had Hannah, Feb. 9, 1693, who married Thomas Robinson ; Sarah, Nov. 1695†; Elisabeth, Dec. 19, 1702, who married Isaac Penfield ; Isaac, Feb. 18, 1706 ; Abigail, June 3, 1709, who married —— Bishoop ; Lydia, Dec. 1711† ; Mary, 1713, who married Stephen Pardee ; John, Dec. 24, 1714 ; Lydia, March 8, 1717, who married Dan Moulthrop ; Naomi† and Bathsheba, April 20, 1720.

ISAAC, married Thankful Rogers. They had Thankful, Dec. 1731† ; John, May 22, 1734 ; Hannah†, Elisabeth, Sarah† ; Isaac and Andrew and William, died at sea ; Joshua, Samuel, John, *was killed at Fort Hale.* [†*These died of consumption.*]

HUGHES,

HENRY FREEMAN, married Lydia Tuttle, July 19, 1749. They had Henry, July 7, 1751 ; Freeman, John, Abigail, who married Stephen Rowe, 1781 ; Daniel, June 17, 1759.

FREEMAN, married Mary Richards, Nov. 24, 1774. They had Mary, Hannah.

JOHN, married Mary Grannis, Oct. 10, 1778. They had Lydia, Aug. 17, 1779 ; Lois, Sept. 12, 1782 ; Russel, Nov. 6, 1784 ; Huldah, Nov. 25, 1787 ; Polly, June 20, 1789 ; Henry, John†, Abigail.

DANIEL, married Lue Grannis. They had Sarah Rosewell, Daniel†.—2d wife, Sarah Atwater, had Aaron Atwater, Jan. 20, 1797.

BORDWELL, married Mercy Collins, 1763. They had Rebekah†, Anna Collins, Rebekah, Israel, Joseph.

COLLINS, married Abigail Bradley, Jan. 2, 1790. They had Huldah, June 18, 1793 ; Nancy, May 11, 1796 ; Collins, Jan. 24, 1798† ; Sarah Bradley, June 28, 1801† ; Susan, John†.

HUNT,

JOHN, married Elisabeth Tomline. *They came from London,* and had Frederic William, Dec. 16, 1772† ; John, April 10, 1775 ; Grace, May 20, 1776 ; Ann Maria, Dec. 5, 1777 ; Sarah, Dec. 16, 1779† ; Emily, Dec. 18, 1780 ; William Henry, Sept. 13, 1782 ; Elisabeth, Sept. 14, 1783 ; James Richard, March 29, 1785 ; Woodward Hervey, Jan. 19, 1787† ; Charles Augustus, May 27, 1789†; Sarah, Nov. 10, 1790† ; Samuel Bradley Horatio, Dec. 4, 1792.

JOCELIN,

NATHANIEL, married Abigail Abbot, March 15, 1720. They had Nathaniel, Dec. 19, 1721 ; Abraham, Sept. 29, 1723 ; Abigail, July 23, 1725, who married Nathaniel Porter ; Joseph, Jan. 31, 1726 ; Anner, July 29, 1729, who married Elijah Atwood ; Mary, 1731, who married Elijah Skinner ; John, May 22, 1723 ; Thomas ; Thankful, who married —— Gibson ; Rebekah, who married John Porter ; Anna, who married Jonathan Hastings ; Sarah, Nov. 5, 1746, who married George Lancraft.

NATHANIEL, JUN. married Ann Wadsworth. They had Amaziah, Sept. 1, 1744 ; Simeon, Oct. 22, 1746.

KING,

GEORGE, married Patience Conklin, Dec. 27, 1756. They had John, Oct. 12, 1760 ; George, Edward.

GEORGE, JUN. married Elisabeth Tuttle, May 30, 1776. They had Elisabeth, Sept. 14, 1785 ; Patience†, Rebekah†, John, Oct. 12, 1780.

LANCRAFT,

GEORGE, married Sarah Jocelin, Feb. 6, 1776. They had Mary, who married Joseph Hill ; George, Nathaniel, Infant†, Abigail, who married John St. John ; Joseph†, Simeon, Thomas, Joseph, Amaziah.

GEORGE, JUN. married Mary Day. They had Sarah, Nathaniel. William, Maria, Almira, Abigail, Lucius.

LANFEAR,

Russel, married Mehitabel Goodsell. They had Sarah Amanda, July 2, 1796 ; Mary Ann, Joseph, Russel, Horace, Nancy, Luezer, George.

LARKINS,

Joshua, married Jerusha Blackman. They had Lemuel, Sarah, Betsey, Nancy, Martha, Samuel, Eunice, Jerusha, John, Lydia, Polly.

LINDSLEY,

Samuel, married Jane Graham. They had William, Henry, Samuel, Robert, Jane Freelandt, Charlest, Jane Freeland, Charles, Lucius, Sarah.

LUDDINGTON,

WILLIAM, *died at the Iron works,* 1662, *and his widow* married George Rose. He had William ; Henry, *died in* 1676 ; Hannah, John, Thomas ; a daughter.

William, jun. married Martha Rose. They had Henry, Eleanor, who married —— Baley ; William, Sept. 25, 1686. —2d wife, Mercy Whitehead, 1690. *Previous to their marriage, it was stipulated by a written Covenant, that the first child which she might have, should be made equal in heirship with his first child, which he had by his first wife; he being entitled to a double share : and that her other children should be made equal to his other children.* They had Mercy, May 31, 1691, who married John Dawson, 1715 ; Hannah, March 13, 1693 ; John, Jan. 31, 1694 ; Eliphalet, April 28, 1697 ; Elisabeth, 1699t ; Dorothy, July 16, 1702, who married Benjamin Mallory ; Dorcas, July 16, 1704, who married James Way.

Henry, married Sarah Collins, 1700. They had Daniel, June 21, 1701 ; William, Sept. 6, 1702 ; Sarah, Feb. 1703t; Dinah, Jan. 16, 1704, who married Isaac Thorpe ; Lydia, Feb. 9, 1707, who married Moses Thorpe ; Nathaniel, April 2, 1708 ; Moses, Oct. 8, 1709 ; Aaron, Jan. 6, 1710, died at sea ; Elisha, Aug. 1712t ; Elisha, Jan. 7, 1716 ; Sarah, March 6, 1714, who married Daniel Mead ; Thomas was drowned.

Daniel, married Hannah Payne, 1726. They had Daniel, Feb. 1727t ; Ezra, Dec. 21, 1728 ; Solomon, Nov. 3, 1732 ; Hannah, Nov. 4, 1734.—2d wife, Susan Clark,

1741 ; had Phebe, Nov. 19, 1742 ; Daniel, May 9, 1744 ; Titus, Sept. 13, 1747 ; Collins†, Collins, John†, John.

WILLIAM, (of Henry,) married Mary Knowles, 1730. They had Submit, Feb. 10, 1733 ; Mary, May 20, 1736 ; Henry, May 25, 1739, who married Sarah Luddington ; Lydia, July 25, 1741, who married Aaron Buckley, 1761 ; Samuel, April 30, 1744 ; Rebekah, May, 1747† ; Anna, June, 1750† ; Stephen, Oct. 18, 1753.—*This family lived in Branford, and their house was burnt in the night of the 20th May, 1754, and Rebekah and Anna were burnt in it.*

NATHANIEL, married widow Mary Chedsey. They had Lucy, who married Russel Grannis.—2d wife, widow Eunice Smith ; had Eunice, who married Matthew Rowe ; Nathaniel, Mary.

WILLIAM, (of William, jun.) married Anna Hodge, March 1, 1711. They had Matthew, April 23, 1712 ; Ruth, June 7, 1713 ; Naomi, Dec. 15, 1716 ; Elisabeth, Feb. 9, 1720 ; Abraham, Nov. 30, 1721 ; Samuel, Aug. 10, 1723 ; Joseph, April 3, 1726.

MATTHEW, married Lydia Smith. They had Joseph ; Mabel, who married Isaac Mallory ; Timothy ; Samuel, who married Desire Barnes, 1787, *no children.*

JOHN, (of William, jun.) married Elisabeth Potter. They had John, Jan. 26, 1723 ; Jude, July 23, 1725 ; Elisabeth, who married John Rose.

JUDE, married Mary ——. They had Elisabeth, March, 1763.

ELIPHALET, married Abigail Collins. They had Jesse, Isaac, Amos ; Asa, *died in the French war ;* Mary, who married Amos Frisbe ; Olive, who married Joseph Grannis ; Amet, Hannah† ; Abigail, who married Enos Barnes.

JESSE, married Mehitabel Smith. They had Lydia, who married Edward Goodsell and Thomas Shepard ; Elam, Eliphalet, Jesse ; Mehitabel, who married Stephen Bradley, jun. ; Abigail, who married Christopher Tuttle ; Amos.

ELAM, married Rachel Tuttle, 1774. They had John, May, 1775 ; Elam, Nov. 2, 1777 ; Rachel, Sept. 4, 1780 ; Mehitabel, April 21, 1783 ; Naomi Smith, March 3, 1787.

ELIPHALET, married Sarah Potter, June 9, 1777. They had Jairus, Sarah, Eunice and Lois, Eliphalet.

JESSE, JUN. married Thankful Chedsey, 1779. They had Betsey, March 22, 1780 ; Caleb Chedsey, Aug. 22, 1790 ;

Lue, July 22, 1794 ; Justin, Aug. 22, 1796 ; and five died young.—2d wife, Sarah Moulthrop ; had Roxana, Wyllys, Sarah, Nancy, Lewis.

AMOS, married Huldah Chedsey, Feb. 2, 1791. They had Huldah†, Fanny, Polly, Amos, Levi, Sarah, Jesse, Almira, Elam, Mehitabel, Huldah.

ISAAC, married Mary Goodsell. They had Appeline ; Mary, who married Isaac Grannis, jun. and Seth Barnes ; Martha, who married Jared Grannis ; Isaac, Asa ; Sarah, who married Joseph Howd ; Anna, who married Jacob Hitchcock ; Jared, married Sarah Goodsell, 1798 ; Ame.

ISAAC, JUN. married Sarah Frisbe. They had Polly, Harriet, Levi, Almira, William, Isaac and Sarah, Asa.

ASA, married Betsey Luddington, 1799. They had Jared†, Henry†, Eliza, Lorinda, Betsey.

AMOS, (of Eliphalet,) married Mercy Thompson, June 7, 1757. They had Sibyl, who married Joel Dawson ; Ame.

ELAM, (of Eliphalet,) married Anna Finch, 1748. They had Anna, Oct. 6, 1751, who married John Chedsey, 3d.

THOMAS, (of the first William,) *removed to Newark ; his oldest son was* John.

JOHN, married Rebekah ——. They had James, Aug. 8, 1703; Rebekah and Abigail, Aug. 23, 1707 ; Elisabeth, Sept. 1710†.

JAMES, married Eleanor Barnes, Jan. 2, 1735. They had Eunice, May 11, 1751 ; Elisabeth, David, Lemuel.

MALLORY,

PETER, *signed the Plantation Covenant of New-Haven,* 1644. He had Rebekah, May 18, 1649 ; Peter, July 27, 1653 ; Mary, Oct. 1655† ; Mary, Sept. 28, 1656 ; Thomas, Sept. 15, 1659 ; Daniel, Nov. 25, 1661 ; John, May 10, 1663 ; Joseph, 1666 ; Benjamin, Jan. 4, 1668 ; Samuel, March 10, 1673 ; William, Sept. 2, 1675.

PETER, JUN. *New-Haven,* married Elisabeth Trowbridge, May 27, 1678. They had Peter, April, 1679† ; Caleb, Nov. 3, 1681 ; Peter, Aug. 1684† ; Elisabeth, April 27, 1687 ; Judith, Sept. 2, 1689 ; Benjamin, April 3, 1692 ; Stephen, Oct. 12, 1694 ; Ebenezer, Nov. 29, 1696 ; Zechariah, May 2, 1699 ; Abigail, Aug. 5, 1701 ; Zipporah, Dec. 15, 1705 ; Peter, March 1, 1708.

CALEB, *New-Haven,* had Caleb, Aug. 3, 1712.

THOMAS, *New-Haven,* married Mary Umberfield, March

26, 1684. They had Thomas, Jan. 1, 1685; Daniel, Jan. 2, 1687.

JOHN, *New-Haven*, had John, Sept. 6, 1687; Elisabeth, May 1, 1691; Rebekah, Sept. 15, 1693; Mabel, Dec. 19, 1695; Silence, Oct. 13, 1698; John, March 1, 1701; Obedience, April 11, 1704.

JOSEPH, married Mercy Pinion. They had Mercy and Thankful, Aug. 1694; Abigail, Aug. 1696; Joseph, Nov. 5, 1698; Benjamin, Nov. 5, 1701; Hannah, Sept. 1, 1709.

BENJAMIN, married Dorothy Luddington. They had David†, Mercy†, Joseph, Isaac, Mary†.—2d wife, Mary O'Neal; had David, Mercy, Levi, Dorothy, John, Mary, Simeon.

JOSEPH, married Thankful Roberts. They had Benjamin, 1751; Elisabeth, 1754; Amos, 1756; Abigail, 1760; Thankful, 1762; Ezra, 1767.—2d wife, Eunice Barnes, 1774; had Noah Woodruffe, 1775.

BENJAMIN, married Eunice Tamadge, Dec. 19, 1774. They had Amasa, Elisabeth, Patty, Zina†.

AMOS, married Abigail Brown, June 4, 1777. They had Amos; Infant†.

ISAAC, married Mabel Luddington. They had Asa, Jared, Lorana and Ame; Lorana married Samuel Shepard, 1782; Ame, married Moses Matthews; Jesse; Adah, who married Caleb Hotchkiss; Jacob; Mercy, who married Jones Curtiss; Lydia, who married Joshua Baker; Lorinda, who married Timothy Way; Hannah†.

ASA, married Huldah Chedsey, Feb. 26, 1778. They had Annis†, Jared†, Hannah, Huldah† Huldah, Jared†.

JESSE, married Hannah Rowe, 1781. They had James, March 26, 1782; Lole, Oct. 3, 1784; Heman, April 12, 1787†; Heman, April 12, 1789; Wyllys, April 6, 1793†; Jesse, March 27, 1796; Wyllys.

JACOB, married Hannah Foot. They had Isaac, Sarah, Jesse, Infant†, Fanny, Emily, Jacob.

DAVID, married Mary Wardell, 1769. They had Sarah, David, Samuel, Polly, Irene, Culpepper.

JOHN, married Miriam Stokes, 1775.

MEW,

ELLIS, married Ann ——. They had Ann.

MORRIS,

THOMAS, married Elisabeth ——. *He signed the Plantation Covenant at New-Haven,* 1639. They had John,

Eleazar, Ephraim† and Thomas, Oct. 3, 1651 ; Hannah, who married Thomas Lupton, 1652 ; Joseph, May 25, 1656 ; Elisabeth.

JOHN, married Anna. She died 1644. He then married widow Elisabeth Lampson ; had John, Dec. 1666†.—3d wife, Hannah Bishop, Aug. 12, 1669. They had Mary, June, 1670†; Hannah, Aug. 10, 1671, who married Joseph Smith ; Mary, Sept. 9, 1673, who married John Heminway ; Elisabeth, 1675, who married —— Maltbie and Rev. John Davenport ; Thomas, April, 1679†; Abigail, Aug. 22, 1683, who married James Peck, 1706 ; Desire, March 25, 1687, who married Stephen Howel, 1708.

ELEAZAR, married Anna ——. They had Rebekah, June 20, 1682, who married Nathaniel Hitchcock, 1702 ; John, Oct. 8, 1684 ; James, Eleazar, Adonijah ; Anna, who married Samuel Smith.

JOHN, married, Elisabeth Alling, Jan. 24, 1713; *no issue.*

JAMES, married Abigail Rowe, Feb. 24, 1715. They had Jemima, Dec. 1715†; Daniel, June 4, 1718 ; Abigail, Jan. 10, 1720 ; James, 1723 ; Amos, 1726.

DANIEL, married Elisabeth Smith. They had Abigail, Aug. 13, 1742 ; Elisabeth, Oct. 1743†; John, Oct. 12, 1745 ; Jemima, Aug. 25, 1747; Elisabeth, May 25, 1749.

AMOS, married Lydia Camp, June 26, 1745. They had Lydia, 1746, who married David Beecher, 1771 ; Ame, Feb. 19, 1748, who married Asa Bradley, 1768, and Eliphalet Fuller, 1783 ; Amos, March 13, 1750 ; Sarah, March 18, 1752, who married Gershom Scott and Edward Brockway ; John, July 22, 1754†; Elisabeth, March 6, 1757†; John, Sept. 2, 1759; Elisabeth, Oct. 13, 1761, who married Stephen Woodward, 1780 ; Esther, Oct. 24, 1763, who married William Collins, 1783 ; Asahel, Feb. 14, 1766 ; Lorinda, June 4, 1768, who married Samuel Hathaway, 1788 ; Anna, July 13, 1773, who married Bela Farnham, 1797.

AMOS, JUN. married Betsey Woodward. They had Amos, July 27, 1780 ; Betsey, Nov. 2, 1781 ; Clarissa, July 6, 1783 ; Susan, Oct. 17, 1784 ; Harriet, April 6, 1786 ; Lydia, June 18, 1787 ; Lucy, April 12, 1789 ; Hezekiah, Aug. 15, 1790†.

JOHN, married Desire Street, 1779. They had Sarah, Feb. 20, 1780†; James, Jan. 5, 1782†; John, Nov. 7, 1783 ;

William, Oct. 3, 1785 ; Stephen, Jan. 13, 1787 ; Nancy, May 28, 1789 ; James, June 25, 1791 ; Sarah, Hezekiah, Lorinda, Anson.

ASAHEL, married Catherine Van Ness. They had Philip, John, Catherine, Henry.

JAMES, had James, Lucy.

ELEAZAR, JUN. married Mercy Ball. They had Stephen ; Sarah, who married Seth Eaton ; Mercy, who married Isaac Holt ; Jacob†, Eleazar†, Mary† ; Mabel, who married Jehiel Forbes.

STEPHEN, married Esther Robinson, June 18, 1741. They had Hannah†, William† ; Hannah, Jan. 1, 1746, who married Samuel Heminway.

ADONIJAH, married Sarah Moulthrop. They had Anna.

JOSEPH, married Esther Winstone, June 2, 1680. They had Thomas, March 23, 1682 ; Esther, Sept. 3, 1684, who married John Peck, 1707 ; Sarah, 1686, who married Joseph Beecher, 1710 ; Joseph, 1688 ; Ephraim, Jan. 1694 ; Dorothy, Sept. 1695 ; Benjamin, April, 1699 ; Mary, June, 1702, who married Joel Munson ; Samuel, July, 1705.

THOMAS, married Sarah Gilbert, May 25, 1708. They had Thomas, March, 1712 ; Daniel, April, 1715 ; Amos, Feb. 20, 1718 ; Asa, Feb. 20, 1721 ; Elisabeth, Feb. 9, 1726.

ASA, married Hannah Brown, March 11, 1758.

JOSEPH, JUN. married Sarah Hotchkiss, Feb. 3, 1709.

EPHRAIM, married Ruth Sperry, Jan. 24, 1717. They had Abigail, Oct. 31, 1717 ; Ruth, Nov. 27, 1718 ; Ephraim, May 23, 1721.

BENJAMIN, had Sarah, March 15, 1737 ; Elisabeth, April 10, 1739 ; John, March 9, 1742.

MOULTHROP,

MATTHEW, married Jane ——. *They removed from New-Haven to Stoney River,* 1662. They had Matthew ; Elisabeth, who married John Gregory, 1663 ; Mary.

MATTHEW, JUN. married Hannah Thompson, 1662. They had Hannah, Jan. 1663† ; Hannah, April 20, 1665 ; John, Feb. 5, 1667 ; Matthew, July 18, 1670 ; Infant, 1673† ; Lydia, Aug. 8, 1674 ; Samuel, June, 1677† ; Samuel, April 13, 1679 ; Keziah, April 12, 1682.

JOHN, married Abigail Bradley, June 29, 1692. They had Abigail, Aug. 12, 1693 ; John, March 17, 1696 ; Mary, 1698† ; Sarah, 1701, who married Adonijah Morris ;

Dan, Dec. 1, 1703 ; Israel, June 7, 1706 ; Joseph, Timothy.

JOHN, JUN. married Sarah ———. They had John, Stephen, Mehitabel ; Sarah, who married Timothy Russel and
John Pardee ; Mary, who married John Dawson, jun. ; Abigail, who married Dan Goodsell.

JOHN, 3d, married Abigail Holt. They had David, John,
Reuben† ; Roxana, who married Abijah Pardee ; Reuben.

DAVID, married Hepzibah Hotchkiss. They had David.

REUBEN, married Hannah Street, Nov. 18, 1792. They
had Daniel Bowen†, Maria, Clarissa, Daniel, Delia, Sydney, Reuben.

DAN, married Hannah Belcher. They had Dan†.—2d
wife, Lydia Howe. They had Charles, *lost at sea ;* Timothy ; Hannah, who married Israel Lindsley, 1673 ; Enoch† ;
Enoch ; Sarah, who married Elisha Andrews ; Eli, married
Mary Moulthrop ; Lydia, Mabel, Infant†.

ENOCH, married Mary Hotchkiss. They had Dan†, Dan,
Lydia, Mary, Betsey, Silas, Timothy.

ISRAEL, married Lydia Page. They had Samuel ; Jacob,
lost in the French war ; Timothy† ; Lydia, who married
John Fuller, 1766 ; Lois, who married Charles Page, 1765.

SAMUEL, married Sarah Denison. They had Josiah, May
30, 1754 ; Desire, Nov. 16, 1756, who married Moses
Thompson, 1775 ; Jared, Jan. 20, 1759 ; Jacob, Aug. 29,
1762 ; Sarah, Jan. 13, 1764 ; Mercy, Sept. 9, 1767 ; Lydia,
Aug. 7, 1769 ; Samuel, Sept. 1, 1773 ; James, Oct. 14,
1776 ; Israel, Sept. 1779†.

JOSIAH, married widow Lydia Smith, July 4, 1792. They
had Desire, April 16, 1793 ; Jared, March 9, 1795 ; Samuel Russel, May 5, 1797.

JACOB, married Abigail Pardee. They had Abigail.—2d
wife, Elisabeth Goodrich ; had Betsey, Eunice, Leonard,
Bela, Sarah, Damaris.

JOSEPH, married Mary Whedon. They had Joseph, Elihu, Jude ; Adonijah, *lost in the French war ;* Hannah, Rhoda, Mary, Lucretia, Abigail.

JOSEPH, JUN. married Lucretia Bradley, 1766. They
had Abijah, Joseph†, Jared, Rhoda, Irene, Chauncey.

ELIHU, married Mary Hotchkiss, Nov. 21, 1770. They
had Jared, Polly, Adonijah, Elihu, Esther.

MATTHEW, 3d, married Mary ———. They had Jane,
Dec. 13, 1694, who married Thomas Hodge ; Matthew,
Sept. 1696† ; Joseph, Oct. 1698† ; Mary, June 1, 1701, who

married Gideon Potter; Martha, Feb. 18, 1703; Matthew, Feb. 1, 1705; Benjamin, March 2, 1707; Asher, Jan. 28, 1710; Dorothy, Dec. 1, 1712, who married Samuel Potter; Keziah, Jan. 6, 1714, who married Isaac Grannis.

Matthew, 4th, married Sarah Grannis. They had Thankful, Nov. 1728†; Joseph, Dec. 1730†; Sarah, Jan. 1732†; Mabel, Sept. 6. 1735, who married Caleb, 3d, 1759; Matthew, 1738†; Matthew, Nov. 9, 1743.—2d wife, Hannah Way; had David, March 23, 1748.

David, married Rachel Swayne. They had John†, Martin, Major, Polly, Swayne.

Benjamin; had Benjamin, July 20, 1735; Elisabeth, Mary, Benjamin.

Benjamin, jun married Thankful Grannis, July, 1761. They had Benjamin, Seba, Mary, Elisabeth.

Asher, married Anna Grannis. They had Desire, April 13, 1737, who married Samuel Thompson; Isaac, Feb. 5, 1739; William, March 5, 1740; Levi, Oct. 8, 1743; Solomon, Oct. 3, 1745. These three were lost at sea. Mary, May 8, 1749, who married Eli Moulthrop. Thankful, June 1, 1750, who married John Crawford and Thomas Shepard; Anna, March 25, 1752, who married Samuel Smith; Joseph; Ashur.

Isaac, married Jemima Granniss, Nov. 11, 1761. They had Levi, Desire, William, Solomon, Ira, Abraham, Jacob, Polly, Anna, Rachel, and two Infants†.

Solomon, married Lois Rowe, Oct. 10, 1765. They had Polly, who married William Bradley, 1785; Lois.

Joseph, married Lorana Grannis, 1774. They had Joseph, Lorana, Anna, Levi, Elihu, William, Henry, Polly, Infant†.

Asher, jun. maried Mary Chedsey, Oct. 13, 1783. They had Isaac.

Samuel, (of Matthew, jun.) married Sarah Barnes. They had Sarah, Feb. 24, 1705; Lydia, May 5, 1707, who married Eliakim Robinson; Hannah, April 10, 1709; Phebe, Oct. 14, 1711.

O'NEAL,

HENRY, married Abigail ——. They had Patience, Aug. 24, 1713; Henry, Aug. 23, 1715; Abraham, Sept. 21, 1717; Charles, Jan. 21, 1720; Abigail, May 27, 1723, who married James A. Broton; Phebe, who married George Mulloon.

ABRAHAM, married Sarah Conklin. They had Charles, Henry, John, Archer, lost at sea ; Hannah, who married Solomon Tompkins, 1776 ; Sarah ; Pamela, who married George Aswell, 1787 ; Esther.

PAGE,

MOSES, married Thankful Grannis, 1731. They had Moses, Sept. 1, 1732 ; Aaron, Sarah.—2d wife, widow Lydia Smith ; had Ichabod.

AARON, married Desire Grannis, May 22, 1758. They had Josiah, Huldah, Thankful, William, Desire.

PARDEE,

GEORGE, was apprenticed to Francis Brown, Tailor, 1644, to stay five years, and was married by the Governor to Martha Miles, Oct. 20, 1650. They had John, Aug. 20, 1651†; John, Dec. 2, 1653 ; George, Jan. 15, 1655 ; Mary, Feb. 18, 1658, who married Joshua Hotchkiss, 1677 ; Elisabeth, June 10, 1660, who married —— Olmsted.—2d wife, Rebekah Lane, Dec. 29, 1662 ; had Joseph, April 27, 1664 ; Rebekah, April 18, 1666, who married Samuel Alling, 1699; Sarah, Feb. 2, 1667 ; Hannah, July 7, 1672, who married Edward Vickars.

GEORGE, JUN. married Mercy Ball, Feb. 10, 1675. They had Mercy, Jan. 16, 1676 ; Eliphalet, Dec. 26, 1678; Martha, March 18, 1680 ; John, Nov. 4, 1683.—2d wife, Mary Denison, Feb. 11, 1685 ; had Stephen, 1686 ; Ebenezer; George, Jan, 1690 ; James ; Sarah, who married John Thompson, 4th ; Mary, who married Isaac Chedsey ; Elisabeth.

ELIPHALET, married Hannah Edwards. They had Samuel, Jan. 1706†; Ebenezer, April 5, 1710 ; Eliphalet, Sept. 1713†; Benjamin, Dec. 9, 1714 ; Hannah, March, 1717 ;† Sarah, Nov. 1719, who married Anthony Thompson, 1758; Noah, Dec. 30, 1721.

EBENEZER, married Eunice Smith, Nov. 22, 1739. They had Hannah, Jan. 18, 1742 ; Sarah, Eunice, Eliphalet, Aug. 1751†; Ruth, Feb. 14, 1753.

BENJAMIN, married Mary Bradley, June 17, 1740. They had Levi, Jan. 14, 1742; Moses, July 24, 1744; Hannah, Dec. 13, 1746 ; Jared, Sept. 28, 1748 ; Lois, May 18, 1751, who married Isaac Barnes; Benoni, Feb. 18, 1754†; Desire, July 7, 1759†; Noah, Jan. 12, 1757; Mehitabel, Jan. 11, 1763.†

Levi, married Sarah Chedsey, 1770. They had Gurdon, June 20, 1771 ; Huldah, Nov. 3, 1773†; Huldah, Nov. 29, 1775 ; Mehitabel, Feb. 7, 1779 ; Aner, Dec. 29, 1782 ; Reuel, 1785†.

Gurdon, married Phebe Judd, Nov. 3, 1799. They had Maria, Levi Judd, Henry Atwater, Chester, Gurdon.

Moses, married Sarah Wilmot. They had Thomas, William, Moses, Polly, Sarah, Betsey, Mehitabel, Julia.

Jared, married Rebekah Brown, July 19, 1784. They had Benjamin, June 6, 1785 ; Stephen Brown, Jan. 10, 1787 ; Polly, June 26, 1789†; Mabel, 1791†; Sarah.

Noah, married Mary Woodruff. They had Mehitabel, Phineas, Benoni.

John, (of George jun.) married Abigail Bracket, July 9, 1712. They had John, June 27, 1713 ; Abigail, April 15, 1717; Martha, Nov. 30, 1723 ; Eliphalet, May 4, 1726.

John, jun. *North-Haven,* married Sarah Frost, Dec. 12, 1744. They had James, March 25, 1746 ; Martha, July 6, 1747; John, Dec. 10, 1750†; Sarah, July 31, 1753 ; Ebenezer, Jan. 27, 1755.—2d wife, widow Sarah Russel, Feb. 18, 1762; had Susannah and Rosannah, Oct. 13, 1762; John, Oct. 24, 1764; Lydia, July 22, 1766.

James, *North-Haven,* married Mary Smith, Nov. 2, 1772. They had Polly,† Sarah, Mabel, Polly, Isabel, James.

Ebenezer, *North-Haven,* married Jemima Barnes. They had Lyman, Samuel, Betsey, Lucinda, Ebenezer, Jairus, Abigail, Hannah, Nancy.

John, 3d, *North-Haven,* married Elisabeth Bracket. They had Rhoda, Esther, Harriet, John, Betsey.

Eliphalet, (of John, sen.) *North-Haven,* married Mary Blakesley, April 8, 1756. They had Jesse, June, 1757†; David, Aug. 8, 1759; Abigail, Mary, Hannah.—2d wife, widow Mary Bishop; had Jesse, April 12, 1771.

Stephen, married Mary Howe. They had Stephen, May 30, 1725 ; Mary, 1731 ; Elisabeth, 1735.

Stephen, jun. married Mabel Russel. They had Stephen, Samuel, Mercy, James†, Eli, James, Asahel, Mary, John, Amos,† Elisabeth, Amos.

Stephen, 3d, married Abigail Smith, 1768. They had Samuel, Sarah.

Ebenezer, (of George, jun.)—had Hannah, March 28, 1728; James, Dec. 27, 1729.

George, 3d, married Sarah Bradley. They had Isaac,

13

Nov. 3, 1722; Lydia, Jan. 10, 1725; Jacob, 1727; Mercy, 1730.

ISAAC, married Sarah Leavit. They had Leavit, Isaac and Joseph, Anna, Jemima.

LEAVIT, married Sarah Heminway, 1782. They had Samuel, Sarah, Jared, Anna, Leavit,† Infant.†

JOSEPH, married Sarah Fields, 1783. They had Isaac, Laban, Betsey, Hezekiah, Almira.

JACOB, married Mary Heminway. They had Abijah, Sarah,† Jacob, Chandler, Sarah, who married Daniel Austin; Mary, John, Eunecia, who married Timothy Thompson; Abraham,† Elisabeth Lovisa, Abraham.

ABIJAH, married Roxana Moulthrop, 1777. They had Abigail, Isaac Holt, Polly, Clarissa†, Abijah, Maria, Sarah†, George†, Anna, Sarah.

JACOB, JUN. married Lydia Heminway, Nov. 3, 1777. They had Jacob†.

CHANDLER, married widow Lydia Hotchkiss, Feb. 4, 1790. They had Reuel†; Reuel, Sept. 4, 1792; Eunecia, Aug. 20, 1794.

GEORGE, SEN. *gave his son Joseph land in New-Haven a few days before his marriage.*

JOSEPH, married Elisabeth Yale, Jan. 30, 1689. They had Joseph, Aug. 9, 1693; Thomas, Oct. 26, 1695; John, Feb. 6, 1697; Mary, April 9, 1700.—2d wife, Elisabeth Payne, Dec. 2, 1703; had Elisabeth, Sept. 16, 1704; Daniel, Nov. 28, 1706; Rebekah, March 26, 1708; Josiah, Sept. 14, 1711; Ebenezer, Nov. 4, 1714; Samuel, Aug. 3, 1718; Sarah, Aug. 1, 1721.

PENFIELD,

ISAAC, married Elisabeth Howe. They had Elisabeth, Jan. 2, 1717, who married Isaac Goodsell; Hannah, Feb. 19, 1724.

PINION,

NICHOLAS, married Elisabeth. They had Ruth, Hannah, Mary, Thomas, Robert.

THOMAS, married Mercy ——. They had Christiana, who married Samuel Downe; Mercy, who married Joseph Mallory; Abigail, who married Samuel Cande, 1703.

POTTER,

John and William, brothers, signed the Plantation Covenant, New-Haven, June 4, 1639.—WILLIAM had Nathaniel, Joseph, Hope, Rebekah.

JOHN, had John, Samuel.

JOHN, JUN. married Hannah Cooper. They had Hannah, 1661†; John, June, 1663†; Hannah, June 26, 1665; John, Aug. 4, 1667; Samuel, July, 1669†; Infant, Feb. 1671†; Mary, March 1673†; Samuel, Jan. 2, 1675.—2d wife, widow Mary Russel, Dec. 29, 1679; had Abigail, who married Samuel Thompson.

JOHN, 3d, married Elisabeth Holt, Feb. 23, 1692. They had John; Elisabeth, Sept. 24, 1697, who married John Luddington; Gideon, June 3, 1700; Daniel, June 15, 1701; Enos, Dec. 12, 1706; Samuel, Joseph.

GIDEON, married Mary Moulthrop. They had Mary, Aug. 17, 1724, who married David Smith; Gideon, April 24, 1726; Thankful, July, 1728†; David, Jan. 12, 1732; Dorothy, Dec. 1733†; Desire, May, 1736†; Stephen, Jan. 12, 1739; Jerusha, July, 1741†; Jared, Sept. 25, 1742; Thankful, Aug. 1746†.

GIDEON, JUN. married Keziah Leavit, 1752. They had Thankful, Nov. 10, 1753, who married James Spencer; Lois, July 15, 1756, who married Nehemiah Smith; Lydia†, Gideon†.

DAVID, married Mary Wright. They had Levi, Nov. 1751†; Levi, Jan. 1, 1757; Desire, Jan. 25, 1755, who married Daniel Goodsell; Isaac, died in a prison ship.

LEVI, married Sarah Thompson, 1778. They had Samuel, May, 1779;† Levi and Sarah,† Feb. 24, 1781; Polly, April 9, 1783; Elisabeth, Oct. 1785;† Elisabeth, Jan. 17, 1787; James, Sept. 19, 1789; Anna, Feb. 4, 1792.

STEPHEN, married Sarah Lindsley, July 3, 1766. They had Lucinda, April 4, 1767; Sarah, James, Matilda, Mary, Frederic.

JARED, married Sarah Forbes, April 19, 1764. They had Sarah, Mary.

DANIEL, married Hannah Holbrook, Sept. 12, 1728. They had Nathan, July 28, 1729; Eunice, 1731;† Phineas, Jan. 1733;† Hosea, March, 1735;† Lois, Dec. 1737;† one 1739; Elam, Jan. 1, 1742. [† These 4 and the mother died in 11 days.]

ENOS, married Sarah Heminway. They had Sarah, 1732;† Anna,† Isaac,† Israel, Abner, who died at sea; Hannah, who married Levi Chedsey.

ISRAEL, married Mary Dawson, Feb. 4, 1761. They had Sarah, who married Eliphalet Luddington ; Hannah, Anna,† Joel, Asahel, Anna, Enos.

SAMUEL, married Dorothy Moulthrop, 1738. They had Samuel, Sept. 10, 1739; Jacob, June 29, 1741.

JOSEPH, married Thankful Bradley, March 11, 1729. They had Joseph, Aug. 9, 1730 ; Titus, April 1, 1734 ; Mercy, Dec. 18, 1737; Thankful, Aug. 26, 1739; Sibyl, Sept. 1, 1741 ; Jesse, May 21, 1743; Elisabeth, Aug. 1, 1745.

REDFIELD,

WILLIAM, married Rhoda Tucker. They had William, Mary, George, Julia.

ROBERTS,

WILLIAM, married Joanna ——. They had William, Zechariah, Alice and Lydia, Anna, who married Samuel Butler, 1712 ; Abigail.

WILLIAM, JUN. had Thomas.

THOMAS, had Joseph, Dec. 1727; John, Nov. 14, 1729 ; Ebenezer, Dec. 4, 1731 ; Elisabeth, Oct. 17, 1733 ; Eunice,† Mary,† Anna.†

EBENEZER, married Elisabeth Jacobs, 1756. They had Anna, Susan.

JONATHAN, had Molly, Rebekah, Thankful, Jonathan.

JONATHAN, JUN. married Jemima Abbot. They had William,† William, Hannah, Pamela, Betty, Eli, Jemima.

ROBINSON,

JACOB, married Sarah Hitchcock, 1690. They had John, Dec. 3, 1691 ; Thomas, Dec. 5, 1693 ; Sarah, Dec. 24, 1695, who married Samuel Bradley ; Hannah, Feb. 24, 1698, who married Thomas Dawson; Mary ; Eliakim, April 2, 1706.

JOHN, married Mary Barnes, Nov. 28, 1720. They had Jacob, Oct. 20, 1721 ; Mary, Sept. 5, 1724, who married Moses Santford, 1746 ; John, Aug. 16, 1729 ; Miriam, Dec. 1, 1731 ; (Hannah, July 29, 1745 ; Stephen, March 20, 1748 ; Levi, March 17, 1751 ; Amos, June 15, 1754. *It is doubtful whether the 4 last were children of this John, unless he had a second wife.*)

JACOB, married Elisabeth Bracket, July 14, 1747. They had Moses, July 14, 1754 ; Adah, Aug. 8, 1760.

JOHN, JUN. married Lois Santford, 1755. They had Mary, Aug. 8, 1755 ; Desire, Jan. 2, 1758 ; John, Nov. 12,

1760; Justin, Dec. 6, 1765; Harmon, July, 1767;† Harmon, July 7, 1768; Medad, July 19, 1770; Linas, Feb. 14, 1774; Lois, March 19, 1776.

JOHN, 3d, married Leura Spencer. They had Mary, Aug. 2, 1784; Uriah and Desire, July 6, 1787; Clarissa, Abigail, Susan, Salmon, Erastus.

HARMON, married Lucinda Baldwin. They had Polly, Rodney, Harmon, Jesse, Augustus, Medad, Mary.

THOMAS, married Anna Harrison. They had Benjamin, Dec. 23, 1716; Esther, July 7, 1720, who married Stephen Morris.—2d wife, Hannah Howe. They had Thomas, April 4, 1723; two died young; Hannah, Sept. 1731;† Andrew, Dec. 1733.†

BENJAMIN, married Catharine Durand. They had Esther, Andrew, Mary, Levi, 1757; Benjamin, 1759.

THOMAS, JUN. married Anna Wooster. They had Jehu, Jared, Ziba, Amasa, lost at sea; Abijah, Sarah, who married Aaron Williams, 1758; Lydia, Zurviah.

JEHU, married Elisabeth Auger, 1769.

JARED, married Mary Thompson, 1760. They had Chandler, Jemima, Anna, Sarah, Ziba.

CHANDLER, married Lois Grannis, 1781.

ROWE,

MATTHEW, had Elisabeth, Jan. 1650;† Daniel, Jan. 1651;† John, April 30, 1654; Hannah, Aug. 1656;† Joseph, Nov. 1658;† Stephen, Aug. 28, 1660.

JOHN, married Abigail Alsop, July 14, 1680. They had John, Oct. 23, 1681; Matthew, Feb. 14, 1683; Stephen, July 1, 1687; Abigail, Aug. 13, 1689, who married James Morris, 1715; Hannah, Feb. 11, 1691, who married John Leak, 1720; Sarah, Oct. 15, 1700, who married Eleazar Brown, 1725.

JOHN, JUN. married Rebekah Mix, Feb. 1, 1711. They had John.

MATTHEW, married Rebekah Mix, Feb. 1, 1710. They had Mary, Jan. 27, 1711; Rebekah, 1713, who married Joel Tuttle; John, 1715; Abigail, who married Stephen Ives, 1736; Sarah, who married Daniel Olds, 1759; Hannah, Aug. 8, 1724, who married Stephen Thompson, 1746; Lydia, June 1, 1726, who married Job Smith.

JOHN, married Hannah Smith, 1741. They had Matthew, Feb. 1742;† Mary, March 22, 1744, who married Michael Todd; Lois, March 21, 1746, who married Solomon Moulthrop, 1765 ; Matthew, March, 1748 ;† Hannah, June, 1749 ;† Ezra, April 5, 1752; John, May 31, 1754 ; Matthew, Nov. 28, 1756; Stephen, May 6, 1759 ; Hannah, June 9, 1762, who married Jesse Mallory.

JOHN, married Esther Hotchkiss, Oct. 29, 1778.   *No issue.*

MATTHEW, married Eunice Luddington.   They had Daniel, Aug. 5, 1782 ; Mary, March, 14, 1785 ; Hannah, Sept. 21, 1786 ; Matthew, Sept. 19, 1788 ; Lois, Feb. 28, 1791 ; Stephen, March 22, 1792 ;† Eunice, Jan. 22, 1795 ; Elisabeth, May 26, 1797 ;† Rosewell and Russel, Aug. 7, 1800 ; Elisabeth, Louisa.†

STEPHEN, married Abigail Hughes, Dec. 6, 1781.   They had Stephen, Dec. 6, 1782 ;† Lois, Oct. 17, 1783 ;† John, Nov. 11, 1785 ; Lydia, Dec. 14, 1786 ; Infant,† Infant,† Infant,† Lue, Nov. 11, 1793 ;† Esther, Dec. 14, 1795 ; Eliada, Aug. 12, 1798 ; Infant.†—2d wife, Elisabeth Miles, had Stephen.

STEPHEN, *New-Haven,* (of first John,) had Stephen, Sept. 7, 1716; Joseph, Oct. 7, 1718 ; Daniel, Nov. 7, 1720 ; Mary, Dec. 21, 1722 ; Ebenezer, Feb. 18, 1725.

JOSEPH, *New-Haven,* married Abigail Beecher, Dec. 21, 1743.   They had Joseph, Sept. 27, 1744 ; Ebenezer, Sept. 2, 1748 ; Rebekah, June 29, 1750 ; Mary, Jan. 28, 1753 ; Eunice, June 29, 1755 ; Stephen, Jan. 31, 1758.

JOHN, 3d, of *New-Haven,* married Esther Carrington, June 22, 1736.   They had John, July, 1737 ;† Mary, Oct. 7, 1741 ; Catherine, Feb. 28, 1744 ; John, Dec. 13, 1765 ; Esther, March 7, 1768.

RUSSEL,

JOHN and Ralph, *were brothers, and appear at the Iron works about the year* 1664.——JOHN *died in* 1681 ; and Hannah, his widow, married Robert Dawson. They had Hannah, 1670, who married Joseph Grannis, 1702 ; William, Sept. 1676 ;† one, Aug. 1679 ;† John, Nov, 1, 1680.

RALPH, married Mary Hitchcock, Oct. 12, 1663.   They had John, Dec. 14, 1664 ; Joseph, March 20, 1667 ; Edward, Feb. 1673 ;† Samuel, 1671.

JOHN, married Hannah Moulthrop, Aug. 17, 1687.   They had Hannah, Feb. 18, 1689, who married Benjamin Gregory; Lydia, Sept. 18, 1692, who married Abraham Utter, 1715 ; John, Jan. 15, 1695 ; Edward, April 19, 1698 ; Abigail, May 19, 1701, who married Abraham Hodge ; Rachel, Dec. 15, 1703, who married —— Beecher ; Mabel, July 14,

1706, who married Samuel Utter; Sarah, Feb. 25, 1712, who married John Shepard.

JOHN, JUN. married Mary Forbes, May 17, 1717. They had Mary, May 22, 1718, who married Benjamin Smith, 1742; Sarah, Sept. 27, 1720, who married Caleb Bradley; Lydia, March 1, 1726; Mabel, May 7, 1728, who married Stephen Pardee, jun.; John, July, 1730;† Mehitabel, April, 1733;† Ame, Jan. 17, 1735, who married John North, 1763; Joseph, July 4, 1740; Mehitabel, March, 1744;† Levi, July, 1747.†

JOSEPH, married Abigail Grannis, Nov. 7, 1764. They had Abigail, Aug. 28, 1765, who married Joseph Shepard, 1787; Mary, Jan. 3, 1767;† John, March 7, 1769; Mehitabel, Jan. 8, 1771;† Joseph, May 27, 1772;† Truman, June 2, 1774;† Truman, Feb. 26, 1776; Major, July 20, 1778; Mary, Aug. 15, 1784.

JOHN, married Elisabeth Russel, 1796.—2d wife, Olive Grannis; had two Infants,† John, Eliza, Ai, Rothilda, Olive, Polly, Sherman, Barlow, Joseph.

TRUMAN, married Elisabeth Davidson. They had Abigail, Joseph, Betsey, Almira, Leonard, Jane Elizabeth.

EDWARD, married Catherine Utter. They had Catherine, June 22, 1724; Hannah, May 20, 1726, who married Phineas Curtis, 1759; Edward, Oct. 3, 1729; Mary, April 20, 1732, who married Robert Dawson and Ebenezer Chedsey; Benjamin, Feb. 2, 1736.

EDWARD, JUN. married Mary Pardee. They had Mary, who married James Stanclift; Catherine, who married Gideon Allen; Benjamin; Hannah, who married Asaph Hotchkiss; Edward; Elizabeth, who married John Russel.

EDWARD, JUN. married Lois Bibbins. They had Sarah, Catherine, Mahala, Deforest, Edward Kneeland.

BENJAMIN, married Mary Utter. They had, Infant.† *He died a prisoner in the French war.*

SAMUEL, married Esther Tuttle, Feb. 27, 1695. They had Samuel, 1696; Esther, May 4, 1699; Mary, Jan. 1700;† Infant, Aug. 1702;† Ralph, Aug. 1703;† Joseph, Dec. 1706;† Daniel, Abel.

SAMUEL, JUN. married Mary Heminway, May 13, 1719. They had Samuel, Feb. 2. 1720; Timothy, Sept. 29, 1722; Stephen; Ichabod; Eunice, who married Thomas Smith 4th and Nathaniel Luddington; Esther, who married Joseph Hotchkiss.

TIMOTHY, married Sarah Moulthrop. They had 4 children, which died young, and were buried at two funerals, two and two in a grave.

ABEL, married Eunice Luddington. They had Abel.

JOSEPH, (of Ralph,) married Jane Blackman, 1687. They had Joseph, Nov. 1687;† Samuel, April 23, 1697.

SHEPARD,

THOMAS, married Hannah. *They became members of the Church in Branford, 1709, and in 1717 removed to East-Haven.* They had John, Thomas, Ruth, Elisabeth, Hannah, Sarah, who married Richard Darrow.

JOHN, married Sarah Russel. They had Sarah, March 11, 1728, who married John Chedsey, jun. 1745 ; Mary, Sept. 1731 ;† Elisabeth, July 20, 1734, who married Enos Hotchkiss ; John, Feb. 1737 ;† Stephen, April 17, 1740 ; John, Oct. 27, 1743 ; Mary, Sept. 30, 1746, who married David Grannis ; Levi ; Huldah, who married Elias Townsend.— 2d wife, widow Mary Potter ; had David, May, 1762.†

STEPHEN, married Ame Grannis, March 13, 1765. They had Sarah,† Sarah, Ame, who married Thomas Potter; Stephen, Isaac, Jared, Huldah.

STEPHEN, JUN. married Sarah Grannis, 1799. They had William, Willet, Merit, Henrietta, Orchard, Rosetta, Stephen, Nancy.

JOHN, JUN. married Elizabeth Bradley, April 18, 1765. They had John, Jared, Benjamin, Ziba, Levi, William, Rosewell, Irene, who married Holt Dawson, 1793 ; Betsey.

JOHN, 3d, married Ame Goodsell. They had Jeremiah, Nancy.

THOMAS, JUN. married Sarah Hotchkiss. They had Samuel, Aug. 22, 1730 ; Thomas, Jan. 16, 1733 ; Abigail, June 15, 1736, who married Elias Forbes and Jonathan Goodsell ; Isaac, 1738 ;† Jacob, who married Patience Bradley ; Mary.

SAMUEL, married Elizabeth Pardee. They had Hannah, who married Timothy Way ; Thomas, Joseph, Mary, Elisabeth, Sarah, Samuel, who married Lorana Mallory, 1782 ; Mabel, Amos, Abraham.†

THOMAS, 3d, married Widow Lydia Goodsell, Feb. 4th, 1783. They had Elihu, March 9, 1785 ; Elias, Lydia, Jacob.†

JOSEPH, married Abigail Russell, Nov. 1, 1787. They had Elizabeth, Hezekiah, Joseph.—2d wife, Huldah Thompson ; had Harriet, Amos.

SLAUGHTER,

MEDAD, married Martha O'Neal, Feb. 16, 1758. They had Anna, Nov. 1759 ;† David, Anna, Medad.

SMITH,

THOMAS, married Elizabeth Patterson, the only child of EDWARD P. 1762. They had John, March, 1664 ;† Anna, April 1, 1665 ; Infant, 1667 ;† John, June 14, 1669 ; Thomas, Aug. 1671 ;† Thomas, Jan. 31, 1673 ; Elisabeth, June 11, 1676 ; Joanna, Dec. 17, 1678 ; Samuel, May 24, 1681 ; Abigail, Aug. 17, 1683 ; Lydia, March 24, 1686, who married Theophilus Alling, 1708 ; Joseph, 1688 ; Benjamin, Nov. 21, 1690, died a young man.

THOMAS, JUN. married Sarah Howe. They had Thomas, Joseph, Samuel, Dow, Benjamin.—2d wife, widow Abigail Thompson, had Elisabeth, who married Daniel Morris.

THOMAS, 3d, married Abigail Goodsell. They had Thomas, July 27, 1719 ; David, Nov. 15, 1721 ; Stephen, Nov. 28, 1724.

THOMAS, 4th, married Eunice Russel, March 11, 1741. They had Thomas, Dec. 10, 1742; Enos, Nov. 2, 1744 ; Abigail, Feb. 3, 1747, who married Stephen Pardee, 1768 ; Jacob, July 7, 1749 ; Eli, Nov. 8, 1751 ; Elisabeth, May 21, 1754, married Jesse Upson, 1775.

THOMAS, 5th, married Anna Smith, Nov. 20, 1766. They had Betsey, who married Oliver Todd, 1786 ; Louisa, Lament and Infant.†

DAVID, married Mary Potter. They had David, Isaac, Simeon, Gideon, John, Abigail, Mary, Desire, Hervey.

STEPHEN, married Jemima Parmaly, 1747. They had Jemima, Sept. 12, 1748; Stephen, 1751 ; Caleb, Oct. 10, 1753 ; Orphana, 1756, who married Samuel Cook.—2d wife, Sarah Dawson, Oct. 20, 1760, had Thomas, Nov. 29, 1761.—3d wife, Comfort Picket, had Sarah, 1768, who married Giles Bracket.

STEPHEN, JUN. married Hannah Lindsley. They had Daniel, June 18, 1780 ;† Betsey, Jan. 14, 1783 ; Daniel, 1785.†

CALEB, married Sarah Russel, Oct. 10, 1782. They had Edward Russel, Oct. 12, 1783; Sarah, April 1, 1787 ; Caleb, June 28, 1794 ;† Almira.

THOMAS, married Desire Thompson, Oct. 16, 1792. They had Stephen, Sept. 18, 1793; Samuel, Oct. 21, 1795; Warren, Sept. 9, 1798 ; Willard, Sept. 12, 1800 ; Alvin,

Nov. 17, 1802 ; Caleb Alfred, March 9, 1805 ; Sarah, Thomas, Merwin, Charlotte, Nancy.

SAMUEL, (of Thomas, jun.) married Eleanor Thompson. They had Samuel,† Lydia,† Infant,† Enos,† Isaac,† Isaac.— 2d wife, widow Mary Russel ; had Lydia, Samuel.

ISAAC, married widow Mabel Chedsey, 1762. They had Ira, June 2, 1763 ; William, May 25, 1765 ; Eleanor, Nov. 29, 1767, who married William Ottee, and had Mary and Nancy ; Isaac and Caleb, July 15, 1770 ; Sarah, Oct. 12, 1772, who married John Tyler ; Huldah.

IRA, married Sarah Davenport, 1784. They had Isaac, Twins,† Lorinda, Hezekiah.

WILLIAM, married Ame Chedsey. They had Isaac.

CALEB, married Lydia Chedsey, May 29, 1794. They had Julina, James, Huldah,† William,† Huldah, Elisabeth, William, Desire Chedsey, Jacob Chedsey, Desire, Harriet Maria, Mary Emily.

SAMUEL, JUN. married Mary Dawson, April 11, 1765. They had Samuel, Jared, Lydia, who married Isaac Chedsey, 1791.—2d wife, Didamea Grannis, 1773 ; had Isaac, Mary, Ame, Desire, Roger, Ransom.

Dow, married Kezia Barker. They had Jordan, Sept. 1, 1733 ; Sarah, Aug. 31, 1736 ; Joseph, April 12, 1739 ; Lydia, Jan. 1, 1743 ; Dow, May 21, 1745 ; Daniel, Jan. 23, 1748 ; Keziah, Aug. 28, 1751 ; Isaac, April 21, 1754.

JORDAN, married Sarah. They had John, 1782 ; Jerusha, 1784.

JOSEPH, married Lydia Harrison, Feb. 24, 1762. They had Simeon, Dec. 29, 1762.

Dow, jun. married Anna. They had Sarah, Anna, Hannah, Dow Chester.

BENJAMIN, married Sarah Russel, Dec. 2, 1742. They had Mary, Dec. 19, 1743, who married Samuel Smith ; John, Benjamin, Alling.

ALLING, married Elisabeth Rose, 1775. They had Benjamin, John, Betsey, Hannah, Polly, Thomas.

SAMUEL, (of first Thomas,) married Anna Morris, 1708. They had Patterson, Oct. 17, 1709; Abel, Nov. 4, 1711 ; James, June 14, 1713 ; Benjamin, Sept. 20, 1716 ; Anna, May 17, 1719, who married Daniel Holt and Timothy Andrews; Thankful, Aug. 27, 1722, who married Stephen Bradley ; Sarah, April 6, 1725, who married James Denison ; Daniel, Aug. 6, 1727; Samuel, June 1, 1732.†

PATTERSON, married Sarah Thompson. They had John,†

Samuel,† John, May, 1745 ;† Jacob,† Sarah, Jan. 31, 1748, who married Jared Bradley, 1768 ; Jacob, July 6, 1751.

JACOB, married Lois Bishop, July 15, 1778. They had Lois ; Jacob, Jan. 22, 1783 ; Sarah.

ABEL, married Lydia Ball, March 17, 1737. They had Lydia, Jan. 27, 1738, who married Samuel Basset; Samuel, Oct. 10, 1739 ; Abel, June, 1742 ;† Anna, Aug. 22, 1744, who married Thomas Smith, 5th ; Oliver, Feb. 21, 1749 ; Lucy, Aug. 16, 1751, who married David Bishop ; Sarah, who married John Bracket.—2d wife, widow Lydia Tuttle, June 25, 1767. They had Jude, May 22, 1768 ; Lyman.†

SAMUEL, married Mary Smith. They had Abel, Polly, Benjamin, Lydia,† Desire.†

OLIVER, married Thankful Bracket, Nov. 17, 1774. They had Esther, Samuel, Lyman, Sydney, Justus, Oliver, Leveret, Hervey.

JUDE, married Olive Foot. They had Anna, Lucy, Maria and Melinda.—2d wife, Ruth Basset; had Olive, Julia, Jude. —3d wife, widow Hannah Mason ; had Lyman, Amelia, Polly.

JAMES, married Lydia Todd, March 26, 1747. They had Mary, Dec. 22, 1747, who married James Pardee ; James, Aug. 30, 1750 ; Benjamin, 1753 ;† John, June 14, 1756 ; Thomas, Oct. 10, 1761 ; Eli ; Mabel, Jan. 20, 1769, who married Merriam Munson.

JAMES, jun. married Martha Frost. *No issue.*

JOHN, married Anna Cooke. *No issue.*

THOMAS, married Sarah Frost. They had Thomas, Sarah, Sibyl,† John,† John.†

ELI, married Hannah Howd. They had Lydia, Benjamin. —2d wife, Polly Whitney ; had Benajah, Eli and Hannah.

BENJAMIN, married Desire Denison, 1743. *No issue.*

DANIEL, married Hannah Atwater, 1749. They had Samuel, Dec. 14, 1749 ; Anna, Aug. 25, 1751, who married Abraham Heminway, 1771 ; Joseph, Nov. 4, 1754 ; Benjamin, Aug. 12, 1757 ; Dorcas, Feb. 23, 1760, who married Timothy Andrews and John Thompson ; Daniel, Sept. 23, 1762; Laban, Aug. 14, 1765 ; Hannah, May, 1770.

SAMUEL, married Anna Moulthrop, March 9, 1775. They had Polly†; Polly, May 6, 1778, who married Abraham Thompson ; Desire, 1780†; Levi, 1782† ; Levi, March 14, 1784 ; Asahel, Dec. 10, 1787 ; Anna, March 17, 1792.

JOPEPH, married Lydia Grannis, Feb. 4, 1777. They had Samuel, lost at sea ; Lydia, Nancy.

BENJAMIN, married Lydia Gates. They had Desire ; Benjamin, lost at sea ; Esther, Marvin, Daniel, Lydia, Eve Ely.

DANIEL, JUN. married Rachel Bishop, Nov. 12, 1781. They had Joseph, Fanny.—2d wife, widow Anna Ford, Dec. 21, 1793 ; had Infant†, George, Mary.

LABAN, married Mary Bradley, Feb. 12, 1789. *No issue. There is a feeble family tradition that John Smith was connected with the preceding family. If so, he must have been the oldest son of the first Thomas that lived, and was 49 years old when he married. This, however, is probable ; but as it is somewhat doubtful, I have placed him after Thomas and Samuel, instead of before them, according to the order observed in respect to other families. Joseph, the son of Thomas, was a house Joiner, and his father requested the Town to grant him a certain lot upon which he might build his shop. This is the only notice I can find on record respecting him.*

JOHN, married Martha Tuttle, Feb. 5, 1718. They had Hannah, Dec. 26, 1718, who married John Rowe, 1741 ; Martha, Aug. 17, 1721, who married Caleb Barnes, 1742 ; Job, Nov. 10, 1722 ; John, June 30, 1724 ; Mehitabel, April 17, 1726, who married Jesse Luddington ; Josiah, July 17, 1728 ; James, April, 1730† ; Lois, Sept. 1732† ; Ichabod†.—2d wife, Lydia Fields ; had James, May 2, 1738, *died in the French war.*

JOB, married Lydia Rowe, 1747. They had Ambrose, March 12, 1748 ; Nehemiah, March 28, 1750 ; Lydia, Dec. 8, 1753, who married Solomon Barnes ; Martha, May 15, 1756, who married Nathaniel Grannis, 1777 ; Elijah, Aug. 27, 1758† ; James, Nov. 1, 1760† ; Job, Aug. 11, 1763 ; John, 1765.

AMBROSE, married Mary Smith, Nov. 14, 1771. They had Amasa, Sept. 1772† ; Esther Hull, March 4, 1774 ; Miles, March 21, 1776 ; Lole, March 12, 1778 ; Ambrose, Jan. 3, 1780 ; Elijah, March 12, 1784 ; Rowe, Dec. 1785 ;† Asenath, Ichabod.†

NEHEMIAH, married Lois Potter, 1775. They had Gideon, Stephen, Nehemiah, Sarah,† James,† John.†—2d wife, Irene Bradley, 1773 ; had Lois, Mary, John.†

JOB, JUN. married Lucretia Smith, 1785. They had Loring,† John, Enos, William, Loring, Infant.†

WILLIAM, *a British Seaman, accidentally fell in compa-ny with Mary Collins at Saybrook, and they were mutuall captivated.* They *however parted, without any expectation of meeting again.* She came home by water, *and when she* arrived at her *father's house,* SMITH was there. *After much opposition, they were married, and had* Lydia, Feb. 4, 1712, who married Matthew Luddington ; Sarah, Oct. 1, 1714.

STREET,

Rev. NICHOLAS, *was ordained Teacher in the first Church at New-Haven, 1659, and died April* 22, 1674 ; he had Samuel ; Susannah, who married —— Mason ; Sarah, who married James Heaton, 1662 ; Abiah, who married Daniel Sherman, 1664 ; Hannah, who married —— Andrews.

Rev. SAMUEL, married Anna Miles, Nov. 3, 1664. *He was graduated at Cambridge College, 1664, and ordained Pastor of the Church at Wallingford, 1674, and died Jan.* 16, 1717. They had Anna, Aug. 1665† ; Samuel, July, 1667† ; Mary, Sept. 1670† ; Nicholas, July 14, 1677; Sarah, Jan. 15, 1681.—2d wife, Mardline Daniels, Nov. 1, 1684 ; had Samuel, Nov. 8, 1685 ; James, Dec. 28, 1686 ; Anna, Aug. 26, 1688.—3d wife, Hannah Glover, July 14, 1690 ; had Eleanor, Dec. 3, 1691 ; Nathaniel, Jan. 19, 1693 ; Elnathan, Sept. 2, 1695; Mary, April 16, 1698 ; John, Oct. 25, 1703.

NICHOLAS, *Wallingford,* married Jerusha ——. They had James, Feb. 10, 1708 ; Elisabeth, April 24, 1709.

SAMUEL, *Wallingford,* had Samuel, May 10, 1707.

ELNATHAN, *Wallingford,* married Damaris Hull, 1721. They had Benjamin, May 18, 1722 ; Samuel, Jan. 1725† ; Samuel, Dec. 8, 1728 ; Nicholas, Feb. 21, 1730 ; Elnathan, Feb. 20, 1732 ; Anna, Feb. 16, 1734 ; Mary, June 28, 1738 ; Jesse, April 17, 1741.

Rev. NICHOLAS, *was graduated at Yale College, 1751 ; was ordained Pastor of the Church at East-Haven, Oct.* 8, 1755, and married Desire Thompson, Dec. 6, 1758. They had Eunecia, Oct. 27, 1759, who married Rev. Stephen W. Stebbins, 1783 ; Desire, Aug. 16, 1761, who married John Morris, 1779 ; Lucinda, July 17, 1763, who married Darius Hickox and Titus Alling and Theophilus Miles.—2d wife, Hannah Austin, April 24, 1766 ; had Hannah, March 8, 1767, who married Reuben Moulthrop, 1792 ; Moses Augustine, Jan. 29, 1769† ; Moses Augustine, April 3, 1770 ; Nicholas, March 22, 1772 ; Elnathan, Feb. 16,

1774; Justin Washington, Nov. 4, 1777; Mary, Oct. 6, 1782.

Moses A. married Lois Smith, 1797. They had Amanda, Lois Marina.

Jesse, *Branford,* married Lois Cooke. They had Sarah, 1776; Horatio Gates, Thaddeus, Benjamin, Lucretia, Anna.

STEVENS,

JAMES, had Eliphalet, Sept. 6, 1718; Samuel. *This family lived at Dragon, and was almost destroyed by sickness and suffering in the hard winter of* 1740.

Eliphalet, had William, March 9, 1739; Hannah, Jan. 29, 1743.

THOMPSON.

John and Anthony Thompson, *brothers, signed the Colony Constitution, New-Haven, June,* 1639, *and in* 1647, *their brother* William *is mentioned.* Anthony *had a son* John. *In* Anthony's *Will, dated* 1647, *he mentions his brothers* William *and* John. *In* 1654, Anthony, jun. *by Will, gave all his lands to his brother John. One* John, *died in* 1674. *In* 1682, William *made his Will and names his sister Ellen, his brother* Anthony's *son* John, *his cousins* John *and* William, *sons of his nephew* John, *and other relatives.* Ebenezer, *who settled in Guilford, was of the New-Haven family, and had a son* John, *who died in* 1676. *The* John *that settled at Stoney River, was also of this family, and was called Farmer* John, *in distinction from* John *at New-Haven, who was a Seaman.*

JOHN, married Eleanor. They had John; Mary, who married John Cooper, jun.; Hannah, who married Matthew Moulthrop, jun. 1662; Rebekah; Sarah, who married Alling Ball, jun. 1678.

John, jun. married Priscilla Powel, March 29, 1666. They had John, Aug. 6, 1667; Priscilla, Aug. 7, 1671, who married Ebenezer Chedsey, 1689; Samuel, Jan. 1673†; Samuel, May 1, 1677; Abigail, Feb. 24, 1679, who married Daniel Collins; Anna, March 20, 1683.

John, 3d, married Mercy ——. They had John, Oct. 11, 1692; Abigail, Oct. 1694; Mercy, Feb. 21, 1696, who married Joseph Tuttle; Moses, Nov. 1, 1699; Eleanor, April 28, 1702, who married Samuel Smith; Samuel, Sept. 30, 1704; Bathsheba, Jan. 24, 1707, who married Joseph Grannis, jun. and Abraham Chedsey; Joseph, March, 1709†.

John, 4th, married Sarah Pardee. They had Sarah, Jan.

17, 1718, who married Patterson Smith ; John, Oct. 21, 1721 ; Stephen, Dec. 25, 1723 ; Timothy, Dec. 26, 1727; Joseph, Jan. 31, 1730 ; James, 1735.

JOHN, 5th, married Mary Hoadley. They had John, Levi, Wyllys, Anna.

STEPHEN, married Hannah Rowe, 1746. They had Amos†; Amos, Aug. 2, 1751 ; Moses, Dec. 28, 1754 ; Hannah† ; Stephen, Jan. 11, 1760.—2d wife, widow Mary Baldwin ; had James.

AMOS, married Mary Thompson. They had Hezekiah†, William, Elisabeth, Isaac, Mary, Susan, Philemon, Asenath, Huldah†, Hezekiah, Esther†.

MOSES, married Desire Moulthrop. They had Hannah, who married John Heminway ; Desire, Anna, Charles, Clarissa, Sylvester†, Betsey†, Betsey, Sarah†, Sarah†.

STEPHEN, JUN. married Lois Bradley, 1779. They had Augustus, Silas†, Hannah†, Orlando†, Ransom†, Sarah†, Hannah, Wyllys.

JAMES, married Lydia Chedsey. They had Stephen, Mary, Leonard, Nathaniel, Henry, Elizur, James, Abraham Chedsey†, Abraham, Edward Ellsworth, Haynes Heminway.

TIMOTHY, married Esther Perkins. They had Sarah, Aug. 1, 1750, who married Abijah Bradley and Samuel Heminway ; John, April 27, 1753 ; Desire, May 26, 1756†; Esther, Aug. 12, 1759, who married Elijah Bradley ; Huldah, June 25, 1762, who married Joseph Shepard, 1798 ; Timothy, Dec. 1, 1766 ; Abraham, Feb. 10, 1772.

JOHN, married widow Dorcas Andrews, 1783. They had John†, George, Desire, Lucy, James†, Lue, James, John, Daniel Atwater.

TIMOTHY, JUN. married Eunecia Pardee. They had Jacob, Sarah, John, Esther†, Willet, Infant†, Esther.

ABRAHAM, married Mary Smith, Nov. 16, 1797. They had Julia Amanda, William, Desire Smith, Samuel, Mary Ann, Abraham, Asahel, Joseph, Sarah†.

JOSEPH, married —— Gilbert. They had William, Phebe, Jared, Lydia, Joseph, Sarah, Tryphena, Rebekah and Betsey.

JAMES, married Elisabeth Bishop. *No issue.*

MOSES, married Desire Heminway. They had Moses† ; Desire, July 5, 1745, who married Rev. Nicholas Street, 1758.

SAMUEL, married Hannah Heminway. They had Mercy, 1728†; Samuel, 1732† ; Mary, 1735†; Samuel, Aug.1, 1737 ;

Moses ; Mercy, who married Amos Luddington ; Mary, who married Jared Robinson ; Abigail, who married Amos Ford, 1774 ; Esther, who married Zacheus Howe, 1771.

SAMUEL, JUN. married Desire Moulthrop, Sept. 12, 1759. They had Jared, Joel ; Samuel, March, 1768 ; Desire, Nov. 19, 1771, who married Thomas Smith, 1792.

JARED, married Lydia Blakesley, Oct. 12, 1786. They had Isaac†, Lorinda, Lydia, Isaac.—2d wife, Grace Hunt; had Nancy, Harriet, Emily, Desire.

JOEL, married Lois Chedsey, 1782. They had Sarah, Huldah, Mary, Anson, Horace, Nancy, Reuel, Lue, Lorinda, William.

SAMUEL, married Sarah Holt, 1786. They had Samuel, Desire, Miles, Sarah, William, Dan, Asenath, Nancy, Almira, Albert.

SAMUEL, (of John, jun.) married Abigail Potter. They had Abigail, Oct. 1704† ; Sarah, Nov. 28, 1706, who married John Taintor ; Mary, April 30, 1790, who married Samuel Forbes ; Samuel, June 3, 1711 ; Mehitabel, May 3, 1713, who married Thomas Grannis.

SAMUEL, JUN. married Elisabeth Denison, Sept. 18, 1738. They had Elisabeth, Feb. 21, 1740, who married Azariah Bradley, 1759 ; Samuel, May 8, 1743 ; John, May 11, 1746; *these two died unmarried ;* Sarah, May 27, 1749, who married Levi Potter, 1778 ; Abigail, 1753, who married Samuel Bradley, 1777, and Joseph Heminway, 1786.

TOWNSEND,

SAMUEL, married Sarah Tradeway. *No issue.*

TUTTLE,

WILLIAM, married Elisabeth —. *They were among the first settlers at Stoney River, about the year* 1645. They had Thomas, Jonathan, Sarah, Joseph, Simon; Nathaniel, Feb. 24, 1652.

THOMAS, married Hannah Powel, May 21, 1660. They had Hannah, Feb. 24, 1661 ; Abigail, Jan. 17, 1663 ; Mary, Jan. 14, 1665 ; Thomas, Oct. 27, 1667 ; John, Dec. 5, 1669 ; Esther, April 9, 1672 ; Caleb, Aug. 29, 1674 ; Joshua, Dec. 19, 1676.

THOMAS, JUN. married Mary Santford, 1692.

JOHN—*doubtful whether this is the son of Thomas or John ;* had Ephraim, April 2, 1690; John, Sept. 5, 1692 ; Nathaniel, Jan. 20, 1694 ; Mary, Dec. 26, 1696.

CALEB, had Enos, Nov. 11, 1711 ; Timothy, Feb. 21, 1713 ; Eliphalet, March, 1716.

ELIPHALET, married Desire Bradley. They had Mary, March 23, 1741 ; Desire, May 5, 1743 ; Mehitabel, March 20, 1745 ; Esther, Feb. 19, 1747.

JONATHAN, married Rebekah ——. They had Rebekah, Sept. 10, 1664 ; Mary, Feb. 7, 1666 ; David, Nov. 14, 1668 ; Jonathan, April 6, 1669 ; Simon, March 11, 1671 ; William, May 25, 1673.

JOSEPH, married Hannah Munson, May 2, 1667. They had Joseph, March 18, 1668 ; Samuel, July 15, 1670 ; Stephen, May 20, 1673 ; Timothy, Sept. 1676 ;† Susanna, Feb. 20, 1679 ; Elisabeth, July 12, 1683 ; Hannah, May, 1685 ;† Hannah.

JOSEPH, JUN. married Elisabeth Santford, Nov. 10, 1691. They had Joseph, Nov. 10, 1692 ; Noah, Oct. 12, 1694 ; Elisabeth, July 27, 1705 ; Thankful, Sept. 3, 1709.

JOSEPH, 3d, married Mercy Thompson. They had Joel, Oct. 28, 1718; Mary, Dec. 22, 1720, who married John Heminway, jun. 1738 ; Ame, 1726 ;† Mercy, Sept. 17, 1730, who married Abraham Heminway, jun. 1746 ; Comfort, 1732 ;† Joseph, 1734 ;† Samuel, 1741.—2d wife, widow Sarah Washburn ; had Joseph, Ame, Benjamin.

JOEL, married Rebekah Rowe, 1743. They had Stephen, 1744 ; Joel, Aug. 21, 1746 ; Daniel, Sept. 29, 1749 ; Abraham, Nov. 17, 1750 ; Mercy, April, 1752, who married Joshua Barnes, 1781 ; Rebekah, Dec. 20, 1755, who married Joseph Bracket, 1782 ; Christopher, Sept. 26, 1759 ; Mary, April 11, 1764.

STEPHEN, married Rhoda Coe. They had Amasa, Mary, Joel, Sarah, Abraham,† Maria.

JOEL, JUN. married Anna Woodward, Jan. 6, 1774.—2d wife, Elisabeth Fowler, Oct. 15, 1778 ; had Sarah, July 12, 1779 ; Elisabeth and Anna, March 11, 1782; Rebekah, Feb. 22, 1785 ; Polly, Sept. 6, 1787 ; Julia, June 8, 1790 ;† Joel, May 8, 1792.

DANIEL married Ame Grannis, March 24, 1785. They had Rebekah.

ABRAHAM, married widow Anna Thomas. They had Julia ; Abraham Rowe.

CHRISTOPHER, married Abigail Luddington, March 24, 1786. They had Mercy, Joseph, Smith,† Smith, Abigail, Miles, Sarah Smith.†—2d wife, Mary Dawson ; had Sarah Smith.

14 *

SAMUEL, married Bethiah Miles, Sept. 6, 1761. They had
Amasa, Aug. 27, 1762 ;† Samuel, Aug. 6, 1763 ;† Bethiah
Miles, Jan. 22, 1765 ;† Samuel Amna, Sept. 18, 1767 ;† Sarah Miles, Feb. 2, 1770, who married Russel Pierpont, 1790 ; .
Bethiah, March 22, 1772 ;† Samuel, June 23, 1773 ; Ammi,
Dec. 17, 1775 ; Zurviah, Feb. 22, 1777 ; Phebe Amna, Dec.
6, 1780; Eunecia, Sept. 10, 1783 ; Frederic William, May
30, 1786.

NOAH, married Rachel Hoadley, Dec. 1, 1720. They had
Lydia, Jan. 27, 1722, who married Freeman Hughes ; Timothy, April 3, 1724 ; Desire, 1726 ;† Elisabeth, Jan. 8, 1728 ;
Desire, Sept. 17, 1730 ; Joseph, July 18, 1734 ; Rachel,
1737 ; Abigail, Sept. 12, 1740.

TIMOTHY, married Anna Washburn, Jan. 12, 1743. They
had Mary, May 31, 1744 ; Timothy, Dec. 14, 1746 ;† John,
Nov. 5, 1749 ; Sarah, 1752, who married Levi Forbes ; Rachel, who married Elam Luddington and David Burnham ;
Anna ;† Elisabeth, who married George King.

JOSEPH, married Mary Granger. They had Josiah, Sept.
4, 1762 ; Mary, March 9, 1765 ; Daniel, Oct. 10, 1767 ; Anna, who married John Monroe ; Joseph, Asahel, Timothy.

JOSIAH, married Eve Ely Gates, 1795. They had Mary
Granger, Lydia Caroline, John.

ASAHEL, married Mary Colone. They had Thomas,† Asahel, Mary, Eliza Ann, Thomas, Jane, Joseph, Charles,
Francis.

JOHN, married Catherine Lane, Nov. 8, 1653. They had
Hannah, Nov. 2, 1655 ; John, Sept. 15, 1657 ; Samuel, Jan.
9, 1659 ; Daniel and Mary, April 13, 1664 ; Elizabeth, Nov.
21, 1666 ; David, Nov. 14, 1668.

TYLER,

JOHN, married Mabel Bradley, April 20, 1786. They had
Amma, Feb. 20, 1789 ; John, June 29, 1792 ; Twins, June
1796 ;† William, June 26, 1799 ; Jerusha Louisa.

UTTER,

ABRAHAM, married Lydia Russel, June 27, 1715. They
had Abraham, March 7, 1716 ; Lydia, July 24, 1720 ; John,
Dec. 18, 1722 ; Isaac, Feb. 22, 1725.

WANTWOOD,

BENJAMIN, had Benjamin, July 20, 1712 ; Jeremiah, Feb.
20, 1714.

WALKER,

JAMES, married widow Abigail Everton, They had John,

Oct. 15, 1764; William, Feb. 6, 1766 ; Mary, Jan. 29, 1770, who married Allen Frost and Chandler Pardee.

WILLIAM, married Eunice Chedsey, Dec. 9, 1787. They had John, William, James.

WAY,

THOMAS, married Anna ——. They had Daniel, Ebenezer, Elisabeth, John, David, Mary, Hannah.

DAVID, had Esther, Sept. 1720 ;† Mary, March, 1722 ;† David, July 25, 1723 ; Mary, Feb. 13, 1725; Hannah, May 6, 1727 ; Thomas, Oct. 25, 1728.

JAMES, married Dorcas Luddington. They had Mercy, Aug. 30, 1728 ; Hannah, 1735 ;† Mary; James, Jan. 5, 1741 ; Timothy, March 16, 1745.

TIMOTHY, married Abigail Dawson, Oct. 4, 1765. They had Abigail, Dec. 7, 1766.—2d wife, Rhoda Rose ; had Timothy, Dorcas,† James, Jared, Rufus, Rhoda, and 7 more, who died young.—3d wife, Hannah Shepard, 1792 ; had Dorcas, Elisabeth, Thomas, William, Ame, Infant.†

WHEDON,

DANIEL, married Abigail Granger. They had Sarah, who married Jedediah Darrow ; Lucretia, who married Saul Root ; Grace, who married Henry Hughes ; Denison, who married Mary Parish ; Abigail, who married —— Hopson ; Asenath.

WEDMORE,

CHARLES, married Lydia Grannis, April 4, 1786. They had James, Charles, Daniel, Nathaniel.—2d wife, Polly Barnes ; had Sarah, Nancy, Nelson, Wealthy, Mary, Susan, Daniel.

WOODWARD,

Rev. JOHN, *was graduated at Cambridge College,* 1693 ; *was ordained Pastor of the Church at Norwich, Dec. 6,* 1699 ; *assisted in the Council that compiled Saybrook Platform,* 1708 ; *was dismissed from his pastoral charge, Sept.* 13, 1716, *and was admitted an inhabitant of New-Haven, Dec. 24th, of the same year.* He married Sarah Rosewell. They had Lydia, 1706, who married Deodate Davenport, 1730 ; Rosewell, 1708 ; Elisabeth, 1710 ; John, 1712 ; Sarah, 1714, who married Samuel Miles ; Richard, 1716 ; William, Oct. 18, 1718 ; Mary, 1720, who married Joseph Trowbridge.—2d wife, Mary Gaskill, May 5, 1731 ; had Gaskill.

ROSEWELL, married Huldah Hill. *No issue.*

JOHN, jun. married Mary Denison, Sept. 3, 1741. They had John, Oct. 6, 1742 ; Mary, Jan. 23, 1745, who married Gurdon Bradley, 1766 ; Lydia, Oct. 6, 1747, who married Azariah Bradley, 1764 ; Anna, Nov. 30, 1749, who married Joel Tuttle, 1774 ; Elisabeth, Feb. 6, 1752, who married Joseph Heminway, 1769 ; Huldah, June 17, 1754, who married Jared Heminway, 1774 ; Mabel, April 16, 1757 ;† Stephen, June 16, 1758.

JOHN, 3d, married Ruth Curtiss. They had Hezekiah, June 13, 1763 ; John, Dec. 27, 1768 ; Jeremiah, Aug. 5, 1771 ;† Mary, May 8, 1773, who married Eleazer Heminway ; Rosewell, Nov. 7, 1775 ;† James, July 12, 1780.†

HEZEKIAH, married Asenath Bradley, April 13, 1794. They had Mary, Ruth, Asenath, Jeremiah, Jennet,† Jennet, James, Hezekiah, Richard,† Richard.

JOHN, 4th, married Mary Davenport, Jan. 15, 1794. They had, Clarissa, Rosewell, Eliza, Emeline, John,† Lyman and Leura.

STEPHEN, married Elizabeth Morris, Jan. 20, 1780. They had William, Anna, Elisabeth, Lydia, Sarah, Jeremiah, Almira, Harriet, Stephen, Augustus.†

RICHARD, married Susan Deluce. They had Susan, Betsey, who married Amos Morris, jun. ; Richard, Peter, Rosewell, John, Sarah.

WILLIAM, married Mabel Chedsey. They had Sarah, who married Samuel Page ; Mabel, who married Jesse Denison ; Rosewell, William, Josiah, Abraham ; and six died in infancy.

GASKILL, married Anna Butler. *No issue.*

PETER, *brother of Rev. John,* married widow Hannah Pardee, Jan. 5, 1725. They had Samuel, Dec. 11, 1727.

SAMUEL, married Abigail Lampson, Nov. 22, 1750. They had Abigail, July 11, 1754, who married William Day ; Infant,† Mary, who married —— Godard.

N. B.   An omission belonging to page 146, next to the 4th line from top ; which may be added at the end of the family record.

EZRA ROWE married Huldah Chedsey, Feb. 1, 1773. They had Elizabeth, July 11, 1774, who married Heman Hotchkiss ; Elijah, June 18, 1776 ; Samuel, April 8, 1778 ; Levi, March 5, 1780 ; Huldah, April 27, 1783 ; Ezra, Feb. 25, 1786 ; Hervey, Oct. 26, 1788 ; Sarah, June 26, 1790 ; Frances, Oct. 13, 1792.

PART III.

-->>●◉●<<--

CONTAINING AN

ACCOUNT OF THE DEATHS

IN THE

FAMILIES NAMED IN THE SECOND PART.

--◈◈◈◈◈--

THE present place of burial in East-Haven, was sequestered for that use in 1707. Previous to that time, some of the dead were buried on the west side of the Green ; but they were generally carried to New-Haven. And previous to the year 1773, the catalogue is irregular and imperfect. It was collected, principally, from the records of East-Haven, New-Haven, and the monuments of the graves. From the year 1773, it is regular, and generally accurate.

[*N. B.*—d. *stands for days,* w. *for weeks, and* m. *for months.*]

		Age
1647. Thomas Gregson, first white settler in E. Haven.		
1650, Oct. 9, Mary, a child of Deacon John Chedsey,		2w.
1651, Jan. 2, Elizabeth, a child of Matthew Rowe,		8m.
Oct. 6, Ephraim, a twin child of Thomas Morris,		3d.
1652, Sept. 3, Daniel, a son of Matthew Rowe,		20m.
1653, June 28, John, a son of George Pardee,		20m.
1659, Edward Hitchcock, one of the Southend men.		
Joseph, a son of Matthew Rowe,		1
1660, Sept. 8, Son of Henry Lindon.		
1662, May 27, Matthew Rowe, the first of that family.		
June 13, Hannah, a child of John Potter,		6m.
Wm. Luddington, the first of this name & family.		
Jan. 2, Hannah, child of Matthew Moulthrop, jr.		10m.
1663, Jan. 2, James, a son of James Denison,		1
May 26, John, a son of Thomas Smith,		10w.
Aug. 10, John, son of John Potter,		14m.
31, John, son of John Davenport, jun.		7w.
1664, Dec. 4, Anna, wife of John Morris.		
1667, June 4, Daniel, son of Deacon John Chedsey,		10

1667, John Lindon and Michael Delano.
     Elizabeth, wife of Nicholas Pinion.
1668, Oct. 16, John, son of James Denison,   5
     Francis Browne, the first of that family.
     Oct. 21, John son of Eliakim Hitchcock,   2m.
     Rebecca, child of John Cooper, jun.   2
     Dec. 22, Matthew Moulthrop, the father of this name.
     Elizabeth, wife of John Morris.
1669, Aug. 17, Joseph Potter.
     Oct. 31, Edw'd Patterson, one of the Southend men.
     Nov. 16, Samuel, son of John Potter,   1
         Matthias Hitchcock, one of the South-end men.
         A child of John Morris.
1670, William Hunter.
     Dec. 21, Infant son of John Potter.
1672, Jan. 14, Thomas, a son of Thomas Smith,   5m.
     May, Jane, widow of Matthew Moulthrop.
1673, Ap. 27, Benj. Linge, a first settler at Stony River.
     July 11, Eliphalet Ball,   23
         21, Thomas Morris, father of the Morris family.
1674, Ap. 22, Rev. Nicholas Street, father of the Street
            family.
     Dec. 11, John Thompson, father of the East-Haven
            Thompsons.
1675, Jan. 23, Mary, child of John Austin.
     Feb. 10, John, a son of John Austin.   7
     June 15, Hannah, wife of John Potter, in childbed, 36
     Aug. 28, Benjamin Lixon.
1676, March 4, Wm. Andrews, a purchaser of Southend.
     April, Nicholas Pinion.
         Mary, wife of Thomas Barnes.
         Henry Luddington, a young man.
     May 2, Rebecca, wife of Jonathan Tuttle.
     June 3, Thomas, son of William Holt,   23
1677, Elizabeth Rose.
     Oct. 14, Samuel, son of Matthew Moulthrop,   4m.
1679, Ralph Russel, the father of the E. Haven Russels.
1681, John Russel.
     Ann Mew, only child of Ellis Mew.
1683, Ap. 4, Mary, wife of John Austin—and her Infant.
     Oct. 27, Mary, a child of John Austin,   3
     John Pardee,   30
1684, Edward Vickars—and Edmund Tooley.
     Aug. 3, Edward, son of Ralph Russel,   10

1684, Aug. 13, Mercy, wife of George Pardee, jun.

Dec. 30, Elizabeth, wife of William Tuttle.

1687, Joseph, son of Joseph Russel,   5w.

1688, Elizabeth, wife of Deacon John Chedsey.

July 16, Elizabeth, daughter of do.   20

Dec. 31, John Chedsey, Deacon of the first Church,

N. H. and father of all the Chedsey family,   67

1689, Sept. 21, Alling, son of Alling Ball.

Oct. 27, John, son of Joseph Pardee,   7

Nov. 23, John Cooper.

William Roberts.

Dec. 13, John, son of Ebenezer Chedsey.   2

1690, Feb. 22, Dorothy, wife of Capt. Alling Ball.

John Austin, the father of the East and New-Haven family.

John Asbill.

Joseph Tuttle,   62

April 8, Eleanor, widow of John Thompson 1st.

Dec. Mercy Mallory.

1691, Feb. 1, Matthew Moulthrop, jun.   58

15, Thomas Mallory,   30

1692, Jan. 15, Anna, wife of Caleb Chedsey.

1693, Feb. 13, Serg't John Thompson, jun.

John Chedsey,   42

1695, James Tailor.

1699, Aug. 4, Abigail, child of Thomas Goodsell,   2

1700, George Pardee, the father of the East and North-Haven Pardees,   71

1701, Sept. 19, Elizabeth, wife of Joseph Pardee,

Nov. 1, Mary, child of Samuel Russel,   3

1702, June 4, Jane, widow of Thomas Gregson,   above 80

Aug. 17, A child of Samuel Russel.

1703, Dec. 25, Hannah, wife of Caleb Chedsey.

1704, Feb. Ann, widow of Ellis Mew.

May, Eliakim Hitchcock.

Oct. 5, Ralph, son of Samuel Russel,   14m.

1705, Jan. Lieut. Samuel Hotchkiss.

Nathaniel Boykim.

1707, Feb. 19, James, a child of Samuel Hotchkiss,   8d.

July 28, Elizabeth, child of Wm. Luddington,   8

April 22, Lydia, child of Daniel Collins,   2m.

Nathaniel Hitchcock.

Nov. 26, Samuel Potter,   32

Dec. Serg't John Potter, the father of the East-Haven Potters,   70

1707, Dec. 22, Joshua Hotchkiss.
1708, July 1, Mary, a child of John Moulthrop,   10
1709, Feb. 27, Mary, wife of John Hitchcock.
   March 14, Abel, a son of Joseph Chedsey,   7d.
     27, Sarah, a child of Henry Luddington,   6
   May 22, Sarah, wife of John Dawson,   21
1710, Jan. 12, Hannah, wife of John Morris,   59
   Feb. 27, Mary, wife of John Hitchcock.
   July, Capt. Alling Ball, jun.   54
   Oct. 10, Thomas Pinion.
     15, Hannah, wife of Thomas Tuttle.
     19, Thomas Tuttle,   68
1711, May 11, James, a son of Samuel Hotchkiss,   2m.
   July 8, Abigail, daughter of Thomas Smith,   28
   Sept. 20, Samuel Heminway the 1st,   about 75
   Dec. 10, John Morris.
1712, Joseph Chedsey,   57
   Thomas Barnes, jun.   59
   Jemima Wooding.
   Joseph Morris,   56
   Dec. 17, Martha, wife of the Rev. John Davenport,
     Stamford.
     25, Samuel Thompson,   56
     28, Abigail, daughter of do.   8
   Sarah, wife of Eliakim Hitchcock.
1713, Jan. 3, Elisabeth, wife of Issac Bradley,   56
     12, Isaac Bradley, father of the E. Hav. Bradleys, 62
     19, Widow Hannah Hotchkiss,   41
     30, Samuel Moulthrop,   36
   Feb. 20, Deacon Caleb Chedsey,   52
     14, Serg't John Moulthrop,   46
   March 12, Serg't John Potter, jun.   46
   April 22, David Austin,   43
   May 16, Thomas Goodsell,   67
   Oct. 24, Lydia, child of Daniel Collins,   3
   Dec. 13, Elisabeth, child of John Luddington,   3
     17, A child of Richard Darrow,   6m.
1714, Jan. 30, Hannah, 2d wife of Robert Dawson,   40
   May 23, Mary, wife of Thomas Alcock.
   July 14, Silence, of Joshua Austin,   4m.
1715, Feb. 5, Abraham, child of Abraham Heminway,   3w.
   March 12, Elisha, child of Henry Luddington,   7m.
   Elisabeth, widow of John Potter, jun.   42
1716, April 28, Joseph, son of Matthew Moulthrop,   17

1716, June 28, Ebenezer, son of Ebenezer Chedsey,
     killed by the upsetting of a cart,   14
  July 10, Isaac Bradley, jun.
  Oct. 23, Sarah, widow of Capt. Alling Ball, jun. 57
    27, Daniel Chedsey, son of Caleb Chedsey, 21
    24, Lydia, of Daniel Collins, 3
1717, Jan. 16, Rev. Samuel Street, Wallingford, in the
    43d year of his ministry,   above 75
  Feb. 19, James, son of Samuel Hotchkiss, 7w.
  Joanna Jones.
  July 20, Abigail, widow of John Davenport, jun.
  Samuel Thompson,   41
1718, April 24, Sarah, wife of Lieut. Thomas Smith.
1719, May 8, James Denison,   78
  June 4, Hannah, wife of Isaac Penfield, 27
  Dec. 19, Edward Grannis.
1720, Daniel, child of Abraham Chedsey,   1
  April 4, Hannah, child of Eliphalet Pardee, 3
  Oct. 20, Sarah, wife of Rev. John Woodward, 33
1721, April 25, John Thompson, 3d,   54
1722, Aug. 15, Isaac, child of Abraham Heminway, 18m.
1723, March 12, John Potter, 3d,   28
  Sept. 3, Eliphalet Pardee,   45
  Oct. 25, Mehitabel, wife of Thomas Dawson.
  Nov. 12, John Pardee.
  Nov. 22, George Pardee, jun.   58
1724, Feb. 13, Capt. John Russel,   59
  June 26, Samuel Russel,   53
  Nov. 15, Stephen Rowe,   47
    16, Capt. Thomas Smith, the father of the
      Smith family,   about 90
1725, Jan. 1, Amos, son of Daniel Collins,   20
  March 18, Sarah, widow of Thomas Goodsell, 62
  James Morris,   about 39
  Dec. 4, Eliphalet, son of Eliphalet Pardee, 13
1726, Feb. 25, Samuel, son of Samuel Thompson, 6
  April 17, Thomas Morris,   44
    18, Thomas Shepard, the father of the She-
      pard family.
  Priscilla, widow of Sergt. John Thompson, 80
  Sept. 26, Ebenezer Chedsey,   61
    James, son of do.   22
  Oct. 8, Samuel Chedsey,   23
    30, John Luddington.
        15

1726, Thomas Way.
    John Auger,   40
    Dec. 5, Nathaniel Hitchcock,   48
        10, Anna, widow of Eleazar Morris.
1727, Jan. 27, William Bradley,   45
    Thomas Smith, 3d,   30
    Henry Luddington,   48
    John Moulthrop,   31
    Dec. 24, Elisabeth Smith, widow of Thos. Smith, 51
1728, Jan. 1, Priscilla, widow of Ebenezer Chedsey, 57
    April 24, Martha Alcock,   21
    June 29, Joseph, son of Sergt. John Thompson, 18
1729, Rebecca, widow of Nathaniel Hitchcock, 47
    Daniel, son of Abraham Chedsey,   1
1730, James Hitchcock,   27
    Daniel, son of Abraham Chedsey,   6m.
    May 23, Anna, child of Abraham Heminway, 7
    July 1, Hannah, child of Abraham Chedsey.
        19, Hannah, widow of Rev. Samuel Street.
    Nov. 22, Sarah, wife of John Ball,   75
1731, Jan. 1, John Ball,   82
    Feb. 5, Rev. John Davenport, Stamford, 62
    James Pardee,   about 45
    John Denison,   54
1732, Aug. 28, John Dawson,   55
    Nov. 8, John Howe,   65
1733, June 16, John Holt,   88
1734, March 3, Jacob, son of Eleazar Morris, 4
        8, Mabel, wife of Abraham Chedsey, (with
        twins,)   39
    April 3, Samuel, son of David Austin, 2m.
    Nov. 3, Sarah, wife of John Moulthrop, jun. 36
1735, March 5, Mary, child of Abraham Chedsey, 8
    John Luddington,   41

Those that follow, died with the throat ail.

1736, Oct. 13, Abigail, child of James Denison, 5
        27, Andrew, child of Thomas Robinson, 3
    Nov. 9, Mary, child of Thomas Dawson, 10
        11, Dorothy, child of Gideon Potter, 3
        17, Hannah, child of Thomas Robinson, 5
        Hannah, child of John Hitchcock, 19
        20, Ame, of Joseph Tuttle,   10
        27, Comfort, of do.   5

1736, Ichabod, of John Smith, 2
James, of   do. 7
Dec. 25, Lydia, of Samuel Smith, Foxon, 10
    28, Isaac, of   do. 2
    Desire, of Joseph Grannis, jun. 4
    30, Samuel, of Samuel Smith, Foxon, 10
Thankful, of Isaac Howe, 5
David, of Benjamin Mallory, 2
1737, Feb. 8, Joseph, of Thomas Dawson, 2
    Daniel, of Daniel Luddington, 9
    9, Mary, of Thomas Dawson, 4
    Hannah, of James Way, 1
    Infant of Daniel Bradley.
    25, Samuel of Samuel Thompson, (Foxon,) 5
Joseph, of Thomas Roberts, 9
March 12, Mercy, of Samuel Thompson, (Foxon,) 8
Mary, of   do. 2
July 5, Mary, of Eleazar Morris, 11

Those who died with other diseases, in 1736 & '7, are,
Stephen Pardee, 40
A child of Abel Collins.
Matthias Hitchcock, 61
1736, Nov. 11, Elisabeth, widow of Samuel Gaskill.
1737, Feb. 2, Enoch, of Dan Moulthrop, 1
    3, Sergt. John Heminway, 61
    William Luddington, 51
    10, Abigail, wife of Joseph Holt, 49
Child of Edward Cannodis.
April 3, Mary, wife of Abraham Chedsey, 30
John Brown.
Benjamin Moulthrop, 30

1738, March 6, Lydia, wife of Rev. Jacob Heminway, 57
May 28, James, of John Smith, 8
July 11, Samuel Russel, 43
    21, Sarah, wife of Samuel Russel, 42
Joseph Grannis, jun. at sea, 35
Samuel Goodsell, 54
1739, Rebecca, wife of Samuel Barnes.
Feb. 26, Rebecca, wife of David Austin.
Samuel Potter, 31
John Smith, 71
1740, May 12, Matthew Moulthrop, 3d, 70

1740, May 15, Timothy Dawson,   24
          17, Hannah, wife of Daniel Luddington.
Sept. 5, Mary, wife of Joseph Tuttle.
Oct. 16, Samuel, of Samuel Smith, Foxon,   4
Dec. 22, Samuel Hotchkiss,   57
1741, May 3, Abigail, wife of Thomas Alcock,   58
     June 7, Levi, of Daniel Hitchcock,   2
     Oct. 21, Jerusha, of Gideon Potter,   3m.
1742, April 8, Stephen, of Stephen Austin,   7
          ————
     The following died with fever and dysentery.
May 15, Joseph, son of John Howel,   8
Aug. 30, Hannah, child of John Becket.
     20, Mehitabel, of John Russel,   10
Sept. 4, John, of   do.   12
     15, A child of   do.   9m.
     9, A child of Daniel Potter.
     Eunice, of   do.   11
     12, Desire, of John Howel,   4
     Matthew, of Matthew Moulthrop,   4
     Thankful, of   do.   14
     13, Sarah, of   do.   10
     Joanna Mallory,   33
     15, Hannah, wife of Daniel Potter.
     Lois, child of   do.   5
     17, William, of Deodate Davenport,   8
     19, Mercy, of Benjamin Mallory,   6
     Dorothy, wife of   do.   40
     20, Hosea, of Daniel Potter,   7
     Mary, of James Way,   4
     22, Timothy, of Israel Moulthrop,   6
     28, Anna, of Thomas Roberts,   3
     Titus, of John Dawson.   20
     29, Samuel, of Samuel Holt,   2
Oct. 1, Enos, of Samuel Smith, Foxon,   10
     5 Eunice, of Thomas Roberts,   7
     6, Abigail, of Jonathan Austin,   4
     9, Abigail, wife of Edward Cannodis.
     Samuel, & another child of Patterson Smith.
     10, Mary, of Thomas Roberts,   5
     11, Mary, wife of John Dawson,   52
     12, Eleanor, wife of Samuel Smith, Foxon,   41
     18, Mary, child of John Shepard,   12
Nov. 3, Sergt. John Thompson,   51

1742, Nov. 7, Child of Samuel Smith.
      20, Abigail Newman.

1743, Feb. 21, Punderson, of David Austin,   4w.
    March 31, Sarah Luddington,   29
    May 30, Thomas Luddington, drowned,   25
    June 10, Mercy, wife of Joseph Holt,   44
    John Luddington, jun.   20

The names of those who died with dysentery.

Aug. 20, Jesse Denison,   25
    21, Abigail, his wife,   24
    24, Tim, of James Indian.
    25, Thankful, of Gideon Potter,   15
    26, Samuel, of Samuel Heminway,   4
    27, Moses, of Moses Thompson,   17
Sept. 1, Sarah, of Enos Potter,   11
    3, Abigail, widow of John Moulthrop.
    Nancy, servant of John Heminway,   75
    Abigail, 2d wife of Nathaniel Barnes,   22
    4, Joseph, of John Heminway,   15m.
    6, Mercy, wife of Joseph Tuttle,   46
    7, Mary, widow of John Heminway,   71
    10, Sarah, of Hezekiah Camp,   2
    11, Mary, of Abraham Chedsey,   8
    15, John, of John Shepard,   12
    16, Jemima, of Daniel Hitchcock,   13
    19, Josiah, of Jonathan Goodsell,   18m.
    20, Matthew, of John Rowe, jun.   19m.
    22, Esther, of David Way,   23
    28, Mary, of John Shepard,   12
    30, Joan, wife of James Indian.
Oct. 11, Mehitabel, of John Russel,   11
    18, Sibyl, of James Denison,   13
    19, Anna, wife of Capt. Samuel Smith,   57

Nov. 23, Mercy, widow of William Luddington,   75
1744, Jan. 9, Mercy, relict of John Thompson,   77
    Feb. 18, Stephen, of Stephen Austin,   9m.
    June 23, John Howel,   35
    Oct. 15, Josiah, of Jonathan Goodsell,   9m.
    Nov. 19, John Morris,   60
    Dec. 24, Desire, of Gideon Potter,   9
1745, May 30, Serg't Samuel Goodsell,   61
    June 2, Sarah, wife of Matthew Moulthrop 4th,   38

1745, July 19, Jacob, of Patterson Smith.   4m.
      29, Abigail, of John Washburn,   7
   Aug. 3, Matthew, of Matthew Moulthrop,   3
      15, Mary, widow of Matthew Moulthrop 3d, 68
      26, Mary, of Isaac Chedsey,   10
   Two children of Thomas Robinson.
1746, Feb. 14, Rev. John Woodward,   74
   July 1, Jared, of Zebulon Bradley,   2m.
   Sept. 3, Elizabeth, wife of Thomas Whedon.
   Nov. 2, Thomas Goodsell, jun. A. M.   42
1747, Jan. 20, Daniel Potter,   46
1748, April 28, Matthew Moulthrop.
   Samuel Holt—at sea,   35
1749, Jan. 9, Sarah, relict of John Thompson,   54
   April 7, Rachel, wife of Noah Tuttle,   46
   Sept. 1, Sarah, of Enos Potter,   11
      9, Rosewell, of Deodate Davenport,   7
   Oct. 1, Ebenezer, of Ebenezer Darrow,   7
1750, Jan. 15, Loly, of Benjamin Pardee, jun.
   Eleazar Morris,   62
   Aug. 6, Hannah, of Stephen Morris,   6
      17, Amos, of Stephen Thompson,   5
   Dec. 29, Matthew Rowe,   67
1751, Aug. 22, Lois, of Daniel Auger,   2
      Samuel, of Samuel Hotchkiss, Northford, 5
      29, Sarah, of   do.
   Sept. 22, Thomas, of Samuel Holt,   4
      27, Elizabeth, second wife of Sam'l Barnes, 45
      Anna, of Daniel Holt,   10
   Oct. 13, Thankful, of Gideon Potter,   5
      31, David, of Daniel Holt,   7d.
   Nov. 20, Samuel Goodsell, killed at a saw-mill in
      Northford, by a log rolling upon him,   41
   Dec. 19, Elizabeth, wife of John Potter 3d,   78
1752, May 26, Levi, of David Potter,   6m.
   Aug. 11, Abraham Heminway, killed by lightning, 75
      Benjamin Smith, blind and insane.
      15, Eliphalet, of Ebenezer Pardee,   1
1753, Jan. 2, Sarah, wife of Jacob Goodsell,   25
      20, Hannah, wife of Thomas Shepard, jun. 17
      Infant of do.
   Nov. 1, Isaac, of Thomas Shepard,   15
      7, John Luddington,   58
1754, May 21, Noah Pardee,   33

1754, June 10, Lois, child of Joshua Austin.
Aug. 27, John, of Patterson Smith, 10
Sept. 25, Peter Woodward, 58
Oct. 7, Rev. Jacob Heminway, 70
   22, Isaac Penfield, 70
Dec. 26, Thomas Smith 4th, of small-pox, 35
   30, William, of Deodate Davenport, 10
1755, Abigail, second wife of Deacon Thomas Smith, 76
1756, Feb. 17, Isaac, of Enos Potter, 20
March, Dorcas, third wife of Samuel Barnes.
June 10, Jemima, wife of Stephen Smith, 27
   11, Daniel Holt, 45
July, William, of Jonathan Roberts, 2
Sept. 8, Samuel Thompson, 46
   27, John, son of Amos Morris, 3
Mercy, second wife of Caleb Hitchcock, and for-
   merly widow of Samuel Holt, 46
1757, April 2, Thomas Alcock, 80
   20, Capt. Samuel Forbes, 54
1758, March 23, Samuel Bradley, 72
May 7, Mary, wife of Nathaniel Luddington, 62
June 18, Lydia, wife of Capt. Deodate Davenport, 52
Dec. 30, Gideon Potter, 57
1759, Jan. 12, Thomas Dawson, 72
   29, Dan Moulthrop, of consumption, 56
1760, Jan. 13, Capt. Zebulon Bradley, N. York, small-pox, 46
Feb. 12, Lydia, widow of Dan Moulthrop, meazles, 43
March 29, Deacon Joshua Austin, 86
May, Abel, son of Abel Smith, 18
July 25, Elizabeth, child of Amos Morris, 3
Sept. 6, Elizab. daughter of Rev. John Woodward, 50
Dec. 6, Rebecca, wife of Matthew Rowe, 76
   8, Mary, widow of Samuel Goodsell, above 70
Mehitabel, widow of Deac. Joshua Austin.
   22, Lydia, wife of Abel Smith, 45
1761, Jan. 1, Caleb Chedsey 3d, 23
Deacon Daniel Hitchcock, 52
Sarah, wife of John Shepard, 49
Abigail, wife of Caleb Chedsey, jun. 62
   10, Elizabeth, wife of Azariah Bradley, cons. 21
   16, Joseph Tuttle, 68
   22, Samuel, son of Isaac Chedsey, 7
   23, Abigail, widow of Deac. Daniel Hitchcock, 53
   27, Isaac Pardee, 37

1761, Jan. Abraham Chedsey, 60
    Bathsheba, his wife, 53
  Feb. 3, Thankful, of Gideon Potter, 8
    17, Moses Thompson, 63
    William Woodward, 43
    Lydia, widow of Russel Grannis.
    [This winter, there was a great mortality among heads of families, some of which are above named. The disease is said to have been a very malignant pleurisy. Of those who had it, very few survived, and some of the sick died in a few hours.]
  Feb. 24, Benjamin Barnes, 68
  June 1, Eliphalet Luddington, 63
    John Pardee, of North-Haven, 77
  July 5, William, son of Stephen Morris, 2
  Dec. 3, Deacon Deodate Davenport, Esq. 55
1762, April 17, John Heminway, 45
  July 21, Capt. Samuel Barnes, 63
  Sept. 3, Amasa, of Samuel Tuttle, 5d.
  Deacon Thomas Smith, about 90
1763, May 8, Mary, wife of John Russel, 66
  June 10, Lois, child of Joshua Austin, 4
  July 6, A daughter of Abraham Bradley, 6w.
  Aug. 7, Infant of Samuel Tuttle, 1d.
  George Pardee the 3d, 73
1764, March, Ziba Robinson.
  Aug. 29, Abigail, wife of Joshua Austin, 31
  Oct. 23, Sarah, 2d wife of Capt. Stephen Smith, 28
  Nov. 19, Sarah, wife of Dan Bradley, 34
1765, Jan. 6, Capt. Samuel Smith, 84
    27, Desire, wife of Rev. Nicholas Street, 20
  May 7, Jared, son of Abraham Bradley, 4m.
  July 15, Mercy, wife of Samuel Davenport.
    26, Enoch, son of Jacob Hitchcock.
  Dec. 30, Desire, widow of Moses Thompson, 58
1766, June 9, Thomas Robinson, 73
  July 7, Mary, child of Joel Tuttle, 3
    12, Stephen, of Joseph Bishop, 3
  Dec. 15, Abigail, wife of Timothy Way, 23
1767, Jan. 8, Elizabeth, widow of Isaac Penfield, and
    wife of Caleb Chedsey, jun. 62
    18, Rebecca, wife of Abel Collins, 65
  Feb. 4, Lieut. Isaac Blakesley, 63

1767, March 19, Gideon Potter, 41
    May 28, Samuel, son of Samuel Thompson, 24
    Aug. 9, Lydia, of Samuel Smith, (Foxon,) 22
    Sept. 5, Mary, wife of do. 65
       9, Gideon, of Gideon Potter, 3
1768, Jan. 25, Jesse, of Eliphalet Pardee, North-Haven, 10
    July 7, Levi, son of Samuel Goodsell, jun. 23
    Sept. 21, Eleazar Brown, 72
1769, March 5, Abigail, child of Jacob Hitchcock.
      4, Jacob, child of   do.
    April 18, Penfield Goodsell, 27
    May 3, Moses Augustine, son of Rev. N. Street, 14w.
    Sept. 14, Joseph Bishop, 64
1770, March 21, Widow Mary Pardee, N. Branford.
    Aug. 31, Anna, child of Timothy Tuttle, 16
    Abigail, wife of Nathaniel Jocelin, 70
    Samuel Smith, (Foxon,)   above 70
    Oct. 3, Bethiah Miles, child of Samuel Tuttle, 7
    Nov. 2, Mary, wife of William Luddington, colic, 60
1771, April 10, Samuel, child of John Chedsey, 10
    June 16, Deborah, widow of Samuel Chedsey, 77
    Sept. 29, Enos Pardee, Northford, 81
1772, April 5, Bethiah, child of Samuel Tuttle, 14d.
    May 2, Dorcas, child of Timothy Way, 2
    Sept. 9, Elizabeth, child of Samuel Barnes, 17m.

The number of deaths in the preceding catalogue, is 507.

—⧜—

IN the following catalogue, no names are mentioned, but those that belonged within the town of East-Haven. The other names are placed in the Appendix.

A part of the following catalogue was recorded by Rev. Mr. Street; and he generally dated on the day of burial. This error in date, I have in some instances corrected.

DEATHS, DISEASES, AND AGES.

1773.

Jan. 9, Huldah, wife of Rosewell Woodward, consump. 60
    21, Elizabeth, child of Benjamin Bishop, 2
    26, Mary, wife of Samuel Smith, (Foxon,) childbed, 28
Feb. 7, Patterson Smith, fit, 63
    17, Hezekiah, son of Ichabod Barnes, croup, 5
    24, John, son of John Fuller, canker rash, 4

Feb. 28, John, of David Moulthrop, croup,   3
March 8, Sarah, of John Fuller,   } canker rash,   6
     Lois, of do. buried together, }   4
    12, Abraham, of Jacob Pardee,   1
     Chloe, a black child of Sam'l Thompson, c. rash,   4
    29, Abel Collins, fit,   67
April 21, Edward Russel, pleurisy,   75
May 6, Thomas, of Thomas Allen,   2
June 18, Samuel Amna, of Samuel Tuttle, croup,   6
    30, Mehitabel, wife of Daniel Bradley, dysentery,   71
July 2, Sarah, wife of James Denison, dys.   47
    7, Sibyl, child of Jacob Bradley, dys.   15
    10, Dorothy, of James Denison,   } dys.   10
     James, of do. buried together, } dys.   5
     Mary, of Stephen Bradley, dys.   10
    30, Thankful, wife of Joseph Mallory, dys.   43
Aug. 15, Infant of John Goodsell,   2d.
    21, John, son of John Barnes, dys.   6
    27, Lydia, of Abraham Chedsey,   1
Sept. 10, Rosewell Woodward, fit,   66
    17, Sarah, wife of Caleb Hitchcock.
    23, Abigail, child of Josiah Bradley,   8m.
    27, A child of Stephen Moulthrop,   6
Oct. 4, Infant, of Noah Tucker,   1d.
Nov. 19, Jared, of Elisha Andrews, dys.   3
Dec. 2, Edward Veal,   80
    25, Cajoe, servant of Amos Morris, drowned,   45
    30, John Deliverance, died at sea,   30

                   1774.

Jan. 4, Thomas, of Ichabod Barnes,   4
Feb. 11, Benjamin, son of James Smith,   20
    16, Child of Russel Grannis,   5
    26, Elisabeth, of Samuel Holt, cholera,   5m.
March 2, Mary, widow of Rev. John Woodward,   82
    12, Diana, wife of Richard Darrow,   84
Sept. 16, Lois, of widow Lois Moulthrop, dys.   4
     Charles O'Neal, at sea,   29
    27, James Denison, lock jaw,   55
Oct. 12, John, of Azariah Bradley, c. rash,   6m.
    18, Lieut. John Russel, consump.   80
     Desire, daughter of Timothy Thompson, dys.   18
    22, Martha Slaughter, dys.   48
    25, Lucretia, child of William Bradley, dys.   8
Nov. 7, Desire, wife of Benjamin Smith, dys.   51

Nov. 10, Huldah, of Levi Pardee, dys.   1
    12, Mehitabel, of Benjamin Pardee, dys.   12

1775.

Jan. 1, David Penn Gaylord,   77
Feb. 5, Trueman, of Joseph Russel, c. rash,   8m.
March 17, Child of David Mallory, c. rash,   1
    19, Richard Darrow,   94
April 30, Jacob Goodsell, burnt in a fish house,   52
May 1, Job Smith, consump.   58
    4, Infant of Thomas Allen,   2d.
    9, Timothy, of Elisha Andrews, cholera,   2
July 12, David, of Joseph Bishop, by lightning,   17
Aug. 10, Amos, of Dan Goodsell, gravel,   24
Oct. 28, Stephen Morris, dropsy,   60
Nov. 7, Hannah Howe, consump.   28
    11, Child of William Bradley,   18m.
Dec. 3, Child of Stephen Pardee,   18m.
    Lyman, of Abel Smith,   5

1776.

April 26, Edward Russel, jun. pleurisy,   47
    27, Joseph Hotchkiss, consump.   50
Aug. 15, James, of Job Smith, consump.   15
Sept.   Elijah, of Job Smith, in battle on Long Island,   18
    Samuel Smith. (half-mile,) dys.   37
    John, of Elam Luddington, c. rash,   15m.
    Benjamin Bishop, consump.   30
    Thomas Smith, burnt in a fire ship,   34
Oct. 16, Amasa, of Ambrose Smith, fever,   7m.
    18, Child of Gershom Scott,   2
    Anna, of James Broton,   4
Nov. 12, Hannah, wife of Stephen Thompson, nerv. fev.   52
    Nathan Andrews, died a prisoner, N. Y.   32

1777.

Jan. 6, Ame, wife of Jedediah Andrews, jun. and infant,
    in child-bed,   18
March 30, Caleb Hitchcock,   65
April 5, John Mallory,   24
    19, Timothy Tuttle, jun. fever,   17
    20, Street Chedsey, pleurisy,   20
    24, Mary Forbes,   70
May 24, Infant of Joseph Mallory,   3w.
July, Black child of John Woodward, whooping cough,   1
    17, Russel Grannis, consump.   50
Sept. 1, Lydia, wife of Deac. Amos Morris, mortification,   50

Oct. 25, Deac. Samuel Heminway, Esq. dropsy,   63
Nov. 12, Samuel, of Levi Chedsey, kicked by a horse,   3
Dec. 1, James Thompson, pleurisy,   42
     Isaac Potter, British Prison Ship, N. Y.   18
   3, Abigail, of Samuel Goodsell, c. rash,   2m.
  14, Eli Heminway, drowned,   24
1778.

Jan. 17, Sarah, wife of Samuel Bradley,   83
March 6, Polly, of Samuel Smith, jun.   2
July 19, Hannah, of Isaac Mallory,   11m.
Aug. 20, Tony, nervous fever,   27
Oct. 22, Capt. Timothy Tuttle,   54
  29, Amos, of Amos Mallory,   2m.
Nov. 17, Mary, wife of Samuel Holt,   37
Dec. 31, Daniel Granger, fever,   22
1779.

Jan. 12, Capt. Ezra Fields, consump.   48
  17, Mary, widow of John Heminway, b. colic,   58
May, Infant of Jared Bishop.
June 29, Mehitabel Pardee, of Levi, croup,   5m.
July 5, Isaac Pardee, killed at the British invasion of
     East-Haven,   22
Oct. 21, Zebulon Bradley, killed in battle at sea,   26
     Richard Paul,*   16
     Jacob Pardee, jun.*   21
     Asa Bradley,* small pox,   33
     Abijah Bradley,*   29
Oct. 28, Isaac, of Capt. Isaac Chedsey, consump.   3
1780.

Feb. 12, John Thompson, died at sea,   26
  25, Orphana, wife of Samuel Cook, consump.   24
March 18, Samuel of Levi Potter, c. rash,   10m.
May 18, John Shepherd,   84
     Medad Slaughter, prison ship, New-York,   20
Oct. 25, Timothy, of Levi Forbes, scalded,   2
Nov. 25, Asher Moulthrop, fever,   71
Dec. 9, Rosewell Bradley, at sea,   25
  13, Daniel Bradley,   84
1781.

Jan. 17, Azel, son of Abraham Chedsey, drowned,   12
Feb. 15, Mary Mallory, consump.   38

* These four were taken at the same time, and perished in the
prison ship the following winter.

March 19, Giduo, servant of John Woodward, consump. 65
April 18, John Howe, at Fort Hale, 45
May 26, James, of John Woodward, c. rash, 10m.
June 3, Daffe, child of Rose, fever, 3
    8, John Walker, in battle, Long Island, 16
    18, Child of Rose, c. rash, 5
July 3, Stephen, of Joseph Bishop, lock-jaw, 14
    7, Sarah O'Neal, nervous fever, 20
    Hannah, widow of Thomas Dawson, 82
Aug. 5, Lois, 2d wife of Capt. Amos Morris, consump. 48
Dec. 25, Edward Goodsell, consump. 32
    28, Hannah, wife of Matthew Moulthrop, 74
1782.
Jan. 9, Lydia, widow of Caleb Hitchcock, 60
    10, Isaac Luddington, consump. 40
    Infant of Jesse Luddington, 2d.
Feb. 1, Mehitabel, widow of Samuel Heminway, pleur. 68
    16, Samuel Bradley, dropsy, 32
March 17, Anna, widow of Timothy Tuttle, consump. 50
    Caleb Bradley, 68
April 17, Mary, of Stephen Bradley, jun, fit, 15d.
    19, Daniel, of Daniel Brown, whooping cough, 7
    20, Widow Mabel Utter, 75
May 2, Child of Cuffee, 10m.
June 10, Catherine Russel, 85
    20, Enos Bradley, fall from mast-head, 20
July 4, Benjamin Pardee, mortification, 69
    11, Jared Heminway, consump. 33
Aug. 18, Benoni Pardee, king's evil, 25
Oct. 27, Abigail, wife of Nathaniel Barnes, colic, 63
    Joseph, son of Daniel Bradley, W. India fever, 19
    Elihu Moulthrop,   do. 35
Dec. 20, Child of Peter and Betty, 14m.
1783.
March 5, Desire, wife of Ephraim Chedsey, childbed, 27
    9, Cate, servant of Deac. Stephen Smith, 11
    20, Asahel, infant of Abraham Chedsey, 7d.
April 1, Levi, son of Samuel Smith, 8m.
    2, Elisabeth, wife of Samuel Shepard, a rupture, 48
    6, Mary Abbot, 70
    7, Peggy, servant of widow Pardee, 30
    8, Infant of Joseph Smith, meazles, 4w.
May 2, Samuel, of Levi Chedsey, 1w.
    12, Sarah, of Samuel Barnes, meazles, 9
16

June 1, Anna, wife of John Chedsey, leprosy, 55
July 22, Jeremiah, of Samuel Barnes, small pox, 17
Aug. 29, Daniel Smith, gravel, 56
Sept. 7, Emily, of Amos Mallory, c. rash, 2
 17, John Chedsey, bilious fever, 63
 19, Isaac Bradley, nervous fever, 65
 20, Dan, of Edmund Bradley, 2
Oct. 20, William Day, bilious fever, 40
 21, Mary Pardee, dropsy, 57
Nov. 22, Polly, of Elihu Grannis, croup, 5
   1784.
Jan. 7, Benjamin Smith, cancer, 68
 14, Jedediah Andrews, 3d day ague, 76
 Infant of Thomas Shepard, 1d.
 29, Mehitabel, of Joseph Russel, consump. 19
March 14, Isaac Grannis, jun. nervous fever, 27
June 21, Isaac, of Isaac Barnes, scalded, 18m.
July 12, Susannah, a twin child of Gurdon Bradley, 2w.
Sept. 29, Elisabeth, widow of Jedediah Andrews, tertian ague, 60
Oct. 1, Elam Lu[i]dington, cholera, 30
 Isaac Hotchkiss, fever at sea, 30
 20, Joseph Smith, small pox at sea, 36
Nov. 4, Jemima Pardee, pleurisy, 84
 7, Jacob Smith, hurt by lifting, 32
Dec. 9, Infant of Jesse Luddington, 6w.
   1785.
Jan. 1, Infant of Sarah Moulthrop, 1d.
Feb. 3, Child of Jehiel Arnold, 2m.
May 6, Darius Hickox, consump. 26
 14, David Grannis, drowned off Southend, 42
 David Mallory, do. do. 36
 22, Desire Pardee, nervous fever, 23
July 10, Jared Heminway, consump. 36
Aug. 30, Daniel Chedsey, small pox, 17
 Nancy, of Enos Heminway, c. rash, 4
Sept. 6, Caleb Chedsey, 89
 23, James, of Nehemiah Smith, by opium, 1
 28, Elisabeth, wife of Joseph Heminway, consump. 34
Dec. 27, Elisabeth, wife of George, fever, 22
   1786.
Jan. —, Patience, child of George King, dys. 8
 13, Samuel Thompson, peripneumony, 81
 26, Rebecca, of George King, dys. ?

Jan. 27, Sarah, widow of Patterson Smith, fit, 67
Feb. 28, Elisabeth, of Levi Potter, fits, 4m.
    Benjamin Curtiss, consump. 21
April 1, Abigail, widow of Henry O'Neal, 100
March 10, Joseph, of George Lancraft, worms, 9
June 27, Susannah, wife of Joshua Austin, fever, 50
Aug. —, Infant of Jesse Luddington, 1w.
    28, Reuel, of Levi Pardee, consump. 10m.
Sept. 27, Elisabeth, wife of Daniel Auger, pleurisy, 65
Nov. —, Mary, widow of John Thompson, 85
    Rowe, of Ambrose Smith, 1
Dec. —, A twin child of Ira Smith, 1d.
    Huldah, of Asa Mallory, worms, 2
    Israel, of Samuel Moulthrop, worms, 7
    Thomas Allen, nervous fever, 40
    20, Isaac Mallory, small pox, 55
1787.
Jan. 6, Benjamin Ford, shot by his own gun, 35
    8, Jared, of John Shepard, 18
    9, A twin child of Ira Smith, 5w.
Feb. 17, Hannah, wife of Samuel Heminway, consump. 34
April 22, Noah Pardee, yellow fever, 30
June 29, Thankful, wife of Robert Dawson, consump. 60
July 12, Susannah, dys. 15d.
Sept. 8, Justus, of Stephen Bradley, jun. dys. 4
Oct. 24, Widow Mary Higgins, 76
Nov. 15, Infant of Jesse Luddington, 5d.
Dec. 8, Elisabeth, widow of Eben'r Roberts, pleurisy, 60
1788.
Jan. 21, Mary, widow of Capt. Ezra Fields, consump. 55
    26, Moses Page, 84
March 22, Woodward Hervey, of John Hunt, worms, 2m.
    30, Stephen Pardee, jun. small pox, 63
May 4, Infant of Jared Thompson, 4w.
    7, Olive, wife of Joseph Grannis, small pox, 56
July 9, A twin child of Edward Bradley, 4w.
    30, Abigail, wife, and her Infant, of Jacob Moulthrop, consump. 26
Aug. 8, Elizabeth, wife of Samuel Shepard, consump. 22
Aug. 28, Jared, son of Asa Mallory, cancer, 10
Sept. 14, Esther, widow of Joseph Hotchkiss, putrid fev. 59
    Loring, of Job Smith, 3
    20, Uriel, son of Edmond Bradley, 2
    Sarah, of John Hunt, kicked by a horse, 9

Oct. 9, Daniel Brown, hurt by lifting,   45
    15, Israel Moulthrop,   82
    30, Gideon Hotchkiss, diarrhœa,   19
Dec. 6, Gideon, of Asaph Hotchkiss,   3w.
    Sarah Clark, fever,   18
    12, Caleb, of Jesse Luddington, cholera,   6

1789.

Jan. 11, John Rowe, dropsy,   74
Feb. 18, Hannah Luddington, asthma,   68
March 17, Andrew, servant of Capt. Isaac Chedsey,
    dropsy,   28
    27, James, of John Morris, worms,   8
April 23, Jeremiah Bradley, killed in raising the Church
    house,   22
June 30, Joel Tuttle, cramp,   71
Aug. 25, Mary, of William Bradley, worms,   2
Sept. 7, Hannah, widow of John Rowe, consump.   71
    24, Joseph, of Daniel Bradley,   3
Dec. 7, Widow Lydia Grannis, a rupture,   60
    15, Adah, of Edmond Bradley,   16m.
    23, Mary, wife of Isaac Chedsey, consump.   77

1790.

Feb. 17, Esther, widow of Stephen Morris, palsy,   69
March 9, Eben Tyler, of Moses Heminway, kicked by
    a horse,   4
    21, Mehitabel, widow of Thomas Grannis, palsy,   77
April 5, Phyllis,   90
    Child of Dick,   3m.
May 1, Samuel Moulthrop, consump.   60
    Mary Russel, consump.   17
    3, Mercy Pardee, dropsy,   60
    20, Lieut. Isaac Smith, pleurisy,   50
July 17, Infant of Leavit Pardee,   7d.
    27, James A. Broton, fit,   73
    27, China, scalded,   35
Aug, 25, Tabitha, wife of Philemon Auger, consump.   33
Sept. 3, Isaac, of Jared Thompson, worms,   3
    19, Abraham, of Stephen Tuttle, consump.   2
    Russel, of Nathaniel Grannis, worms,   2
Dec. 12, Abigail, widow of Eliphalet Luddington,   90
    23, Mary, wife of Ambrose Smith, childbed,   39
    31, Elisabeth, widow of Samuel Thompson, palsy, 80

1791.

Jan. 9, Hannah, widow of Isaac Bradley, jaundice,   66

Feb. 18, Sarah, of John Hunt, mortification, 4m.
April 16, Reuel, of Chandler Pardee, nervous fever, 4m.
May 10, Lois, of Matthew Rowe, whooping cough, 10w.
 25, Thomas, Mr. Street's servant, consumption, 57
  John Woodward, jun. 79
June 25, Mary, wife of John Hughes, consumption, 30
July 23, Wyllys, of Daniel Austin, cholera, 9m.
Sept. 8, Lois, widow of Solomon Moulthrop, consump. 45
 12, Mehitabel, widow of Isaac Mallory, consump. 57
Oct. 13, Henry Freeman Hughes, consump. 68
 24, Joseph Russel, jun. consump. 19
Nov. 1, Hezekiah ,of Amos Morris, jun. cholera, 18m.
 7, Susanna Roberts, consump. 34
 17, Mary, widow of John Woodward, jun. fit, 76
Dec. 26, Daniel, of Daniel Hughes, consump. 6m.
1792.
March 24, Huldah, child of Amos Thompson, cholera, 1
May 10, Abigail, wife of Dan Goodsell, gravel, 65
 14, Sarah, of Stephen Thompson, jun. worms, 2
June 16, Lois, wife of Nehemiah Smith, consump. 36
Aug. 13, A child of Ebenezer Holt, 1
Nov. 6, James, of Nehemiah Smith, 1
 15, Electa Lucas, consumption, 18
 Nancy, of Amos Broton, 13w.
1793.
Jan. 3, Keziah, wife of Isaac Grannis, 79
Feb. 2, Ichabod, of Ambrose Smith, 8
 3, Miles, of Sam'l Tuttle, yellow fever, W. Indies, 17
 Isaac Smith, nervous fever, 30
 11, Infant of Samuel Goodsell, whooping cough, 6w.
March 8, Comfort, wife of Deac. Stephen Smith, dropsy, 66
April 18, Jehiel Forbes, consumption, 60
June 1, Anson, a twin child of Edmond Bradley, 2w.
Aug. 24, Anna, the other twin of do. 2m.
July 15, Sarah, of John Morris, canker rash, 13
 25, Timothy Andrews, palsy, 77
 30, Hezekiah Thompson, consumption, 21
Aug. 12, Capt. Isaac Chedsey, 84
 18, Jeremiah, of Jonathan Goodsell, cholera, 1
 20, Joseph, a twin child of Joseph Heminway, dys. 6
Oct. 19, Mehitabel, wife of Jesse Luddington, consump. 69
Nov. Joseph, of Joseph Moulthrop, at sea, 18
 14, Priscilla, widow of Daniel Holbrook, 86
 23, Child of Cuffee, 9
16 *

Nov. Daniel Tuttle,   yellow fever, W. Indies,   25
    Abraham Eggleston,   do.   do.   20
Dec. 23, Jeremiah Woodward, do.   do.   22

1794.

Jan. 6, Jenny,   70
   22, Eleazar Forbes,   20
   25, Reuel, of Joseph Heminway, canker rash,   9
   30, Infant of Jared Grannis,   3d.
Feb. 6, Lydia, widow of Matthew Luddington,   82
   7, Abigail, servant of John Woodward,   78
   21, Mary, of Moses Heminway, canker rash,   15
March 2, Charles Langdon, canker rash,   6
   6, Mary Roberts,   77
   7, Hannah, wife of Timothy Way, jun. childbed, 22
   22, Benjamin Smith, nervous fever,   37
   29, Infant of Capt. Grannis,   3d.
April 14, Hannah, of David Green, canker rash,   3
   19, James, of Amos Broton, canker rash,   1
May 16, Twins of Edmond Bradley,   2d.
   20, Hannah, of John Fuller,   2d.
   21, Desire, of Abraham Chedsey, dysentery,   8
June 17, Mary, of Isaac Bradley, canker rash,   15
July 30, Hannah, of do.   do.   5
Aug. 2, Lydia, of Freeman Hughes,   78
   21, Charlotte, of John Chedsey, canker rash,   18m.
   22, Abraham, of Simeon Bradley, pleurisy,   14
   25, Hannah, wife of Joseph Holt, yellow fever,   52
Sept. Levins, of Levi Forbes, died at sea,   18
Oct. 31, Lydia Pardee, consumption,   64
Nov. 20, Smith, of Christopher Tuttle, canker rash,   2
Dec. 8, Betsey, of Amos Bradley, croup,   1
   19, Samuel Barnes, died at sea,   32

1795.

Jan. 7, Mary, wife of Eleazar Heminway, childbed,   21
   16, Lydia Russel, pleurisy,   68
July 20, Ambrose Smith, lost at sea,   45
   26, Anna, wife of John Forbes, childbed,   21
   28, Richard Woodward,   80
   29, Dan Goodsell,   71
   Twins of Jacob Moulthrop,   2d.
Aug. 22, Thankful, wife of Stephen Bradley, a rupture, 72
   31, Samuel Townsend, consumption,   53
Sept. 2, Jared Barnes, dysentery,   17
   26, Rosewell Woodward, dys.   20

Sept. 30, Child of Dick, dys. 7
Oct. 6, Child of Dick, dys. 8
  7, Heminway, of Nathaniel Barnes, dys. 1
  8, John, of John Hughes, dys. 4
 14, Jacob Bradley, dys. 61
 20, Sarah, of John Chedsey, dys. 15
 23, John, of John Thompson, dys. 12
 24, Hannah, widow of Daniel Smith, dys. 67
 29, Desire, of Samuel Smith, dys. 15
Nov. 4, Thate, servant of Capt. Woodward, dys. 70
  5, Hannah, of Ichabod Bishop, dys. 18
   Ransom, of Stephen Thompson, jun. dys. 9
  8, David, of Widow Mulford, dys. 3
 12, Leavit, of Leavit Pardee, dys. 8
 15, Mehitabel, of Jared Pardee, dys. 5
 21, A child of Zebulon Bradley, dys. 2m.
 24, Levi Forbes, consumption, 56
Dec. 7, Hannah Bradley, consump. 36
 15, Matthew Moulthrop, 90
 31, A child of Richard Wilson, worms, 8
      1796.
Jan. 3, Abigail, wife of Joseph Shepard, childbed, 35
March 3, Harriet, of Isaac Forbes, 3w.
 13, A child of Cuffee, 2m.
May 6, Elizabeth, wife of John Russel, childbed, 22
  Jared Smith, died at sea, 24
  Jesse Bradley, lost at sea, 30
  John Pardee, dysentery, 27
June, Twins of John Tyler, 1 & 2w.
July 12, Rebecca, wife of Jared Pardee, consump. 40
 25, A child of Richard Wilson, 2
Aug. 22, Rachel, of Andrew Davidson, dys. & wh. cough, 1
 26, Eudocia, of Daniel Bradley, dys. & wh. cough, 5
 25, James, of Amma Bradley, dys. & wh. cough, 17m.
 30, Julia, of Thomas P. Cotterel, 3
Sept. 9, Rebecca Roberts, pleurisy, 75
  1, Justus, of Stephen Bradley, 2
 11, Sarah, of Daniel Bradley, dysentery, 2
 13, Jared, of Amos Bradley, 1
 21, Caleb Moulthrop, dysentery, 23
Oct. 25, Thankful, wife of Jesse Luddington, consump. 37
 22, Nancy, of Amos Broton, dropsy, 10w.
      1797.
Jan. 26, Rebecca, widow of Wm. Bradley, pleurisy, 59

Feb. 22, Stephen Bradley, diabetes,   73
  28, John Heminway, jaundice,   58
March 9, Esther, of Amos Thompson, croup,   1
  14, Child of Isaac Forbes, jun.   3w.
April 10, Jacob Barnes, nervous fever,   37
May 6, Titus, servant of widow Mary Pardee, consump.   18
  23, Lydia, wife of Josiah Moulthrop, childbed,   41
  25, Hannah Brown, consumption,   24
June 1, Elizabeth, wife of Deac. Stephen Smith, pleur.   63
  16, Anna, widow of Asher Moulthrop,   84
  17, John Woodward, consumption,   46
  30, John, of Nehemiah Smith, fits,   2
Aug. Penfield Goodsell, lost at sea,   24
Nov. 3, Abraham Barnes, quinsy,   20
  30, Amos, of Samuel Barnes, fever, W. Indies,   18

1798.

Feb. 27, Capt. Samuel Forbes, consumption,   67
  Amos Shepard, fever, W. Indies,   25
March 9, Infant of Timothy Way, fits,   1d.
June 5, Nathaniel Bradley, fever, W. Indies,   20
Sept. 2, Elizabeth, of Matthew Rowe, cholera,   15m.
  10, A child of Nathaniel Yale, cholera,   3
Oct. 8, Abraham O'Neal,   82
Dec. Infant of John Russel,   3d.
  Nathan Andrews, by a fall from a mast,   19
  7, Anna, widow of Timothy Andrews,   80
  10, Nathaniel Barnes,   92
  13, Caleb, of Capt. Caleb Smith, croup,   4
  31, Rinda, of Asaph Hotchkiss, croup,   4
  Margaret Jacobs,   80

1799.

Jan. 26, Robert Dawson,   81
Feb. 8, Jesse Luddington, dropsy,   77
March 14, Levi Mallory, fits,   50
  23, James, of John Thompson, dropsy in the head, 5
June 5, Jacob, of Thomas Shepard, dysentery,   7
July 21, Mary, widow of David Mallory, consump.   57
Sept. 2, Wyllys, of Jesse Mallory, drowned,   6
  25, Penfield, of John Goodsell, nervous fever,   21
Oct. 2, Jedediah Andrews, consumption,   48
  9, Huldah, of Caleb Smith, 2d, croup,   10m.
Nov. 10, Mary Pardee, dropsy,   82
Dec. 29, Esther, wife of Stephen Heminway, consump.   27

1800.

March 13, Infant of Edmond Bradley; one of triplets, 1d.
  30, The other two, buried together, 17d.
May 26, Cuffee, dropsy, 71
June 9, Lydia, of Elisha Andrews, 24
  10, A child of Titus Santford, worms, 2
Aug. Eli Farren, yellow fever, W. Indies, 21
Sept. Capt. Joseph Shepard,* 38
  Rosewell Shepard,* 20
  Abiud Barnes,* 19
  Abraham Shepard,* 18
Dec. 24, Joseph Moulthrop, mortification, 47
  26, Sarah, widow of Caleb Chedsey, bilious fever, 80

1801.

Feb. 17, Sarah, widow of Samuel Townsend, fit, 64
April 2, Betsey, of Richard Spinks, 7
  6, Annis Mallory, consumption, 22
  12, Infant, of Jared Grannis, 1d.
  11, Lydia, wife of Samuel Holt, dropsy, 55
May 22, Isabel, wife of William Everton, dropsy, 67
June 16, Stephen, of Matthew Rowe, drowned, 9
Aug. 11, William, of Caleb Smith, 2d, croup, 13m.
Sept. 25, Martha, wife of Moses Heminway, bilious fev. 49
  28, Betsey, of Moses Thompson, killed by a cart, 12
Oct. 3, Catherine, widow of Benjamin Robinson, 80
  30, Abraham, of Philemon Auger, dysentery, 4

1802.

Jan. 18, Isaac Shepard, nervous fever, 25
Feb. 9, Stephen Thompson, jun. consumption, 40
  26, Nanne ———, perished in a snow-storm, 75
April 6, Mary, of Isaac Forbes, jun. croup, 2
May 19, Mary, wife of Jacob Pardee, dropsy, 68
June, A child of Job Smith.
July, Esther, of Timothy Thompson, meazles, 2
  22, Simeon Bradley, insanity, 71
  25, Samuel Heminway 2d, fever, at Halifax, 24
Aug. 5, Elizabeth, widow of Jacob Bradley, dysentery, 64
Sept. 27, Maria Bradley.
Oct. 9, Hannah, wife of Rev. Nicholas Street, bilious, 61
  Jennet, of Hezekiah Woodward, cholera, 8m.
  23, Clarissa Pardee, consumption, 16
  Gideon Smith, died at sea, 27
Dec. 17, Amos Wilcox, a twin child of Bela Farnham, 3w.

* These four were all lost at sea, in a gale, with the vessel.

1803.

Jan. 25, Sarah Smith, palpitation,	22
Feb. 18, Daniel Auger, fever,	88
20, John, of Nehemiah Smith, cholera,	2
March 9, Elizabeth, widow of Zebulon Bradley,	87
14, Henry, of Asa Luddington, cholera,	1
April 23, Esther, wife of Timothy Thompson,	74
June 6, Jared, of Asa Luddington, drowned,	3
23, Samuel Holt, jun. fits,	33
July 1, Lydia, wife of Charles Wedmore, consumption,	34
9, Elizabeth, wife of Ebenezer Chedsey, consump.	62
18, James Davidson,	22
Aug. 4, Amos Broton, small-pox,	31
A child of John Forbes, dysentery,	2
16, Amos Mallory, consumption,	45
Sept. 1, George, of Abijah Pardee, dysentery,	8
Oct. 15, Holbrook Everton, dysentery,	22
17, Desire, of Ebenezer Chedsey, putrid fever,	24
Nehemiah Smith, lost at sea,	24
Roger Smith, do.	20
David Grannis, do.	20
Nov. 5, A child of Edmond Bradley, dysentery.	
Betsey, of Samuel Forbes, dys.	2
Elvira, of Samuel Goodsell, dys.	7
Dec. 11, Rachel Smith, consumption,	42
21, Mary, wife of Deacon Samuel Davenport, fit,	66
22, Lucy, widow of Russell Grannis, jun.	71
26, Isaac Grannis, fit,	36
Loly, wife of Thomas Barnes, consumption,	27

1804.

Jan. 23, Pamela, wife of Levi Fuller, childbed,	25
A child of Levi Cooper,	1
May 15, Moses Thompson, dropsy,	40
Sept. 3, A child of ―― Jenkins, by a carriage,	1
19, A child of Samuel Grannis, rupture,	5w.
Oct. 26, Charles Bishop, fit,	69
Orlando Thompson, yellow fever, W. Indies,	20
Nov. John Chedsey, jun. the same,	24
10, Lemuel Barnes, consumption,	22
Dec. 7, Mary, wife of John Hughes, consump.	47
18, Mary Britton, fit,	29

1805.

Jan. 21, Daniel, of Samuel Bradley, consumption,	1
28, Catherine Russel, consumption,	84

Jan. 30, Infant of Timothy Thompson, 3d.
Feb. 1, Samuel Shepard, 75
March 24, Sarah Bradley, of Collins Hughes, dropsy, 4
    29, Sarah, of Widow Parks, croup, 5
May 8, Matilda, of Jacob Chedsey, canker rash, 3
Aug. 3, Widow Hannah Barnes, 84
    Anson, of Enos Heminway, drowned, 18
Sept. 11, Sarah Smith, of Christopher Tuttle, cramp, 17m.
    29, Flora, servant of James Chedsey, dropsy, 15
Oct. 16, Eliza Louisa, of Matthew Rowe, consump. 2
    26, Hannah, wife of John Heminway, fever, 30
Nov. 9, Samuel, of Isaac Brown, croup, 5
    10, Almira, of Isaac Brown, croup, 10m.
Dec. 3, Zabulon Farren, 86
    10, John, of John Heminway, fever, 4
    12, Sarah, of Moses Thompson, dysentery, 10
    16, Sarah, of Zebra Eggleston, 2

1806.
Jan. 7, Rebecca, widow of Joel Tuttle, 87
    29, Infant of Henry Welton, 1d.
    30, Anna, of Abijah Pardee, fever, 8
May 7, Abijah Davidson, yellow fever, W. Indies, 22
    17, Sarah, widow of Anthony Thompson, 87
    29, Abigail Grannis, consumption, 22
July 9, Ebenezer Chedsey, consumption, 69
Sept. 7, Hannah, widow of Isaac Forbes, dropsy, 64
    10, Samuel, of Isaac Brown, cholera, 3w.
Oct. 8, Rev. Nicholas Street, 76
Nov. 1, Infant of Bethuel Flagg, 1d.
    29, Charlotte, of Edward R. Smith, cholera, 8m.
Dec. 20, Phineas Curtis, pleurisy, 35

1807.
Jan. 12, Agnes, wife of Albergin Darrow, consump. 30
    30, Mary, widow of Elihu Moulthrop, 61
Feb. 19, Ruth, wife of John Woodward, dropsy, 66
March 27, John Fuller, consumption, 71
May 20, Hezekiah Bradley, yellow fever, W. Indies, 34
June 8, A child of Albergin Darrow, consump. 1
    Solomon, of William Bradley, dysentery, 14
    13, Desire, widow of Zabulon Farren, dyspepsia, 64
Aug. 10, Jacob Pardee, 80
    14, Daniel Tuttle, dysentery, 58
    11, Maria, of Leveret Bradley, sore mouth, 6w.
Sept. 17, George Landcraft, hurt by lifting, 83

Sept. 29, Mary, widow of Joel Mulford, consump.   50
Nov. 26, Timothy Thompson,   88
    30, Sydney, of Jacob Farren, burnt,   4
Dec. 12, Infant of William Woodward,   7d.

1808.

Jan. 13, Infant of Abraham Farren,   2d.
Feb. 12, A child of Parson Forbes,   6w.
March 13, Eunice, widow of Samuel Britton,   78
    30, Mabel, wife of Justin Bradley, childbed,   21
April 12, Sarah, wife of William Woodward, consump.   25
May 23, Isaac Forbes, consumption,   66
Aug. 1, Infant of De Grasse Maltby,   1d.
    3, Street, child of Widow Mary Curtis, croup,   2
Oct. 12, Jane, of Edward R. Smith, lung fever,   3w.
    A child of Elizabeth Mallory, consumption,   1
Nov. 10, Stephen Thompson,   85
Dec. 16, Sarah, wife of Capt. Isaac Chedsey, fit,   80

1809.

Feb. 16, Elizabeth Pardee, consumption,   34
March 19, Edwin, of Amasa Forbes, consump.   19m.
April 27, Delina, of Elijah Rowe, cholera,   8
June 21, Abigail, wife of Joseph Heminway, consump.   56
Aug. 8, Mary Pardee, consumption,   20
    12, Deborah Chedsey, consumption,   84
Sept. 3, Infant of Isaac Holt Pardee,   1d.
    27, Levi, of Levi Potter, jun. cholera,   6w.
    28, Hiram, of James Heminway, suffocated by a
        bean,   4
Oct. 27, Sarah, widow of Abraham O'Neal,   85
Dec. 27, Infant of Abraham Farren,   4d.

1810.

Jan. 11, Jennet, of Samuel Bradley, 2d, cholera,   2
    20, Benjamin Smith, lost at sea,   27
    Henry Welton, lost at sea,   36
    Harriet, of James Bishop, scalded,   2
March 10, Frances, of Samuel Farren, croup,   4
April 3, Timothy, of Rev. Saul Clark, cholera,   3m.
    28, Abraham Chedsey, jun. consumption,   36
May 11, James Heminway, typhus fever,   33
    18, Abigail, widow of Simeon Bradley, liver com-
        plaint,   68
    29, Laura, of John Heminway, typhus fever,   10
June 2, Charles Thompson, typhus fever,   28
    21, Infant of Lyman Hotchkiss.

July 9, Deacon Samuel Davenport, Esq.   70
Aug. 5, Sylvester Thompson,   20
   22, Michael Harrison, typhus fever,   35
Sept. 4, Daniel, of Aner Brown, cholera,   4w.
Oct. 7, Sarah Potter, consump.   30
      Capt. Heminway Holt, lost in a gale at sea,   38
      Jesse Bradley, lost at the same time,   17
      Capt. Caleb Smith, lost in a gale at sea,   57
      Edward R. Smith, at the same time,   27
      John Moulthrop,   do.   34
      Isaac Grannis,   do.   20
   21, Hannah, wife of Abraham Farren,   40
Nov. 2, John Woodward, diarrhœa,   68
   17, James Chedsey, peripneumony,   65
   18, John Shepard, jun. typhus fever,   46
Dec. 6, Desire Chedsey, of Caleb Smith, 2d. croup,   4

1811.

Feb. 13, Huldah Luddington, fever,   19
March 18, Chauncey Barnes, drowned,   40
   21, Nancy Bradley, consump.   27
April 3, Sophia, wife of Parson Forbes, consump.   28
   4, John Shepard, consump.   68
April 29, Ichabod Bishop, consump.   61
May 15, Willet Bradley, consump.   27
   17, Comfort, wife of Josiah Bradley, palsy, 68
June 9, Anna Potter, consump.   19
   16, Frank Davis, typhus fever,   30
      Hubbard, of Parson Forbes, consump.   6m.
   26, Infant of Hervey Rowe,   3d.
July 20, Daniel, of Isaac Brown, cholera,   5m.
   27, Huldah, of Isaac Forbes, jun.   4
Aug. 19, Horace, of John Forbes, consump.   1
Sept. 3, Kism, fit,   38
   8, Daniel, of Heman Mallory, cholera,   1w.
   15, Ruth Bishop, burnt,   70
      Asa Luddington, West-India fever,   41
      Isaac Kimberly, West-India fever,   20
      Isaac Smith, lost at sea,   37
Dec. 3, Henry, of James Bishop, croup,   10m.

1812.

Jan. 1, Lois, widow of Jacob Smith, consump.   57
   12, Infant of ——— Todd,   3w.
Feb. 7, Joseph Grannis,   77
March 17, Mary Hughes, consump.   22

March 28, Abraham Chedsey, apoplexy,   74
April 4, Azariah Bradley, palsy,   78
     7, Huldah Hughes, consump.   19
May 24, Lydia, wife of Chandler Pardee, dropsy,   55
Aug. 3, Wyllys, of Amasa Mallory, consump.   5m.
Sept. 11, David Eggleston,   81
     28, Jennet, child of Samuel Bradley, 2d, wh. cough, 5w.
Oct. 10, Olive, wife of John Eggleston, dys.   56
1813.

Feb. 23, Matthew Rowe, fever,   56
     24, Richard, of Hezekiah Woodward, sore mouth, 3w.
March 28, Nehemiah Perkins, consump.   24
April 15, Desire, wife of Stephen Thompson, putrid fev. 30
May 8, Elisabeth, widow of John Shepard, jr. putrid fev. 67
     17, Amy, widow of John Shepard, 3d, putrid fev.   46
June 4, Huldah, of Willet Forbes,   3d.
July 3, William Everton,   80
     Infant of Amos Bradley,   1d.
     6, Sarah, wife of Isaac Brown, child bed,   32
     10, Orpha, wife of Solomon Dewy, fever,   32
Aug. 2, Levi, of Levy Potter, jun. cholera,   18m.
     15, Elisabeth Isaacs, of Rev. Elijah G. Plumb, dys. 18m.
     23, Lydia, wife of Thomas Shepard, liver com.   67
     26, Eben, of Asahel Bradley, 2d, dys.   8
Sept. 2, Merit, of Abner Bradley, dys.   5
     4, Desire Chedsey, dys.   70
     5, Josiah Heminway, dys.   12
     7, Infant of —— Harrison,   1d.
     8, Martha Elisabeth, of Hervey Heminway,   2
     10, Hannah, wife of Abner Bradley, dys.   31
     14, James, of Amma Bradley, dys.   12
     16, Eli Moulthrop, dropsy,   61
     22, Charles, of Samuel Lindsley, dys.   2
     24, Stephen Augustus, of Stephen Woodward, dys. 5
     27, Abraham, of James Thompson,   1
     30, Jared, of Asahel Bradley, 2d, cholera,   9m.
     Jane, of Samuel Lindsley, dys.   6
Oct. 1, Henrietta, of Stephen Shepard, jun. dys.   5
     4, Esther, widow of Deacon Amos Morris, dys.   77
     6, Mary, wife of Isaac Bradley, bilious fever,   60
     14, Harriet, of Abner Bradley, diarrhœa,   1
     17, Jennet, of John Larkins, diarrhœa,   1
     22, Benjamin, of Joseph Bishop, dys.   7
Nov. 6, Lois Marina, of Moses A. Street, dys.   6

Nov. 10, Abigail, wife of Christopher Tuttle, consump. 49
    21, Deacon Levi Pardee, diarrhœa, 72
     Infant of Jacob Goodsell, 4w.
Dec. 30, Lydia Fields, of Isaac H. Pardee, cholera, 11m.

1814.

Jan. 14, Joseph Hawkins, peripneumony, 52
    29, Timothy Way, dropsy, 69
Feb. 6, Edward, of Tyler Heminway, cholera, 3m.
    14, Wyllys, of Isaac Moulthrop, consump. 4m.
    16, Justin Bradley, consump. 27
July 29, Reuben Moulthrop, diarrhœa, 51
    30, Capt. Isaac Chedsey, dropsy, 83
Aug. 11, Reuel Barnes, at Edenton, N. C. typhus fev. 21
    29, Levi Potter, jun. consump. 34
Sept. 8, Frances, of Rev. Saul Clark, meazles, 10w.
Dec. 16, Hezekiah Thompson, in the army, 21
    31, Desire, wife of Samuel Thompson, 78

1815.

Jan. 10, Jesse Denison, gravel, 69
    11, James Potter, consump. 25
Feb. 16, Sarah Andrews, consump. 35
March 23, Lovisa, wife of Joel Bradley, head disease, 43
    24, Anna, wife of Isaac Forbes, consump. 41
April 7, Mehitabel, widow of Ichabod Bishop, fit, 60
May 21, Hezekiah Woodward, fever, 52
June 4, A child of widow Mary Potter, 1
    24, Hannah, widow of Abraham Chedsey, liver affection, 69
Aug. —, Swayne Moulthrop, consump. 24
Sept. —, Anna Maria, of Daniel Rowe, whooping cough, 9m.
    26, Elizabeth Eggleston, dys. 70
    29, Bradley, of Isaac Pardee, a rupture, 8m.
Oct. 2, Frances Abigail, of Jacob Goodsell, cholera, 10m.
    21, Amos Mallory, dys. 11
     Col. Asa Bray, dys. 60
Nov. 2, Mary, wife of Amos Thompson, typhus fever, 62
    3, Barney Nelson, of Daniel Rowe, dys. 8
    22, William, of Willet Heminway, dropsy, 2
Dec. 11, Charlotte, wife of Amos Morris, jun. consump. 32
    15, Julia, of Townsend Bartlett, dysentery, 14m.
     Hannah, wife of Asa Mallory, consump. 67
     Silas Barnes, lost at sea, 26
     Daniel Wedmore, lost at sea, 23
     Collins Hughes, lost at sea, 17

1816.

Jan. 5, Moses Heminway, gravel,   54
     22, Deacon Stephen Smith,   92
     29, John Goodsell, fever,   68
Feb. 3, Amos Broton, of Amasa Mallory, peripneum.   3m.
March 6, Lois, wife of Edward Russell, pleurisy,   45
     Eunice, wife of Benj'n Mallory, peripneum.   65
     10, Hannah, wife of Abraham Barnes, consump.   68
April 19, Leuramah, wife of Jeremiah B. Davidson, cons. 24
May,   John, of Collins Hughes,   10
     6, John Chedsey, peripneumony,   68
1817.
Jan. 14, Asahel Chedsey, consumption,   36
     14, Sarah, wife of Daniel Hughes, cancer,   60
Feb.   Samuel Thompson, peripneumony,   80
May 4, Mary, widow of Levi Potter, jun. consumption, 34
     20, Samuel Tuttle,   78
June 2, Mary, widow of Samuel Thompson, fit,   52
Aug. 12, Infant, of Rosewell Auger.
Sept. 24, Amos Thompson, typhus fever,   66
Oct. 1, Widow Thankful Luddington,   90
     2, Mary Bradley, consumption,   31
Dec. 16, Mary, widow of Stephen Thompson, dropsy,   82
1818.
Jan. 7, Olive, wife of Justin Luddington, childbed,   20
Feb. 4, Elisabeth, widow of Benjamin Smith, jun. cons. 31
     13, Sarah Bradley, dropsy,   46
     Jared Grannis, jun. lost at sea,   19
March 3, Anna, wife of Dan Holt, asthma,   71
     5, Stepner Primus, consumption,   50
April 5, Amos, of Amasa Mallory, lung fever,   7w.
May 11, Mehitabel Russel, dropsy,   73
     15, Abraham Barnes, consumption,   71
Sept. 30, Collins Hughes, consumption,   53
Nov. 1, Joseph Tuttle, consumption,   29
     18, Amma Tyler, yellow fever, St. Kitts,   28
     22, Edward, of widow Flavel, croup,   1
1819.
Jan. 11. Benjamin Mallory, palsy,   68
April 13, Julia Barnes, died instantly,   23
     19, Rosewell, of Wm. Bradley, s. pock, Martinique, 20
     21, Dennis, of William Barnes, consumption,   2
     26, Stephen Woodward, Esq. dropsy,   61
May 7, Mary, wife of Gurdon Bradley, palsy,   75

Aug. 5, Stephen Pardee, consumption, 33
   13, Stephen Shepard, palsy, 80
   26, John Woodward, 51
Sept. 4, Willet, of Willet Heminway, cholera, 1
Oct. 1, Sarah, widow of Samuel Moulthrop, 86
Sept. be- ⌈Alford Warts, lost at sea in a gale, 26
tween 18 | James Smith, do. 22
and 25, ⟨ Warren Smith, do. 21
   | Leman Parker, do. 18
   ⌊Orin Broton, do. 17
Nov. 7, George, of Isaac H. Pardee, diarrhœa, 1
Dec. 13, widow Eleanor Mallory, palsy, 70
          1820.
Jan. 9, John Davenport, apoplexy, 82
   17, Amoret, of Benj'n Pardee, bowel obstruction, 9m.
Feb. 12, Merit, of Milton Finch, bowel obstruction, 3
   15, Samuel Bradley, pleurisy, 45
April 28, Samuel Potter, consumption, 17
July 15, Sherman Kingsbury, consumption, 56
Oct. 5, Samuel Thompson, of Sam'l Bradley, 2d, cons. 11w.
   16, Sarah-Ann, of Russel Hughes, consumption, 18m.
Nov. 11, Mary, widow of Isaac Luddington, 81
          1821.
June 3, Sarah, of Abraham Thompson, 10m.
July 13, Lois, wife of Moses A. Street, 43
Aug. 6, Anna, widow of John Chedsey, consumption, 70
   19, Jonathan Finch, consumption, 62
Sept. 3, Jacob Thompson, by shipwreck, 29
Oct. 16, Anson Todd, typhus fever, 18
Nov. 4, Huldah, relict of Jared Heminway, palsy, 67
   5, John, of widow Mary Woodward, accidental-
     ly shot, 14
   13, Mary, widow of Edward Russel, jun. 90
   16, Capt. Gurdon Bradley, 83
   22, Esther Bradley, typhus fever, 23
   26, Hannah, widow of Timothy Way, palsy, 65
          1822.
Jan. 1, Phebe, wife of Gurdon Pardee, consumption, 42
   2, Jacob Chedsey 2d, consumption, 43
   8, Caleb Smith, consumption, 51
   22, Willard Bradley, consumption, 26
May 24, Samuel Stansbury, insanity, 51
   30, Esther, wife of Josiah Moulthrop, by a fall, 58
June 15, Lydia, of Major Russel, cholera, 2

July 31, Isaac Holt Pardee, typhus fever,   41
Sept. 28, Joseph Heminway, consumption,   77
Nov. 25, Lydia, child of Amos Morris,   2
Dec. 24, Lue Adeline, child of Bela Forbes, burnt,   1

1823.

Jan. 18, Wm. Broton, hurt in a tavern, 4 days after died, 22
March 8, Infant, of Wyllys Mallory,   1d.
   17, Lois, widow of Stephen Thompson, jun. cons. 70
   29, Sarah, child of Samuel Lindsley, lung fever, 2
April 25, Didamea, wife of Sam'l Smith, (Foxon,) dropsy, 75
   29, Maria, of Milton Finch, consumption,   4m.
July 7, Mabel, widow of Joseph Bishop,   91 & 8m.
Oct. 2, Harriet, of John A. Thomas, dropsy,   7
   11, Deacon A. Morris, consumption,   73
   13, Lorana Moulthrop, cholera,   45
   19, Mary, widow of Charles Bishop, consumption, 84
   29, Asenath, of Asahel Bradley, 2d, consumption, 20
Nov. 7, Josiah Moulthrop, mortification,   70
   8, Samuel Smith, (Foxon,) dropsy,   75

Deaths in 1824, *up to the* 20th *of August.*
Jan. 18, Milton Finch, consumption,   35
Feb. 24, Moses A. Street,   53
   29, Mehitabel, widow of Daniel Auger, dropsy,   81
March 21, Lydia, wife of Isaac Moulthrop, fever,   31
April 20, Bethiah, widow of Samuel Tuttle, asthma,   82
   29, Benjamin Gates, of Daniel Smith, cramp,   4d.
May 10, Desire Moulthrop, consumption,   31
   13, Mary, widow of Ebenezer Chedsey,   92
Aug. 19, Widow Abigail Benham, cholera,   70

TABLE OF MORTALITY.

The following table exhibits the annual number of deaths of persons belonging to East-Haven, from the beginning of the year 1773 to the end of the year 1823 :—

In 1773	34	1786	19	1799	12	1812	12
1774	17	1787	11	1800	13	1813	39
1775	15	1788	20	1801	12	1814	12
1776	13	1789	12	1802	16	1815	25
1777	16	1790	19	1803	28	1816	10
1778	8	1791	16	1804	11	1817	11
1779	11	1792	8	1805	19	1818	13
1780	9	1793	22	1806	13	1819	18
1781	14	1794	28	1807	16	1820	9
1782	19	1795	32	1808	12	1821	12
1783	20	1796	22	1809	11	1822	11
1784	14	1797	16	1810	28	1823	14
1785	13	1798	14	1811	22		

Whole number of deaths, 841. The average number annually, has been about 16½ for the last 51 years.

The following table will show the comparative amount of deaths at different periods of life :—

Deaths under one year old, 116
Under two years, 49
Of two years, 38

18 of 3 years,	10 of 19	11 of 34	9 of 50	9 of 65	13 of 80
19 of 4	21 of 20	7 of 35	5 of 51	7 of 66	4 of 81
16 of 5	11 of 21	9 of 36	5 of 52	9 of 67	8 of 82
10 of 6	18 of 22	6 of 37	1 of 53	14 of 68	4 of 83
8 of 7	5 of 23	4 of 38	2 of 54	8 of 69	11 of 84
11 of 8	16 of 24	1 of 39	7 of 55	12 of 70	4 of 85
6 of 9	8 of 25	8 of 40	7 of 56	13 of 71	3 of 86
6 of 10	7 of 26	4 of 41	6 of 57	2 of 72	3 of 87
2 of 11	12 of 27	4 of 42	5 of 58	4 of 73	3 of 88
6 of 12	6 of 28	4 of 43	2 of 59	3 of 74	1 of 89
1 of 13	5 of 29	9 of 45	14 of 60	8 of 75	5 of 90
4 of 14	13 of 30	4 of 46	6 of 61	4 of 76	1 of 91
7 of 15	4 of 31	4 of 47	3 of 62	10 of 77	2 of 92
3 of 16	8 of 32	5 of 48	5 of 63	7 of 78	1 of 94
11 of 17	6 of 33	2 of 49	5 of 64	2 of 79	1 100
16 of 18					

Of seven deaths the ages are not mentioned.

The fatal diseases prevalent in this town are, Dysentery, Canker-Rash, Croup, Pleurisy, Consumption, Nervous and Typhus Fever.— Palsy and Apoplexy have been frequent among the aged.

A large number of men were lost at sea—by sickness in foreign ports, and by war. Employment in navigation has been exceeding fatal to the lives of the seamen of East-Haven.

APPENDIX.

Containing an account of deaths since the year 1773, in the families which are mentioned in the second part, but residing in other towns.

NEW-HAVEN.

1779, David Moulthrop, prison ship, New-York,   26
1787, Feb. 3, Lois, of Stephen Rowe, buried in East-
        Haven, whooping cough,   5
1788, Feb. 3, Lois of   do.   do.   3m.
1789, Jan. 15, Infant of do.   do.   3d.
1790, Dec. 27, Infant of do.   do.   3d.
1793, Feb. 3, Infant of   do.   do.   4w.
1800, Dec. 18, Infant of do.   do.   3w.
1813, Sept. 16, Abigail, wife of do.   52
1816, Sept. 15, Stephen Rowe,   57
1786, Jan. 21, Infant of Solomon Barnes, buried in E. H.1w.
1789, Aug. 9, Lydia, of   do.   do.   whooping cough,   5
1791, May 11, Lydia, of   do.   do.   cholera,   2d.
——— Sept. 1, Infant of   do.   do.   2d
1803, Sept. 16, Lydia, wife of do. consump.   53
1807, June 10, Solomon Barnes, consump.   54
1790, Sept. 19, Russel, of Nathaniel Grannis, buried
        in East-Haven, worms,   2
1803, Oct. 7, Martha, wife of   do.   do.   dys.   47
1809, Feb. 3. Chloe, wife of   do.   46
1812, June 5, Nathaniel Grannis,   57
1811, June 12, Russel Grannis,   45
1799, Jan. 6, Charles, of John Hunt, buried E. Haven,   10
1804, June 7, A grand child of John Hunt,   do.
1818, Aug. 24, Jennet, of John Farren, diarrhœa,   1
        Nov. 1, Jane of do.   do.   1
1789, Sept. 31, Esther, wife of Addereno Forbes, buried
        in East-Haven, consump.   30
1821, Oct. 14, Lue, wife of Laban Pardee, buried in E.
        Haven, typhus fever,   20

BRANFORD.

1794, June 14, Jared, of Jared Bradley, buried in East-
        Haven, c. rash,   16
1814, July 15, Sarah, wife of do.   do.   typhus fever,   66
1818, Oct. 8, John Bradley, New-Haven, typhus fever,   30
1803, Nov. A servant woman of Jared Bradley, E. H.   79
1822, March 22, Elias Bradley, buried in E. H. consump. 36
1794, Sept. —, Josiah, of Jonathan Goodsell, at sea,   19
1821, April 17, Abigail, wife of do.   85

NORTH-BRANFORD.

1788, March, Irene Moulthrop,	21
1789, Sept. Anna, wife of Dow Smith, jun. consump.	42
1793, June 1, Kezia, widow of Dow Smith,	84
1800, Jan. Jordan Smith, consumption,	67
1798, Feb. Sarah, wife of Jordan Smith,	56
1796, Martha, the relict of Thomas Goodsell, jun.	96
1802, Widow Sarah Elliot, their daughter,	62

NORTHFORD.

1774, Aug. 31, Samuel Hotchkiss,	59
1792, Nov. 23, Martha Goodsell, cancer,	42
1786, Jan. 18, Dan, of Stephen Smith,	6
1809, Aug. 7, Dan, of do. yellow fever, N. Y.	24
1784, March 22, Jesse Street,	43
1792, June 19, Anna Street,	17
1799, Jan. 6, Orton, of Jonathan Finch,	4
1774, Oct. 7, Ebenezer Hotchkiss,	16
1779, June 17, Mary Hotchkiss,	34

NORTH-HAVEN.

1788, March 4, Mary, wife of Eliphalet Pardee.	
1789, Nov. Abel Smith, jun. fever.	
1790, April 17, Abel Smith,	79
1809, Oct. 22, Lydia, wife of Abel Smith,	79
1803, April 20, James Smith,	89
1819, Sept. 14, Lydia, 2d wife of James Smith,	93
1815, Feb. 20, Thomas Smith,	53
1800, Oct. 13, Sarah, wife of Thomas Smith,	39
1795, Oct. 4, Sibyl, child of do.	4
May 27, John, of do.	22m.
1801, Oct. 11, John, of do.	15
1801, May 7, Olive, wife of Jude Smith,	37
1808, April 21, Ruth, wife of do.	31
1822, Dec. 14, Thankful, wife of Oliver Smith,	70
1789, Nov. 15, Oliver Smith,	39
1806, July 20, Lois, wife of Oliver Smith, jun.	27
1815, March 27, Oliver Smith, jun.	35
1806, Aug. 18, Benjamin, of do.	7m.
1818, Sept. 27, Sarah, wife of Hervey Smith,	29
1796, Sept. 1, Mary, wife of James Pardee,	49
1821, Aug. 21, Samuel Heminway, buried E. H. fever,	71

PLYMOUTH.

1796, Aug. 25, Deacon Abraham Heminway,	69
1812, Jan. 20, Mercy, widow of do.	89

WALLINGFORD.

1787, May 22, Damaris, wife of Elnathan Street,	87
Nov. 30, Elnathan Street,	92

GUILFORD.

1775, Oct. 2, Anna, wife of Joel Tuttle,	26
1791, March 4, Julia, child of do.	9m.
1803, Jan. 23, Sarah, child of do.	23
182ː, Nov. 30, Joel Tuttle,	76

WOLCOTT,

1813, Oct. 11, Edward, of Rev. L. Hart, buried E. H. dysentary,	1
16, Rev. Lucas Hart, buried E. H. dys.	29
1795, Oct. 3, Daniel B. child of Reuben Moulthrop, Boston,	1
1803, Oct. Jared, son of Dan Holt, at Cayuga, fever,	21
1804, William Lmith, do. fever,	30
1807, Nov. Elijah Bradley, in Georgia, dysentary,	28
1821, Nov. 4, Hannah, wife of Levy Chedsey, Woodbury,	78

Total, 85.

The whole number of deaths noticed in this work, is 1440.

APPENDIX II.

In the preface to this work, the Old and New Style is mentioned. But, as many of those persons who may possess it, are ignorant both of the origin and the reason of the alteration of the Style, they will, doubtless, be gratified with some information on that subject. The following extract from Adam's Roman Antiquities, contains the information desired on that point; and also concerning the origin of the names of the months, and days of the week, now in common use.

"Romulus, (the founder of the city and empire of Rome,) is said to have divided the year into ten months; the first of which was called March, from Mars, his supposed father; the second, April, either from the Greek name of Venus, or because then trees and flowers open their buds; the third, May, from Maia, the mother of Mercury; and the fourth, June, from the goddess Juno, or in honor of the young, and May of the old. The rest were named from their number, Quintilis, Sextilis, September, October, November, December. Quintilis was afterwards called Julius, from Julius

Cæsar; and Sextilis, Augustus, from Augustus Cæsar; because in it he had first been made consul, and had obtained remarkable victories.

Numa added two months, called Januarius, from Janus; and Februarius, because then the people were purified by an expiatory sacrifice from the sins of the whole year; for this anciently was the last month in the year.

Numa, in imitation of the Greeks, divided the year into twelve months, according to the course of the moon, consisting in all of 354 days: he added one day more to make the number odd, which was thought more fortunate. But as ten days, five hours, and forty-nine minutes, were wanting to make the lunar year correspond to the course of the sun, he appointed that every other year an extraordinary month, called Intercalary month, should be inserted between the 23d and 24th day of February. The intercalating of this month was left to the discretion of the Pontiffs; who, by inserting more or fewer days, used to make the current year longer or shorter, as was most convenient for themselves or their friends. In consequence of this license, the months were transposed from their stated seasons; the winter months carried back into autumn, and the autumnal into summer.

Julius Cæsar, when he became master of the state, resolved to put an end to this disorder, by abolishing the source of it, the use of Intercalations; and for that purpose, adjusted the year according to the course of the sun, and assigned to each month the number of days which they still contain. To make matters proceed regularly, from the first of the ensuing January, he inserted in the current year, besides the intercalary month of 23 days, which fell into it of course, two extraordinary months between November and December, the one of thirty-three, and the other of thirty-four days; so that this year, which was called the last year of *confusion*, consisted of fifteen months, or 445 days.

All this was effected by the care and skill of Soginies, a celebrated astronomer of Alexandria, whom Cæsar brought to Rome for that purpose.

This is the famous *Julian* or solar year, which continues in use to this day in all Christian countries, without any other variation, than that of the *old* and *new style*, which was occasioned by a regulation of Pope Gregory, in the year 1582, who, observing that the vernal equinox, which at the time of the Council of Nice in 325, had been on the 21st March, then happened on the 10th, by the advice of astronomers.

caused 10 days to be entirely sunk and thrown out of the current year, between the 4th and 15th October: and to make the civil year for the future to agree with the real one, or with the annual revolution of the earth, which is completed in 365 days, 5 hours, 49 minutes; he ordained, that every 100th year should not be leap year, excepting the 4000th, so that the difference will hardly amount to a day in 7000 years, or according to a more accurate computation of the length of the year, to a day in 5200 years.

This alteration of the *style* was immediately adopted in all the Roman Catholic countries; but not in Britain till the year 1752, when eleven days were dropped between the 2d and 14th of September, so that that month contained only 19 days; and thenceforth the *new style* was adopted as it had been before in the other countries of Europe. The same year, also, another alteration was made in England, that the legal year, which before had begun on the 25th March, should begin upon the 1st January, which took place 1st January, 1752.

The custom of dividing time into weeks among the Romans, as we do in imitation of the Jews, was introduced in the time of the Emperors. Dio, who flourished under Severus, says, it first took place a little before his time, being derived from the Egyptians, and universally prevailed.— The days of the week were named from the planets, as they still are—Dies Solis, Sunday; Luna, Monday; Martis, Tuesday; Mercurii, Wednesday; Jovis, Thursday; Veneris, Friday; Saturni, Saturday."

Mr. Webster, in his letters to a young gentleman, observes respecting the origin of the names of the days of the week now in common use, that our ancestors worshipped many deities, or deified heroes, as *Woden*, or *Odin*, under whose guidance they migrated into Europe; *Thor*, the thunderer, or god of thunder; *Friga*, who answered to *Venus* of the Romans; and from their several deities we received the names of the days of the week. Sunday, Sun's-day; Monday, Moon's-day; Tuesday, Teut's-day, or Tisday; Wednesday, Woden's-day; Thursday, Thor's-day; Friday, Friga's-day; and Saturday, Satur's-day. Thus the ancient heathen gods are still honored by a weekly and regular rotation of their names, fifty-two times in a year.

FINIS.

A

CONFESSION OF FAITH,

COVENANT,

CONSTITUTION AND RULES OF PRACTICE;

ADOPTED BY THE

CONGREGATIONAL CHURCH IN EAST HAVEN.

TO WHICH IS ADDED

A CATALOGUE OF THE

OFFICERS AND MEMBERS OF THE CHURCH,

FROM THE YEAR 1755, TO DECEMBER, 1833.

NEW HAVEN:

PRINTED BY HEZEKIAH HOWE & CO.

1833.

CONFESSION OF FAITH.

ARTICLE 1. We believe in one only living and true God, the Father, and the Son, and the Holy Ghost, who is a spirit, infinite, eternal and unchangeable, in his being power, knowledge, presence, wisdom, holiness, justice, goodness and truth, that it is the duty of all his intelligent creatures to worship him in sprit and in truth; that he created all things, that he preserves and governs all his creatures, and overrules all their actions for his own glory, and that in whatsoever comes to pass, he is accomplishing his eternal purposes, according to the counsel of his own will, in such a way that man is a free agent, and accountable for all his actions.

2. We believe, that God created man upright; that our first parents freely sinned and fell, and that all mankind, in a state of nature, and before regeneration by the spirit of God, are dead in trespasses and sins, and without any holiness and true love to God, and are justly exposed to all the miseries of this life, and the pains of hell forever.

3. We believe, that God in his mercy has not left all mankind to perish forever; but out of his mere good pleasure, has from all eternity elected some to everlasting life; and that he has covenanted to deliver them from sin and misery, and to bring them into a state of salvation by a Redeemer.

4. We believe, that the only Redeemer of God's elect is the Lord Jesus Christ, who is very God and very man, that taking upon him our nature, he suffered and died on the cross; then he arose from the dead, and ascended into heaven, where he ever liveth to make intercession for us; that he alone has made an atonement for sin; and that, without a special interest in this atonement, there is no salvation.

5. We believe, that without a change of heart, wrought in the unregenerate, by the special agency of the Holy Spirit, who is very God, no one can be an heir of eternal life; and that the soul, which is once made a partaker of renewing and saving grace, will never be permitted so to fall away as finally to perish,

4

6. We believe, that adoption, repentance, justification, sanctification and perseverance, are not bestowed as the reward of any merit, in him who receives them ; but all flow from the free and sovereign gift and grace of God.

7. We believe, that there will be a general resurrection, of the righteous and the wicked ; and a general judgment, at which, all the righteous shall be admitted to everlasting happiness, and all the wicked sentenced to misery without end.

8. We believe, that the Lord's Supper and Baptism, are sacraments of the New Testament; and that baptism is to be administered to unbaptized adults, who profess their faith in Christ, and to the infant children of any, who are members of the Church.

9. We believe, that the scriptures, of the Old and New Testament, are given by inspiration of God, and are the sufficient and only rule of faith and practice.

Thus in the presence of Almighty God, you solemnly profess and believe.

COVENANT.

You do now, in the awful presence of the dread majesty of heaven and earth, before Angels and Men, with seriousness, and as you hope, in sincerity of soul, avouch the Lord Jehovah to be your sovereign Lord, and supreme good through Jesus Christ. And solemnly devote and give up yourself, by divine grace assisting you, in the most sacred ties, to observe all God's commandments, seeking his glory and walk in Christian fellowship, and in the performance of Christian duties, in all the ordinances of Christ to be enjoyed in his Church ; and in this particular Church, so long as God in his providence shall continue you a member of it.

Thus in the presence of God, through grace assisting, you solemnly covenant and promise.

Then doth this Church also accept of you. And I declare you, a member of, and in full communion with, the Church of Christ. And this Church doth likewise promise, that in the strength of divine grace, we will walk towards you in all christian watchfulness and love.

CONSTITUTION.

The Church and Society of East Haven, having given Mr. Nicholas Street, a call, to settle with them as a Pastor, in the work of the Gospel ministry among them, and he accepting the call; the Church called a meeting of the brethren to discourse of Church Government, and of the manner in which they propose to be governed, which was held in East Haven, Sept. 3, 1755. And at said meeting, it was voted and agreed to, that SAYBROOK PLATFORM, should be the CONSTITUTION, by which they and their Pastor, would be governed, with this understanding it in the following respects.

Viz. 1. That no person be admitted a member of this Church, without the vote and consent of the major part of the brotherhood. 2. That no person be censured without the vote and consent of the major part of the brotherhood.

This voted in the affirmative, and signed by the Church's Committee, with the concurrence of Mr. Nicholas Street, called to be Pastor of said Church and people.

THOMAS SMITH,
DEODATE DAVENPORT, } *Committee.*
DANIEL HITCHCOCK,
NICHOLAS STREET.

Dec. 4, 1755. The Church voted that the Lord's Supper be administered once in two months; and that the fragments of the bread and wine be presented to the Minister after the Sacrament as his perquisites.

ARTICLES OF PRACTICE ADOPTED MARCH 2, 1832.

1. Every person coming from a Church, not in Communion with this Church, in case of admission, shall be propounded and admitted in the usual way. And every person coming from other Churches, in order to be admitted as a member of this Church, must furnish such evidence of good character and good standing in the Church to which he belonged, as shall be satisfactory to this Church.
2. Members of sister Churches in good standing may be admitted to occasional communion with this Church, one year. But after that term, they must produce a letter of

1*

dismission from the Church, to which they belong ith a view to unite with this Church, in order to a continued enjoyment of Church privileges.

3. In all cases of private offences, the rule as given in the 18th Chap. of Matthew, 15, 16, 17, verses is to be observed.

4. In cases of public and notorious offences, against the laws of religion and morality, the Church as a body may call the offender to an account, by a Committee appointed for that purpose, who shall report to the Church.

STANDING COMMITTEE.

There shall be a standing Committee of this Church, consisting of four or more members, as the church may judge proper, who with the pastor shall have the powers, and perform the duties, as follows, viz.

1. It shall be the duty of this committee to enquire after all public offences in this church, which may come to their knowledge by complaint or otherwise.

2. It shall be the duty of this committee to ascertain the facts in each case that may come before them, and to make reports to the church, both of the facts and the measures proper in their opinion, to be taken in their case.

3. This committee shall have power to summon before them all members of the church, accused of any offence, to examine them, and to give them such brotherly counsel, as may, in their judgment, tend to reclaim offenders.

4. This committee shall have power to call upon any of the brethren of the church, to aid them in the discharge of any of their duties.

But this church declares, that in appointing this committee, they do not discharge or lessen the obligations of individual members of this church, to watch over, admonish and reprove one another.

This Church was gathered and organized Oct. 8, 1711.

OFFICERS OF THE CHURCH.

PASTORS.

Rev. JACOB HEMINWAY, began to preach in East Haven in November, 1704 ; and was ordained pastor, October 8, 1711 ; and died October 7, 1754, aged 70.

Rev. NICHOLAS STREET, was ordained pastor, October 8, 1755 ; and died October 8, 1806, aged 76.

Rev. SAUL CLARK, was ordained pastor, Jan. 13, 1808; and resigned May 19, 1817.

Rev. STEPHEN DODD, installed pastor Dec. 11, 1817.

DEACONS.

Caleb Chedsey, died Feb. 20, 1713.
Joshua Austin, died March 29, 1760.
Thomas Smith, died 1762.
Daniel Hitchcock, died 1761.
Deodate Davenport, died Dec. 3, 1761.
Samuel Heminway, chosen 1758, and died Oct. 25, 1777.
Abraham Heminway, chosen 1761 ; removed.
Amos Morris, chosen 1776 ; died Dec. 30, 1801.
Stephen Smith, chosen 1778; died Jan. 22, 1816.
Samuel Davenport, chosen 1797 ; died July 9, 1810.
John Morris, chosen July, 1800 ; removed 1806.
Levi Pardee, chosen July 1800 ; died Nov. 21, 1813.
Enos Heminway, chosen 1806 ; removed June 13, 1830.
Amos Morris, chosen 1816 ; resigned 1818.
Bela Farnham,
Amos Morris, } chosen and installed July 1, 1832.
Samuel H. Heminway,

8

A CATALOGUE

Of the members of the Congregational Church in East Haven, from 1755, when Rev. Nicholas Street was ordained Pastor, to the present time, December, 1833.

N B. The persons against whose names this mark * is inserted, are dead. The names of those who are dismissed or who have removed from this town with or without a dismission, are printed in *Italics*. The Names of those from whom the Church has withdrawn fellowship, are omitted as being blotted out. Their number is 14.

* Joshua Austin.
* Mehitabel, wife of Joshua Austin.
* Thomas Smith.
* Deodate Davenport.
* Lydia, wife of Deodate Davenport.
* Sarah Davenport.
* Esther, wife of Stephen Morris.
* John Russel.
* Mary, wife of John Russel.
* *Mary, wife of David Smith.*
* John Chedsey.
* Sarah, wife of John Chedsey.
* Mary, wife of Nathaniel Ludington.
* Sarah, wife of Samuel Bradley.
* Hannah, wife of Isaac Bradley.
* John Shepard.
* Sarah, wife of John Shepard.
* Eunice, wife of Thomas Smith.
* Theophilus Alling.
* Elizabeth, wife of Theophilus Alling.
* Caleb Bradley.
* Sarah, wife of Caleb Bradley.
* Sarah, wife of Dan Bradley.
* Abraham Chedsey.
* Bathsheba, wife of Abraham Chedsey.
* Daniel Hitchcock.
* Abigail, wife of Daniel Hitchcock.
* Daniel Bradley.
* Mehitabel, wife of Daniel Bradley.
* Thankful, wife of Stephen Bradley.
* Elizabeth, wife of Zebulon Bradley.
* Deborah, widow of Samuel Chedsey.

* Dan Moulthrop.
* Gideon Potter.
* Mary, wife of Gideon Potter.
* John Heminway.
* Mary, wife of John Heminway.
* Stephen Thompson.
* Hannah, wife of Stephen Thompson.
* Samuel Heminway.
* Sarah, wife of Abraham Heminway.
* Esther, wife of Timothy Thompson.
* Sarah, wife of Patterson Smith.
* Benjamin Smith.
* Desire, wife of Benjamin Smith.
* Rebekah, wife of Nathaniel Hitchcock, junr.
* Samuel Smith.
* Daniel Smith.
* Hannah, wife of Daniel Smith.
* Sarah, wife of George Pardee.
* Benjamin Pardee.
* Mary, wife of Benjamin Pardee.
* Sarah, wife of Isaac Pardee.
* Mary, wife of Jacob Pardee.
* Mary, wife of Stephen Pardee.
* Mary Pardee.
* Moses Thompson.
* Desire, wife of Moses Thompson.
* Abigail O'Neal.
* Lydia, widow of John Smith.
* Joseph Tuttle.
* Hannah, wife of John Rowe.
* Nathaniel Barnes.
* Mary, wife of Samuel Forbes.
* Thankful, wife of Isaac Howe.
* Elizabeth, wife of Samuel Thompson.
* *Joseph Holt.*
* Mercy, wife of Samuel Holt.
* Abigail, wife of Eliphalet Ludington.
* Anna, wife of Daniel Holt.
* Hannah, wife of Levi Bradley.
* Mehitabel, wife of Jesse Ludington.
* Mercy, wife of Eleazer Morris.
* John Moulthrop.
* Lydia, wife of Israel Moulthrop.

* Samuel Thompson.
* Hannah wife of Samuel Thompson.
* Anna, wife of Asher Moulthrop.
* Mary, wife of Samuel Smith.
* Lydia Robinson.
* Sarah Robinson.
* Elizabeth wife of Isaac Penfield.
* Caleb Chedsey.
* Abigail, wife of Caleb Chedsey.
* Hannah, wife of Thomas Dawson.
* Lydia Grannis.
* Matthew Moulthrop.
* Sarah, wife of Matthew Moulthrop.
* Hannah, wife of Samuel Chedsey, Junr.
* Mehitabel, wife of Thomas Grannis.
* Isaac Chedsey.
* Sarah wife of Isaac Chedsey.
* Joel Tuttle.
* Rebekah, wife of Joel Tuttle.
* Dorothy Tuttle.
* Margaret Jacobs.
* Mary, wife of John Higgins.
* Keziah, wife of Gideon Potter, junr.
* Elizabeth Woodward.
* Mercy Pardee.
* Deborah, wife of Titus Alling.
* Richard Darrow.
* Abigail, wife of Nathaniel Jocelin.
* Thankful, wife of Robert Dawson.
* *Sarah, wife of Rev. Jacob Heminway.*
* Mary, widow of Samuel Goodsell.
* Abigail, wife of Dan Goodsell.
* *Lydia, wife of Ebenezer Darrow.*
* Hannah, wife of Peter Woodward.
* *Eunice, wife of Ebenezer Pardee.*
* *Sarah, wife of Timothy Russel.*
* Esther, wife of Joseph Hotchkiss.
* Gideko and Abigail, blacks.

The above names of members were collected and recorded by Rev. Mr. Street in 1756; Mr. Heminway having left no record.

1757.

Feb. 20. * Mabel, wife of Isaac Mallory.
March 13. * Mary, wife of John Woodward.
            * *Lorana Becket.*
     27. * Mary, wife of John Dawson.
            * Abigail, wife of John Moulthrop.
July 3. * *Abraham Heminway.*
            * *Mercy, wife of Ab: Heminway.*
            * *Zurviah, wife of Joshua Sperry.*

1758.

Sept. 21. * Catherine, servant of John Woodward.

1759.

June 3. * John Davenport.
            * Samuel Davenport.

1761.

May 31. * Mehitabel, wife of Deacon Saml. Heminway.
Nov. 12. * Desire, wife of Rev. Nicholas Street.
            * *Sarah, wife of John Denison.*

1762.

Sept. 19. * Elizabeth, wife of Samuel Shepard.
            * Mary, wife of Edward Russel, junr.

1763.

March 27. * Elizabeth, widow of Ebenezer Roberts.
May 29. * Isaac Chedsey, 2d.
            * *Daniel Whedon.*
Sept. 18. * *Joshua Austin.*
            * Abigail, wife of Joshua Austin.
            * Lydia Pardee.
Oct. 16. * Desire, wife of Samuel Thompson.

1764.

July 15. * Amos Morris.
            * Lydia, wife of Amos Morris.
     21. * Simeon Bradley.
            * Abigail, wife of Simeon Bradley.

1765.

Feb. 24. * Mary Russel.
            * Mabel, widow of Doct. Utter.
            * Mary Mallory, junr.
June 23. * *Amy, wife of Abraham Bradley.*

1766.

Jan. 20. * Mary Mallory.
June. * Elizabeth, wife of Jacob Bradley.
Sept. 21. * John Heminway.

Oct.	* Phineas Curtis.
Nov.	* Sarah, wife of Ezra Fields.

1767.

June.	* Patterson Smith.
Oct. 25.	* Jenny, a black woman.
Dec. 6.	* Anna, wife of Thomas Smith.

1768.

July 24.	* Susannah, wife of Joshua Austin.

1771.

Oct. 13.	* Aaron Page.
	* Stephen Smith.

1772.

June 28.	* Ruth, wife of John Woodward, junr.

1773.

Jan. 24.	* Hannah, wife of Rev. N. Street.
	* Mary, wife of Gurdon Bradley.
Jan. 31.	* Binah and Nanne, black women.
Aug. 15.	* Samuel Holt.
	* Mary, wife of Samuel Holt.
	* Dan Holt.
	* Anna, wife of Dan Holt.
Sept. 19.	* John Fuller.
	* Lydia, wife of John Fuller.
	* Comfort, wife of Josiah Bradley.
	* Jemima, wife of John Heminway.
	* Widow, Mary Richards.
Oct. 10.	* Sarah, wife of Abijah Bradley.
Nov. 17.	Elisha Andrews.
	Sarah, wife of Elisha Andrews.
Dec. 5.	* Lydia, wife of Jacob Goodsell.
19.	* Stephen Tuttle.
	* Rhoda, wife of Stephen Tuttle.
26.	* Nathaniel Ludington.
	* Abigail, wife of John Barnes.

1774.

Jan. 9.	* Mary, wife of Ambrose Smith.
March 27.	* *Hannah, wife of Levi Chedsey.*
April 17.	* Joseph Russel.
	* Abigail, wife of Joseph Russel.
	* Sarah, wife of Isaac Chedsey, 2d.
May 8.	* *Israel Potter.*
	* *Mary, wife of Israel Potter.*
	* Hannah, wife of Joseph Holt.
	* Mary, wife of Isaac Ludington.

May 8.   * Jemima Pardee.
July 17.   * Stephen Shepard.
            * Amy, wife of Stephen Shepard.
            * Thankful Moulthrop.

In Sept. the congregation removed from the old house at the north-west corner of the green, into the new house, now occupied. Then the church was composed of about **140** *members.*

1775.
March 5.   * Joseph Mallory.
            * Eunice, wife of Joseph Mallory.
May 21.   * Lydia, wife of Azariah Bradley.
Dec. 3.   * *Sibyl Denison.*
1776.
March.   * *Timothy Bradley.*
            * *Sarah, wife of Timothy Bradley.*
1777.
Feb. 9.   * Sarah, wife of Jared Bradley.
Aug. 10.   * Mehitabel Russel.
            Mary, wife of David Grannis.
            Abigail, wife of John Goodsell.
            * *Huldah, wife of Elias Townsend.*
Dec. 21.   * Mabel, wife of Stephen Pardee, junr.
            * Widow, Eunice Britin.
1778.
March.   *Amy, wife of Asa Bradley.*
April 5.   * Samuel Smith, junr.
            Anna, wife of Samuel Smith, junr.
            * Widow, Sarah Scott.
            * Elizabeth, wife of David Eggleston.
Oct. 18.   * Widow, Abigail Bishop.
1779.
Jan. 31.   * Widow, Rebekah Bradley.
March 21.   * *Huldah, wife of Ezra Rowe.*
            * *Rachel, wife of Samuel Crumb.*
1780.
Feb. 27.   * Amos Morris, junr.
            * Elizabeth, wife of Amos Morris, **junr.**
July 30.   * Samuel Townsend.
            * Levi Pardee.
            Stephen Smith, junr.
Aug. 6.   * *Eunice Street.*

2

1781.

April 1.   * Abraham Chedsey.
May 20.   * Lydia, wife of Samuel Holt.
    Abigail Hitchcock.
July 29.   *John Morris.*
    * *Desire, wife of John Morris.*
    * James Adkins Broton.
Nov. 24.   * *Mehitabel, wife of Dan Bradley.*
    * Hannah, wife of Isaac Forbes.
1782.

Jan. 27.   * Abigail, wife of James A. Broton.
April 28.   * *Desire, wife of Moses Thompson.*
    * Martha, wife of Moses Heminway.
Aug. 11.   * Widow Lydia Goodsell.
    * Thankful, wife of Jesse Ludington, junr.
Dec. 22.   * Lydia, wife of Isaac Hotchkiss.
    * Mary, wife of Amos Thompson.
1783.

July 6.   * Hannah, wife of Asa Mallory.
Aug. 20.   * *Sibyl, wife of Elihu Bradley.*
Oct. 5.   * Caleb Smith.
    * Daniel Tuttle.
19.   * Elizabeth, wife of Joseph Heminway.
1784.

Feb. 22.   * Esther, wife of John Rowe, junr.
    Temperance, wife of Joseph Hotchkiss.
    Lydia, wife of Edmund Bradley.
March 21.   * *Abigail, wife of Nathaniel Barnes,* junr
Oct. 17.   * Widow Lois Moulthrop.
1785.

Feb. 3.   * *Widow Rachel Ludington.*
1787.

Jan. 25.   * Hannah, wife of Samuel Heminway.
Feb. 8.   * Lois, wife of Nehemiah Smith.
April 22.   * *Leavit Pardee.*
    * *Elizabeth, wife of Leavit Pardee.*
    Sarah, wife of Ira Smith.
May 5.   Elizabeth, wife of Stephen Woodward.
    * Martha, wife of Nathaniel Grannis.
    * Stephen Rowe.
    * Abigail, wife of Stephen Rowe.
20.   * Abigail, wife of Joseph Heminway.
Sept. 2.   *Eunice, wife of Matthew Rowe.*

Nov. 4.   * Eunice, wife of Benjamin Mallory.
1788.
June 1.   *Enos Heminway.*
   Sarah, wife of Enos Heminway.
   * Susannah Roberts.
July 6.   * Anna, wife of John Chedsey.
    13.   Sarah, wife of Levi Potter.
   * Lois, wife of Joel Thompson.
   Amy, wife of Daniel Tuttle.
Sept. 7.   * Tabitha, wife of Philemon Augur.
Nov. 23.   Widow Lucinda Hickox.
1789.
May 24.   * Abigail, wife of Amos Mallory.
1790.
Aug. 15.   * Abigail, wife of Christopher Tuttle.
1791.
Aug. 28.   * Lois, wife of Isaac Barnes.
Nov. 18.   * Desire, wife of Ephraim Chedsey.
1792.
Dec.   * *Hannah, wife of Asaph Hotchkiss.*
1793.
Sept. 22.   Elizabeth, wife of Andrew Davidson.
   Mehitabel, wife of Stephen Bradley, junr.
   * Hannah, wife of Jesse Mallory.
   * Lydia, wife of Solomon Barnes.
Dec. 8.   * *Huldah, wife of Joel Northrup.*
1794.
Oct. 12.   * Reuben Moulthrop.
   Hannah, wife of Reuben Moulthrop.
Oct. 26.   * Abijah Pardee.
   Rosanna, wife of Abijah Pardee.
   Sarah, wife of Joseph Pardee.
1795.
Feb. 15.   Mary, wife of John Woodward, junr.
   Martha, wife of Elam Potter.
Dec. 13.   *Allice, a black woman.*
1796.
April 3.   *Roswell Davenport.*
   Esther, wife of R. Davenport.
   Sarah, wife of Philemon Harrison.
    24.   Desire, wife of Thomas Smith.
   * Rebekah, wife of Caleb Chedsey.
   * Sarah, wife of Samuel Thompson, junr.

July 10.	*Mary, wife of William Bradley.*
Aug. 21.	Dorcas, wife of John Thompson.

1797.

March 19.	* *Rachel, wife of David Moulthrop.*
July 16.	*Sarah, wife of Daniel Austin.*
Aug. 6.	* Widow Sarah Thompson.

1799.

May	* Esther, wife of Stephen Heminway.
26.	* Lois, wife of Edward Russel.
June 30.	*Jacob Heminway.*
	Abigail, wife of Jacob Heminway.
Aug. 4.	* Elizabeth, wife of John Shepard, junr.
	Lydia, wife of Ammi Bradley.
18.	Asenath, wife of Hezekiah Woodward.
	Elizabeth, wife of Amos Bradley.
Sept. 1.	Sarah, wife of Caleb Smith.
Nov. 10.	Widow, Lydia Smith.

1800.

April 24.	* Hannah, wife of Abraham Chedsey.
May 25.	Lorinda, wife of Heminway Holt.
	Amy, wife of William Smith.
June 22.	* John Tyler.
	Mabel, wife of John Tyler.
	Irene, wife of Nehemiah Smith.
	* Eunice, wife of Timothy Thompson, junr.
	Widow, Lydia Bradley.
July 15.	*Lois, wife of Martin Rowland.*

1801.

Jan. 18.	Anna, wife of Bela Farnham.
March 1.	Esther, wife of Elijah Bradley.
May 31.	Lydia, wife of James Thompson.
Sept. 27.	*Amy Beach.*

1802.

Feb. 4.	* *Mary, wife of Philemon Augur.*
	Mary Frost.
	* Hannah, wife of John Heminway.
21.	Hannah, wife of Ephraim Chedsey.
	* Anna, wife of Levi Baldwin.
	* Hannah, wife of Abraham Farren.

1803.

July 24.	*Amy, wife of Joseph Holt, junr.*

1804.

Jan. 29.	*Hezekiah Davenport.*
Aug. 16.	* Samuel Shepard.

Oct. 7.	*Lois, wife of Horatio G. Street.*
	Desire, wife of Philemon Holt.
28.	Mary, wife of Abraham Thompson.

1805.

March 7.	* Nehemiah Smith.
	* Justin W. Street.
July 21.	*Dorcas Way.*

1806.

Jan. 5.	* Sarah, wife of Levi Pardee.
	* Ruth Bishop.
	Lydia, wife of Jacob Farren.
	* Sarah, wife of Isaac Brown.
	* Mehitabel, wife of James Chedsey.
	* Widow Mary Chedsey.
	Widow Abigail Andrews.
	* Mary, wife of Isaac Bradley.
	* Lovice, wife of Joel Bradley.
	Betsey, wife of Samuel Chedsey.
	Jane F. wife of Samuel Lindsley.

Persons received after Mr. Street's death.

* Didamea, wife of Samuel Smith.
Mary Street.
Harriet Morris.
Lucy Morris.
Anna Woodward.

Persons received at different times, by letter, from other churches, and not before recorded.

1807.

March 5.	* Mehitabel Augur.
	* Phebe, wife of William Everton.
	* Eunice, wife of Moses Heminway.
	* Hannah Pardee.
	* Phebe, wife of Gurdon Pardee.
May 7.	* Eunice, wife of Daniel Bradley.
	* *Lois, wife of Silas Bishop.*
April 30.	* Widow Hannah Brown.
	Elizabeth, wife of Amasa Forbes.

Admitted by Mr. Clark.

1808.

| March 5. | *Elijah Rowe, and* } by letter. |
| | *Mary, his wife,* } |

2*

Phebe, wife of John Davenport, by letter.

July 3.　　* Benjamin Mallory.
　　　　　* Joseph Hotchkiss.
　　　　　Isaac Bradley, junr.
　　　　　Sarah, wife of Isaac Ludington.
　　　　　Sarah, wife of Isaac H. Pardee.
　　　　　Lois, wife of Edward R. Smith.
　　　　　Elizabeth, wife of Heman Hotchkiss.
　　　　　Mary Dawson.
　　　　* Mary Barnes.
　　　　　Lydia Morris.
　　　　　Polly Bradley.
　　　　　Amy Bradley.
　　　　* Sarah Bradley.
　　　　　Wealthy Bradley.
　　　　　Abigail Holt.
　　　　* Nancy Shepard.
　　　　　Elizabeth Augur.
　　　　　Orilla Hotchkiss.
　　　　* *Mary Hotchkiss.*
　　　　* *Hannah Goodsell.*
　　　　　Eunice Pardee.
　　　　　Mary Frost, junr.

Sept. 4.　　* *Amy, wife of John Shepard.*
　　　　　Ezra Rowe.
　　　　* Hannah, wife of Jacob Mallory.
　　　　* Asahel Bradley.
　　　　　Bela Farnham.
　　　　　William Woodward.
　　　　　Ezra Rowe, junr.
　　　　　Betsey, wife of Ezra Rowe, junr.
　　　　　Harvey Rowe.
　　　　　Jacob Barnes.
　　　　　Willet Heminway.
　　　　　Clarissa, wife of Elnathan Street.
　　　　　Sibyl, wife of Lyman Hotchkiss.
　　　　* Desire Bradley.
　　　　　Phila Brown.
　　　　　Clarissa Brown.
　　　　　Nancy Davidson.
　　　　　Adah Bradley.
　　　　* Mary Pardee.
　　　　　Sylvia Allen.

	Susan Bradley.
Nov. 6,	*John Rowe.*
	Nicholas Street.
	Betsey, wife of Nicholas Street.
*	James Heminway.
	Elizabeth, wife of James Heminway.
	Levi Rowe.
	Eunice, wife of Levi Rowe.
	Daniel Smith.
	Irene Goodsell.
	Patty Mallory.
	Mary Brown.

1809.

Jan. 1.	Elizabeth, wife of Truman Russel.
	Lydia, wife of James Bradley.
	Asenath, wife of Asahel Bradley, 2d.
	Nancy, wife of Justin W. Street.
	Betsey Heminway.
	Sarah Pardee.
	Eunice Miner.
	Harvey Heminway.
	Eben Tyler Heminway.
	Wyllys Heminway.
March 5.	* *Mary, wife of Asher Moulthrop.*
	* *Huldah, wife of Amos Ludington.*
	Mehitabel, wife of Russel Lanfear.
	Mehitabel, wife of Nathan Andrews.
	Gurdon Pardee.
	Abraham Thompson.
	* Isaac H. Pardee.
	Daniel Rowe.
	Elizabeth, wife of Daniel Rowe.
May 7.	* Asa Mallory.
	Timothy Thompson.
	* *Abigail Baldwin.*
	* Charlotte, wife of Amos Morris, junr.
	Lois Smith.
July 2.	*Elizabeth, wife of Caleb Smith, 2d.*
	* Widow Sarah Davidson.
Sept. 3.	*Mary, wife of George Landcraft.*
	* Mary, wife of Roswell Bradley.
	Widow Amy Bradley.
	Eliza Andrews.

* Huldah Ludington.

Nov. 5.   *Peggy Kism*, a black woman.

1810.

May 20.   *Sophia, Wife of Jacob Goodsell*, by letter.
Nov. 4.   * Widow Mary Thompson.
           * Widow Sarah Landcraft.

1811.

Sept. 11.   Widow Loruhamah Goodsell, by letter.

1812.

May   Widow Abigail Goodsell.
July 5.   Sarah, wife of DeGrasse Maltby.

1813.

Jan. 3.   Grace, wife of Anson Bradley.
May   Elizabeth, wife of Elias Bradley.
Oct. 31.   *Elizabeth, wife of Samuel Bradley, 2d.*

1814.

May 1.   *Widow Mary Thompson.*

1816.

March 3.   * Jacob Goodsell.
           Benjamin Pardee.
           Thomas Landcraft.
           * Lois, wife of Thomas Landcraft.
           * Lovice, wife of Roswell Augur.
           Betsey, wife of John Farren.
           Sarah, wife of John Larkins.
           * Lydia, wife of Isaac Moulthrop.
           Mary Larkins.
           Polly Bradley.
           Hannah Bradley.
           Nancy Thompson.
           Laura Chedsey.
           Eliza Chedsey.
           Statira Rowe.
           * Anson Todd.
May 5.   * Anna, wife of Samuel Holt, by letter from the church in Bethlem.
July 7.   Roswell Augur.

1817.

May 4.   * Widow Elizabeth Smith.

Admitted by Mr. Dodd.

1818.

May 1.   Abigail Ann, wife of Rev. S. Dodd, by letter from the church in Meredith, N. York.

May 3.	Rachel, wife of Daniel Hughes, by letter from the church in Bristol.

1819.

Oct. 31.	* Jared Bradley.

1820.

March 5.	*Widow Lydia Potter.*
Oct. 8.	*James R. Hunt.*

1821.

April 29.	Levi Potter.
	Luey, wife of Caleb C. Ludington.
	Eve Ely, wife of John Tyler, junr.
	Fanny, wife of Matthew Rowe.
	Samuel Russel Moulthrop.
	Daniel Moulthrop.
	* *Roswell Rowe.*
July 22.	Lyman Hotchkiss.
	Sarah, wife of Willet Heminway.
	Luey, wife of Joseph Grannis.
	Nancy, wife of Hezekiah Shepard.
	Widow Mary Tuttle.
	Mehitabel Barnes.
	Abigail Russel.
	Sarah Landcraft.
	Maria Landcraft.
Sept. 16.	*George Landcraft.*
	Jacob Mallory.
	Jesse Mallory, 2d.
	Wealthy, wife of Jesse Mallory, 2d.
	John Larkins.
	Matthew Rowe.
	* *Jesse Mallory.*
	James Mallory.
	Maria Pardee.
	Almena Ludington.
Nov. 4.	*Wyllys Mallory.*
	Huldah Hotchkiss.

1822.

Jan. 6.	Sarah Holt.
Feb. 10.	Elnathan Street.
	Dana Bradley.
	Mehitabel, wife of Dana Bradley.
Nov. 3.	Loly, wife of Aner Pardee.

Aug. 28.	*Charlotte Bradley.*
	Susan Andrews.
	Anna Chedsey.
	Almira Chedsey.
	Charles Woodward.
	Charlotte Delight Todd.
	Lucy Morris Street.
	Harriet Andrews.
	* Ruth Curtis Woodward.
	Asenath Woodward, junr.
Dec. 11.	Stephen Smith, 2d.
	Betsy, wife of Stephen Smith, 2d. and
	Maryette, their daughter.
	Grace Goodsell.
	Elizabeth Morris Bradley.
	1832.
July 1.	* Amanda, wife of Elias Bishop.
Sept. 30.	John Heminway.
	1833.
Nov. 10.	Almira Farren.

SUMMARY.

The number of members in the year 1756, when
Mr. Street collected and recorded the names,   114
    From 1756 to Oct. 1806, the end of Mr. Street's
ministry, were added,   -   -   -   -   230
    Received after Mr. Street's death, and at various
times from other churches,   -   -   -   14
Admitted by Mr. Clark,   -   -   -   11
Admitted by Mr. Dodd,   -   -   -

        Total,   -   -   -   601
Number of deaths and removals since 1756   441

Number of members that remain,   -   -   160